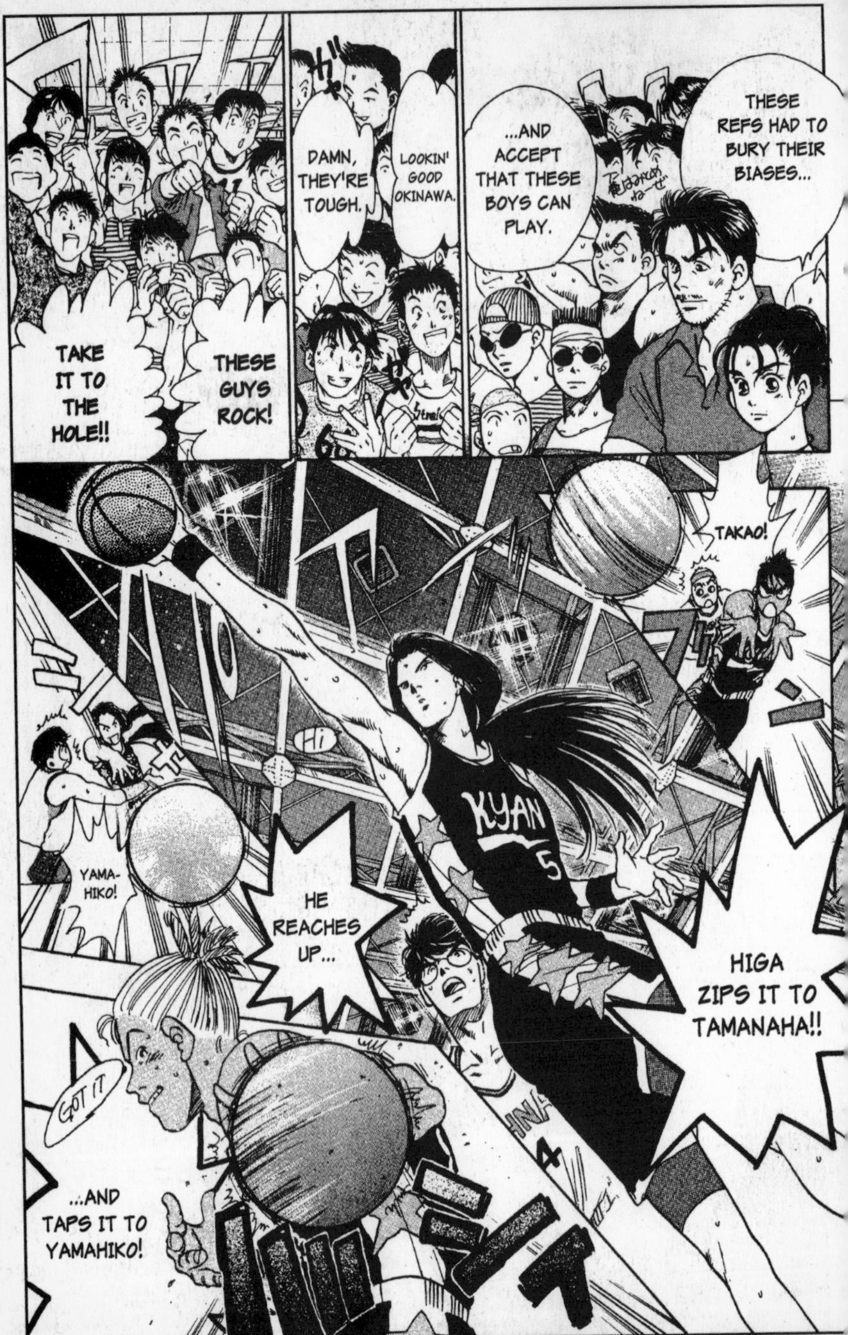
THESE REFS HAD TO BURY THEIR BIASES...
...AND ACCEPT THAT THESE BOYS CAN PLAY.
LOOKIN' GOOD OKINAWA.
DAMN, THEY'RE TOUGH.
THESE GUYS ROCK!
TAKE IT TO THE HOLE!!
TAKAO!
HIGA ZIPS IT TO TAMANAHA!!
HE REACHES UP...
Hi
YAMAHIKO!
GOT IT
...AND TAPS IT TO YAMAHIKO!

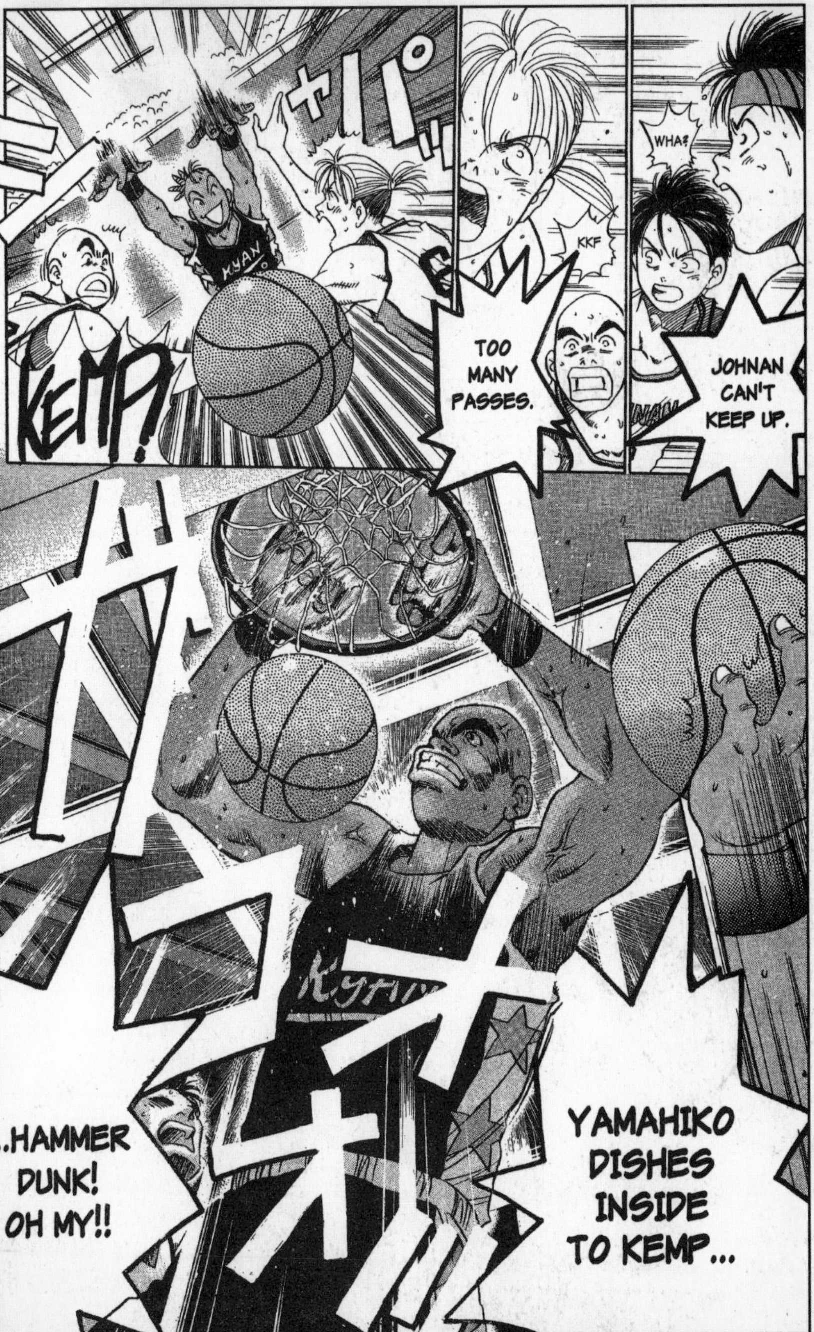
WHA?
JOHNAN CAN'T KEEP UP.
KKF
TOO MANY PASSES.
KEMP!
YAMAHIKO DISHES INSIDE TO KEMP...
.HAMMER DUNK! OH MY!!

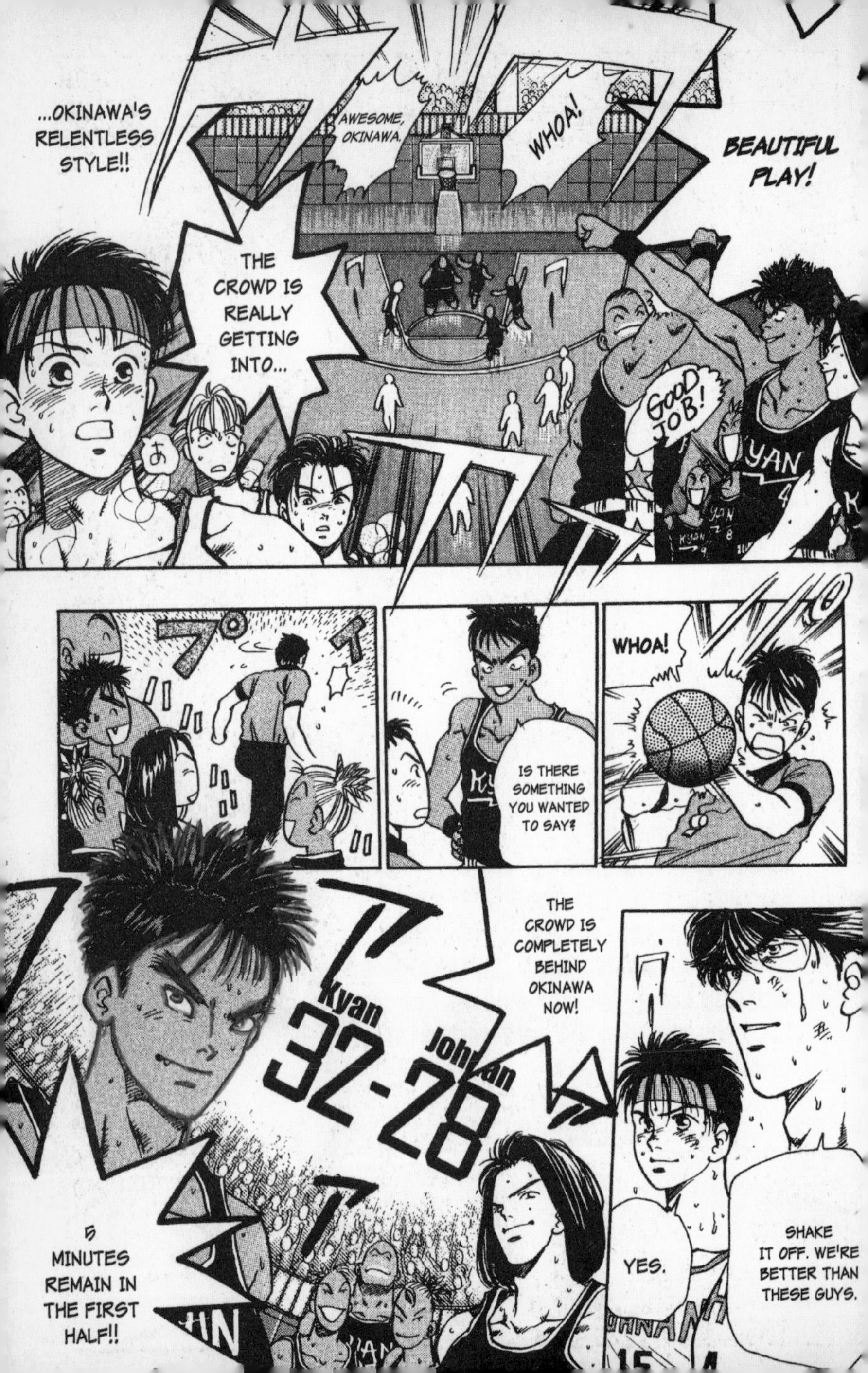
BEAUTIFUL PLAY!
WHOA!
AWESOME, OKINAWA.
GOOD JOB!
THE CROWD IS REALLY GETTING INTO...
...OKINAWA'S RELENTLESS STYLE!!
あ
WHOA!
IS THERE SOMETHING YOU WANTED TO SAY?
プイ
SHAKE IT OFF. WE'RE BETTER THAN THESE GUYS.
YES.
THE CROWD IS COMPLETELY BEHIND OKINAWA NOW!
Kyan 32-28 Johnan
5 MINUTES REMAIN IN THE FIRST HALF!!

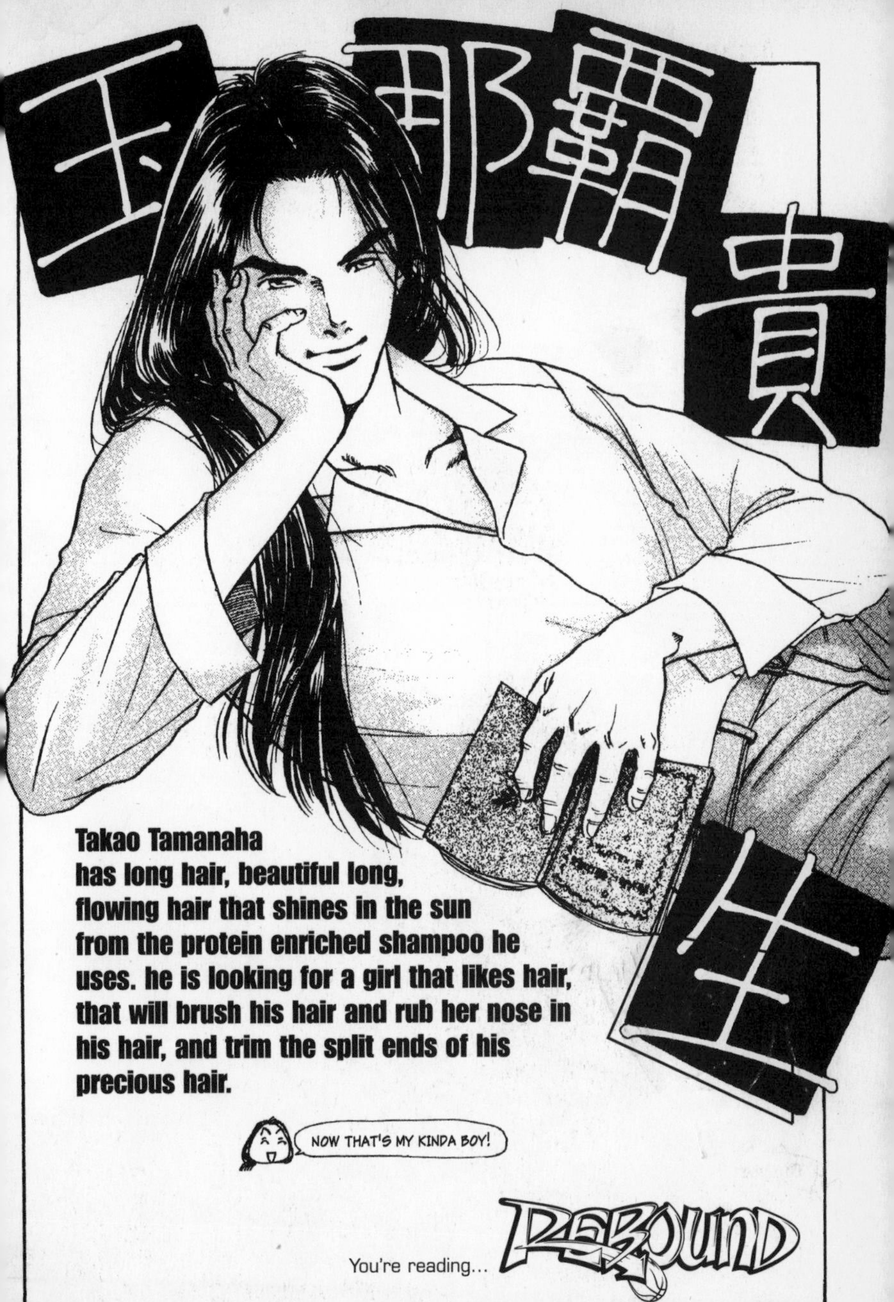
玉那覇貴生
Takao Tamanaha
has long hair, beautiful long, flowing hair that shines in the sun from the protein enriched shampoo he uses. he is looking for a girl that likes hair, that will brush his hair and rub her nose in his hair, and trim the split ends of his precious hair.
NOW THAT'S MY KINDA BOY!
You're reading... REBOUND

REBOUND

Episode 12: Tsunami Offense

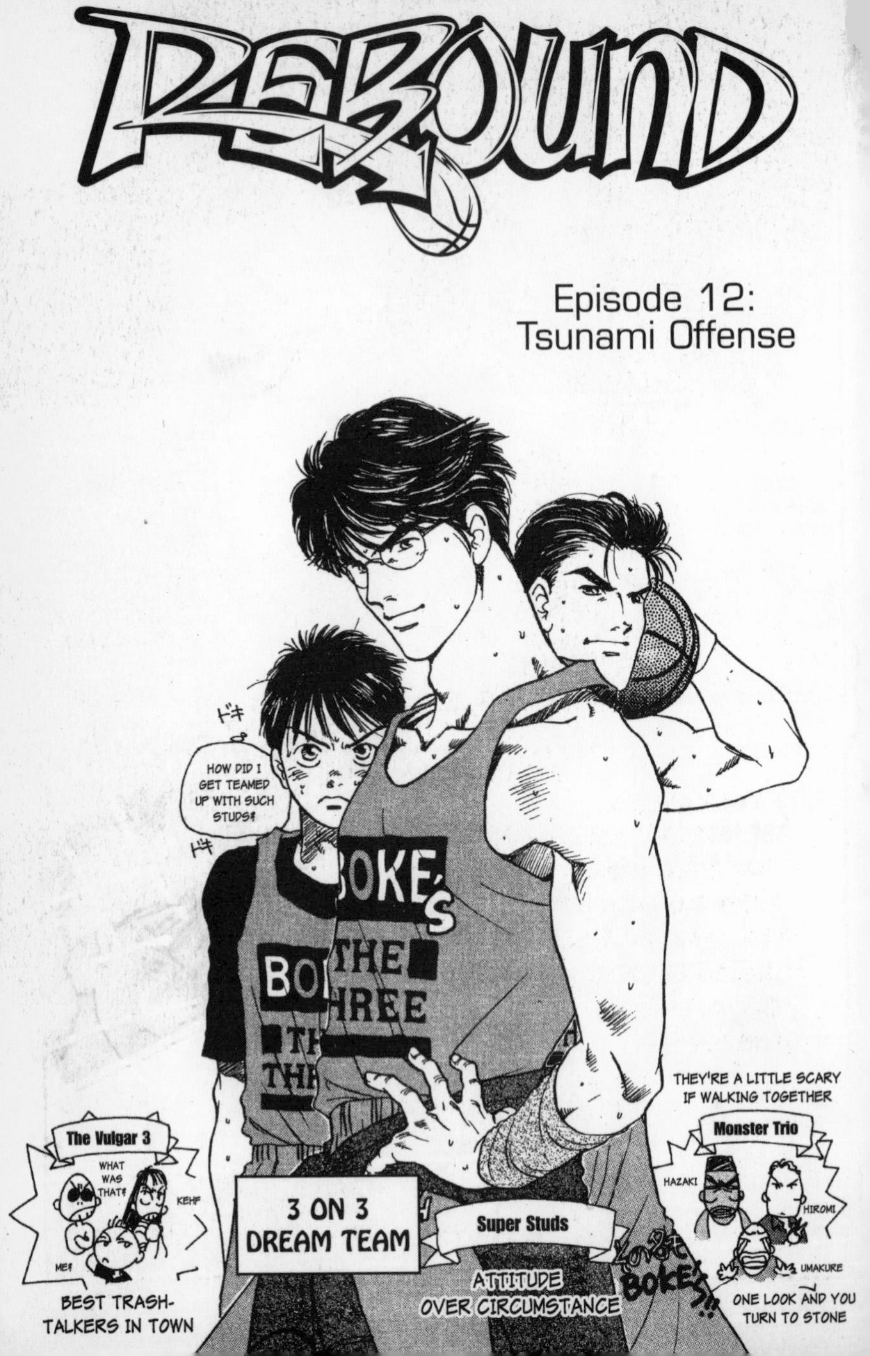
ドキ
HOW DID I GET TEAMED UP WITH SUCH STUDS!?
ドキ
BOKE'S THE THREE
THEY'RE A LITTLE SCARY IF WALKING TOGETHER
Monster Trio
HAZAKI
HIROMI
UMAKURE
ONE LOOK AND YOU TURN TO STONE
BOKE'S!!
3 ON 3 DREAM TEAM
Super Studs
ATTITUDE OVER CIRCUMSTANCE
The Vulgar 3
WHAT WAS THAT!?
KEHF
ME!?
BEST TRASH-TALKERS IN TOWN

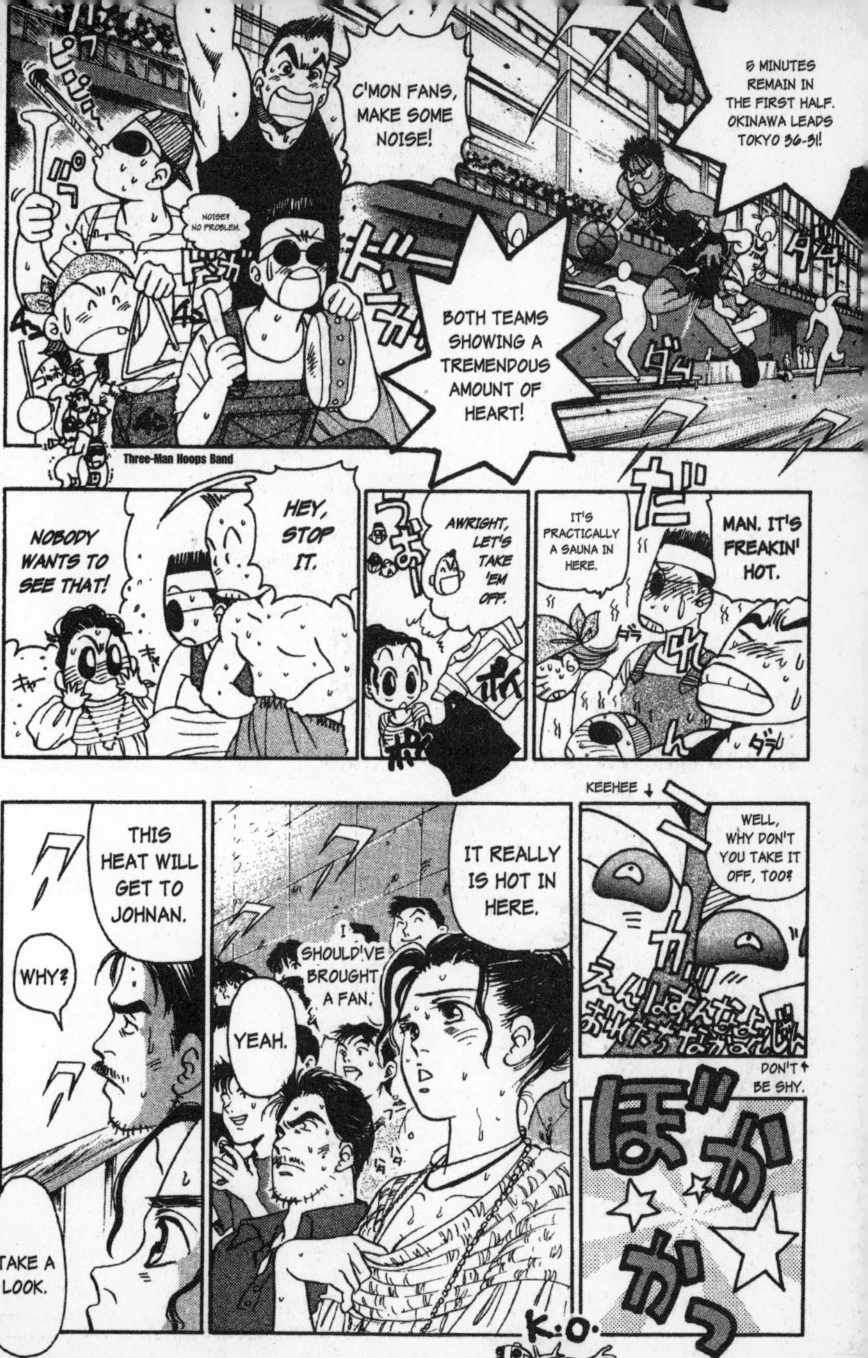
5 MINUTES REMAIN IN THE FIRST HALF. OKINAWA LEADS TOKYO 36-31!
C'MON FANS, MAKE SOME NOISE!
NOISE? NO PROBLEM.
BOTH TEAMS SHOWING A TREMENDOUS AMOUNT OF HEART!
Three-Man Hoops Band
MAN. IT'S FREAKIN' HOT.
IT'S PRACTICALLY A SAUNA IN HERE.
AWRIGHT, LET'S TAKE 'EM OFF.
HEY, STOP IT.
NOBODY WANTS TO SEE THAT!
KEEHEE
WELL, WHY DON'T YOU TAKE IT OFF, TOO?
DON'T BE SHY.
K.O.
IT REALLY IS HOT IN HERE.
I SHOULD'VE BROUGHT A FAN.
YEAH.
THIS HEAT WILL GET TO JOHNAN.
WHY?
TAKE A LOOK.

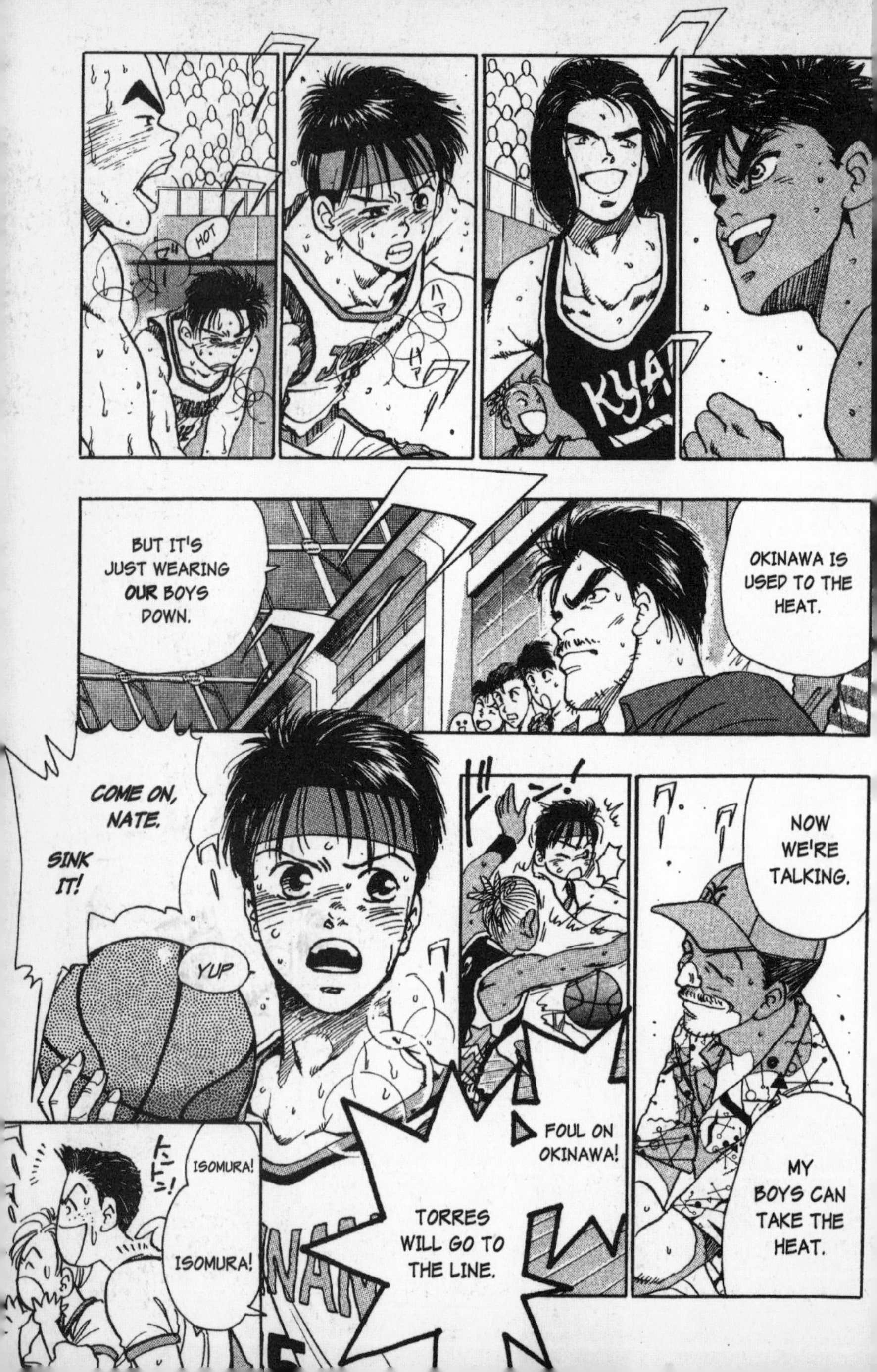
HOT
OKINAWA IS USED TO THE HEAT.
BUT IT'S JUST WEARING OUR BOYS DOWN.
NOW WE'RE TALKING.
MY BOYS CAN TAKE THE HEAT.
FOUL ON OKINAWA!
TORRES WILL GO TO THE LINE.
COME ON, NATE.
SINK IT!
YUP
ISOMURA!
ISOMURA!

We finally see faculty advisor Nishimae.

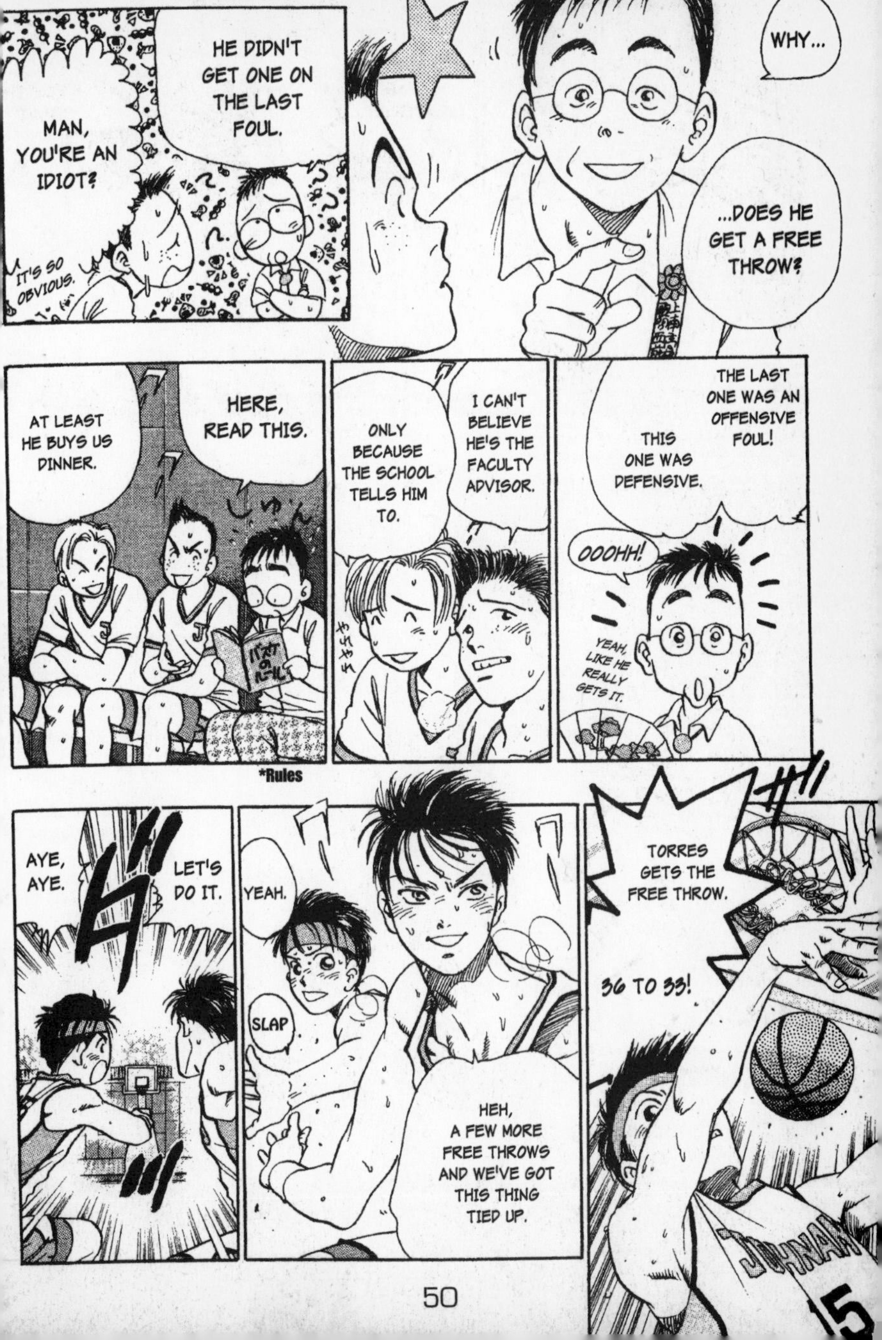
WHY...
...DOES HE GET A FREE THROW?
HE DIDN'T GET ONE ON THE LAST FOUL.
MAN, YOU'RE AN IDIOT?
IT'S SO OBVIOUS.
THE LAST ONE WAS AN OFFENSIVE FOUL!
THIS ONE WAS DEFENSIVE.
OOOHH!
YEAH, LIKE HE REALLY GETS IT.
I CAN'T BELIEVE HE'S THE FACULTY ADVISOR.
ONLY BECAUSE THE SCHOOL TELLS HIM TO.
HERE, READ THIS.
AT LEAST HE BUYS US DINNER.
TORRES GETS THE FREE THROW.
36 TO 33!
YEAH.
SLAP
HEH, A FEW MORE FREE THROWS AND WE'VE GOT THIS THING TIED UP.
LET'S DO IT.
AYE, AYE.

*Rules

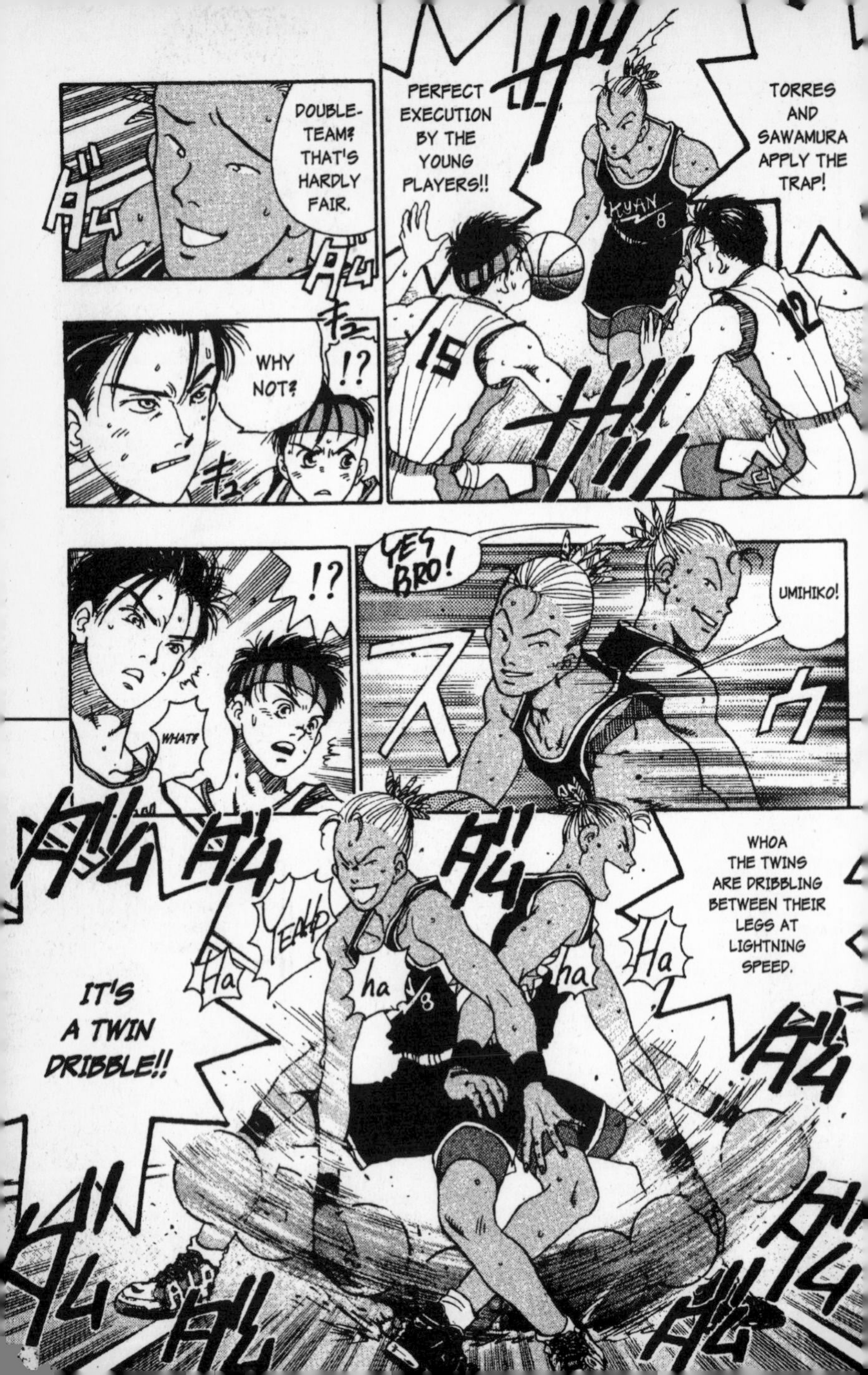
TORRES AND SAWAMURA APPLY THE TRAP!
PERFECT EXECUTION BY THE YOUNG PLAYERS!!
DOUBLE-TEAM? THAT'S HARDLY FAIR.
!?
WHY NOT?
UMIHIKO!
YES BRO!
!?
WHAT?
WHOA THE TWINS ARE DRIBBLING BETWEEN THEIR LEGS AT LIGHTNING SPEED.
Ha
ha
ha
YEAH
Ha
IT'S A TWIN DRIBBLE!!

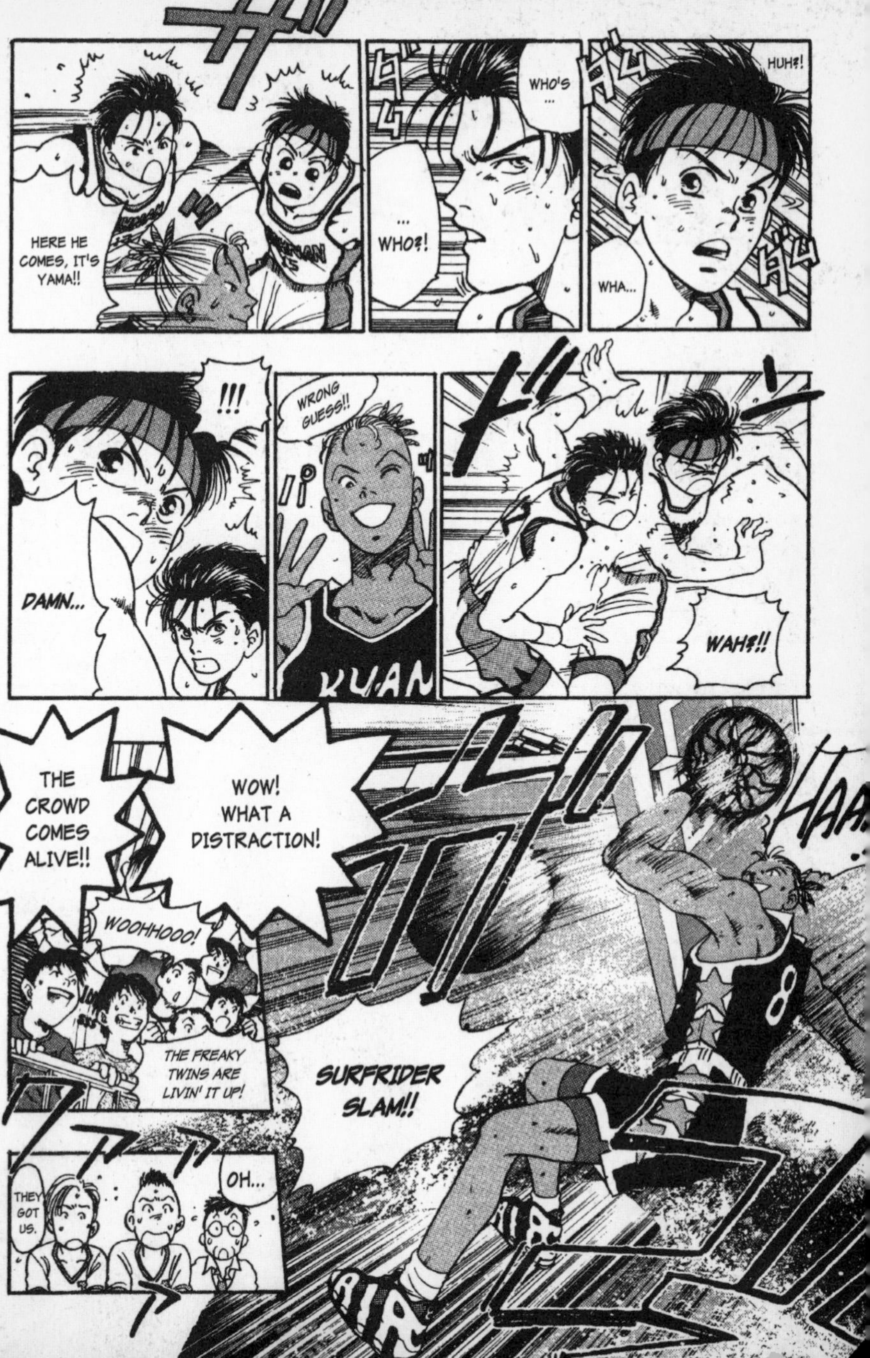
HUH?!
WHA...
WHO'S ...
... WHO?!
HERE HE COMES, IT'S YAMA!!
WAH?!!
WRONG GUESS!!
!!!
DAMN...
WOW! WHAT A DISTRACTION!
THE CROWD COMES ALIVE!!
WOOHHOOO!
THE FREAKY TWINS ARE LIVIN' IT UP!
SURFRIDER SLAM!!
OH...
THEY GOT US.

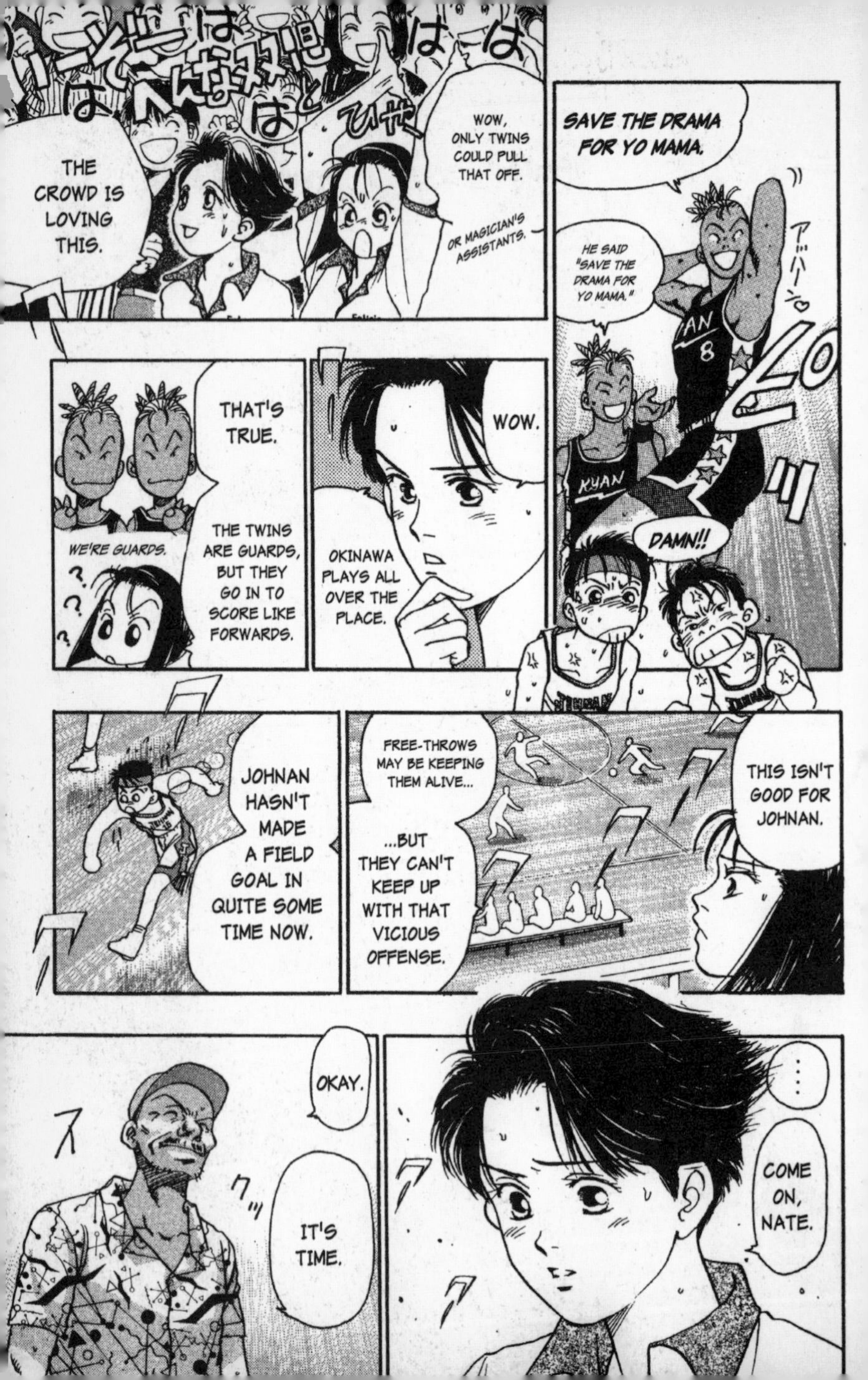
SAVE THE DRAMA FOR YO MAMA.
HE SAID "SAVE THE DRAMA FOR YO MAMA."
DAMN!!
WOW, ONLY TWINS COULD PULL THAT OFF.
OR MAGICIAN'S ASSISTANTS.
THE CROWD IS LOVING THIS.
WOW.
OKINAWA PLAYS ALL OVER THE PLACE.
THAT'S TRUE.
THE TWINS ARE GUARDS, BUT THEY GO IN TO SCORE LIKE FORWARDS.
WE'RE GUARDS.
THIS ISN'T GOOD FOR JOHNAN.
FREE-THROWS MAY BE KEEPING THEM ALIVE...
...BUT THEY CAN'T KEEP UP WITH THAT VICIOUS OFFENSE.
JOHNAN HASN'T MADE A FIELD GOAL IN QUITE SOME TIME NOW.
......
COME ON, NATE.
OKAY.
IT'S TIME.

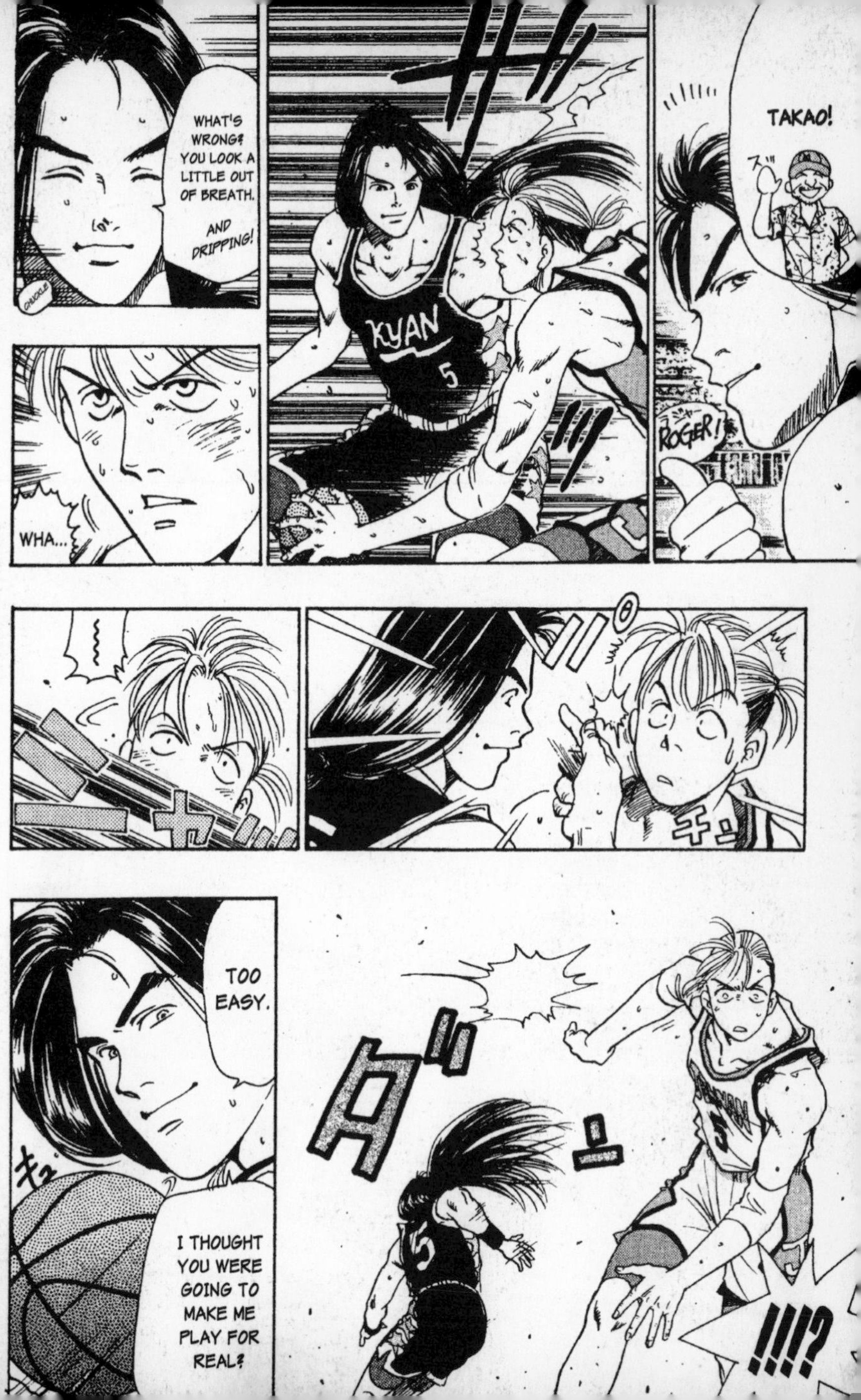
TAKAO!
ROGER!
WHAT'S WRONG? YOU LOOK A LITTLE OUT OF BREATH.
AND DRIPPING!
CHUCKLE
WHA...
!!!?
TOO EASY.
I THOUGHT YOU WERE GOING TO MAKE ME PLAY FOR REAL?

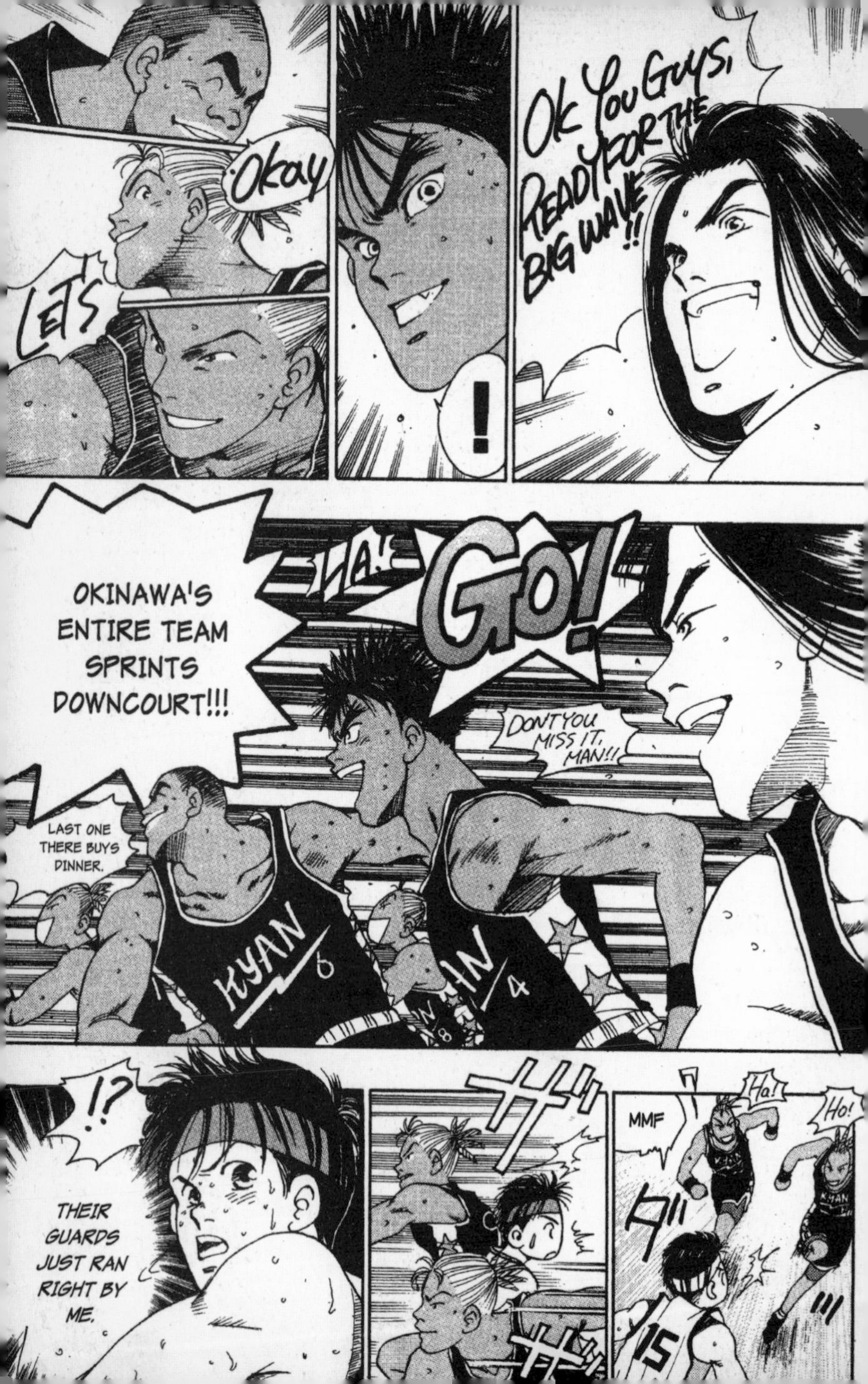
OK YOU GUYS, READY FOR THE BIG WAVE!!
!
Okay
LET'S
HA!
GO!!
DON'T YOU MISS IT, MAN!!
OKINAWA'S ENTIRE TEAM SPRINTS DOWNCOURT!!!
LAST ONE THERE BUYS DINNER.
Ho!
Ha!
MMF
!?
THEIR GUARDS JUST RAN RIGHT BY ME.

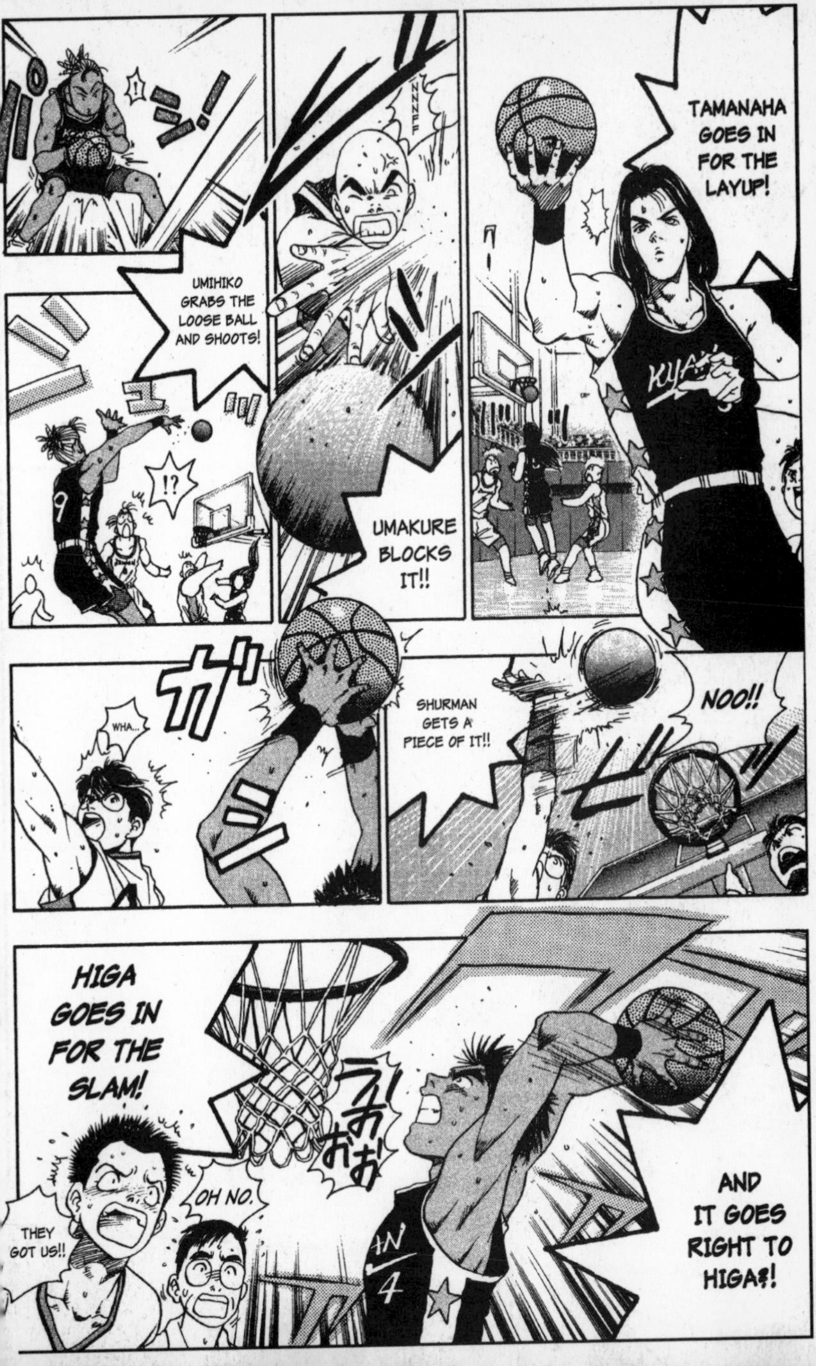
TAMANAHA GOES IN FOR THE LAYUP!
NNNFF
UMAKURE BLOCKS IT!!
!
UMIHIKO GRABS THE LOOSE BALL AND SHOOTS!
!?
SHURMAN GETS A PIECE OF IT!!
NOO!!
WHA...
AND IT GOES RIGHT TO HIGA?!
HIGA GOES IN FOR THE SLAM!
OH NO.
THEY GOT US!!

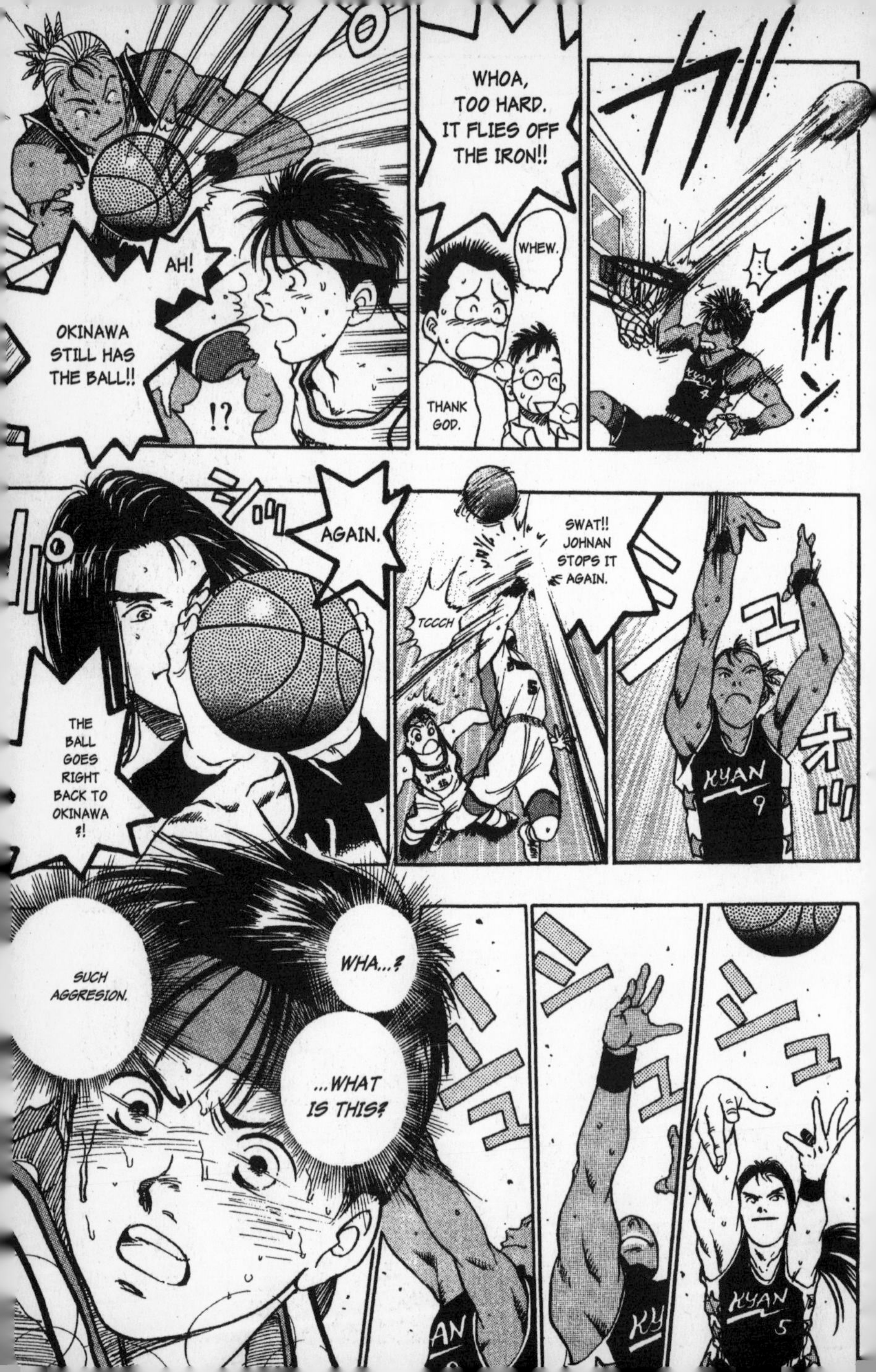
WHOA, TOO HARD. IT FLIES OFF THE IRON!!
WHEW.
THANK GOD.
AH!
OKINAWA STILL HAS THE BALL!!
!?
SWAT!! JOHNAN STOPS IT AGAIN.
TCCCH
AGAIN.
THE BALL GOES RIGHT BACK TO OKINAWA ?!
WHA...?
...WHAT IS THIS?
SUCH AGGRESION.

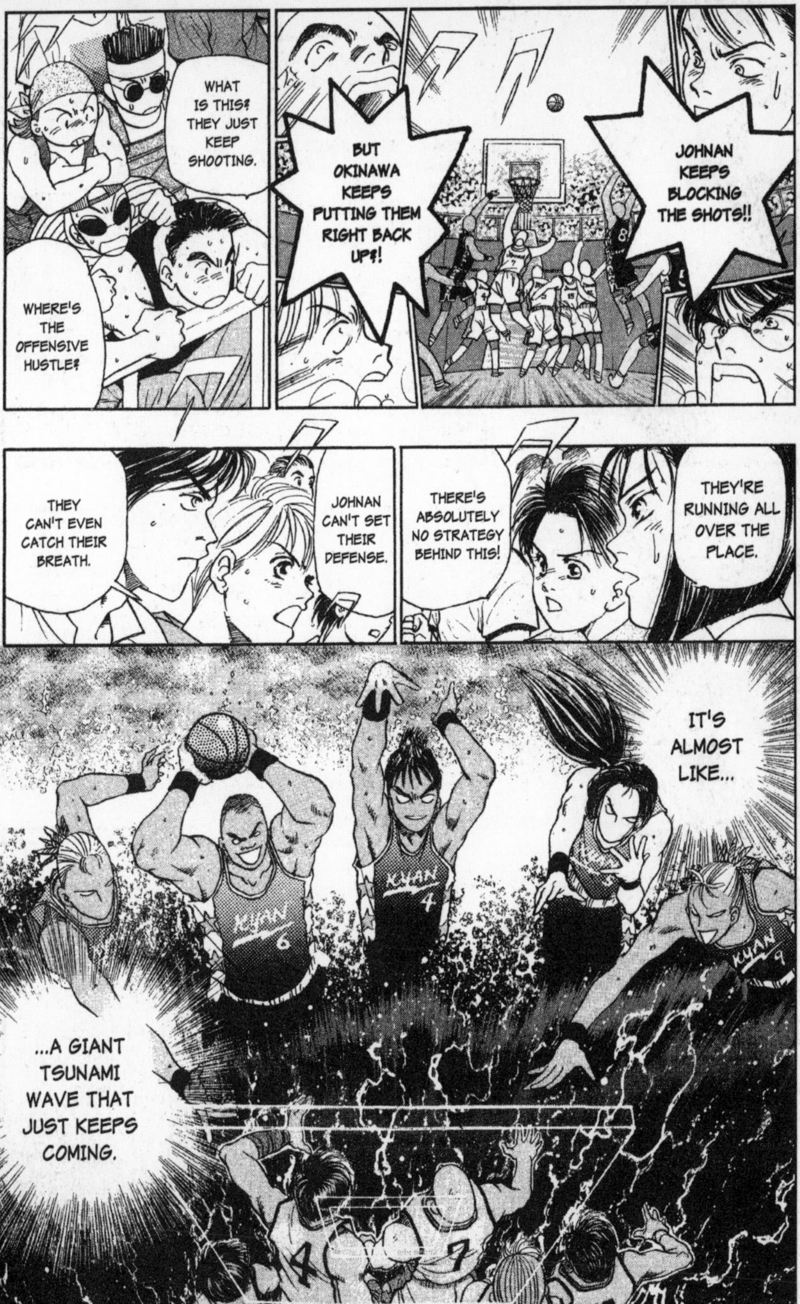
JOHNAN KEEPS BLOCKING THE SHOTS!!
BUT OKINAWA KEEPS PUTTING THEM RIGHT BACK UP?!
WHAT IS THIS? THEY JUST KEEP SHOOTING.
WHERE'S THE OFFENSIVE HUSTLE?
THEY'RE RUNNING ALL OVER THE PLACE.
THERE'S ABSOLUTELY NO STRATEGY BEHIND THIS!
JOHNAN CAN'T SET THEIR DEFENSE.
THEY CAN'T EVEN CATCH THEIR BREATH.
IT'S ALMOST LIKE...
...A GIANT TSUNAMI WAVE THAT JUST KEEPS COMING.

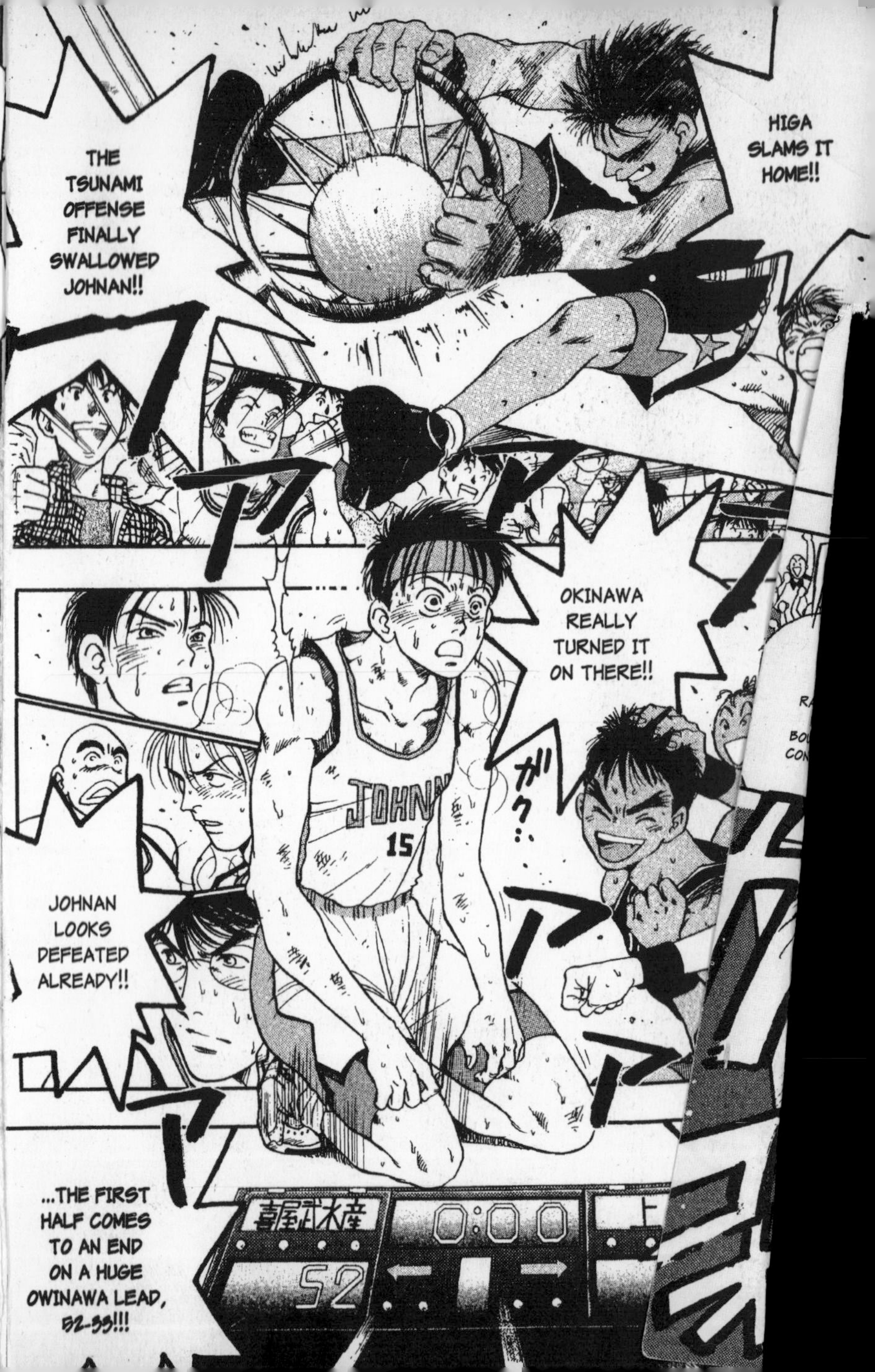
HIGA SLAMS IT HOME!!
THE TSUNAMI OFFENSE FINALLY SWALLOWED JOHNAN!!
OKINAWA REALLY TURNED IT ON THERE!!
JOHNAN LOOKS DEFEATED ALREADY!!
JOHNAN
15
...THE FIRST HALF COMES TO AN END ON A HUGE OWINAWA LEAD, 52-33!!!
喜屋武水産
0:00
上
52

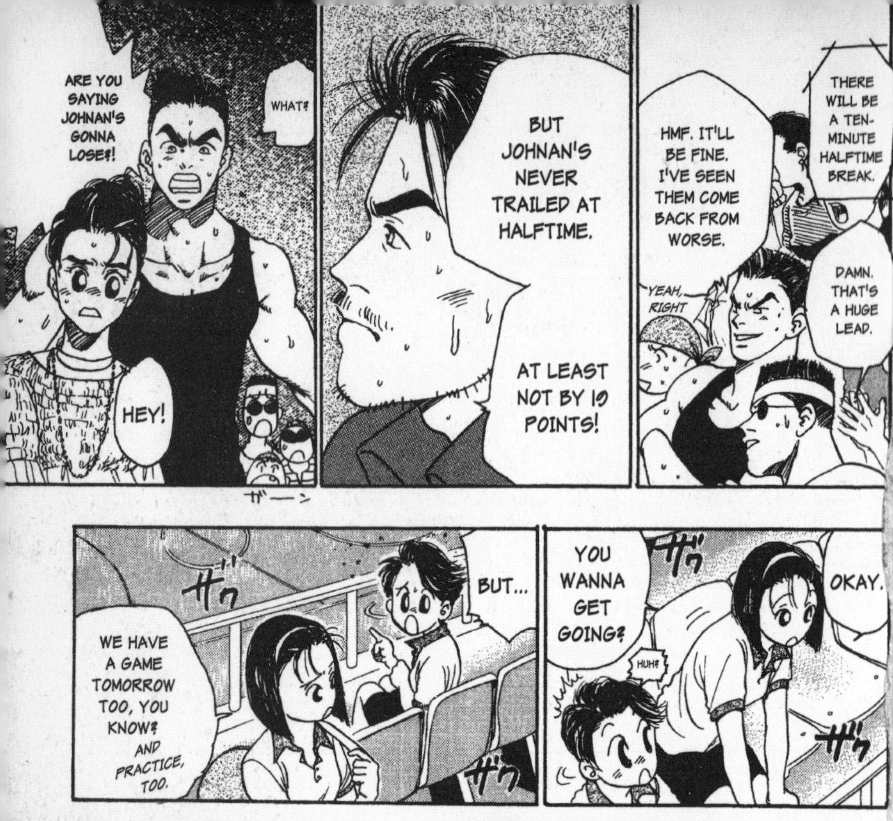
THERE WILL BE A TEN-MINUTE HALFTIME BREAK.
HMF. IT'LL BE FINE. I'VE SEEN THEM COME BACK FROM WORSE.
YEAH, RIGHT
DAMN. THAT'S A HUGE LEAD.
BUT JOHNAN'S NEVER TRAILED AT HALFTIME.
AT LEAST NOT BY 19 POINTS!
WHAT?
ARE YOU SAYING JOHNAN'S GONNA LOSE?!
HEY!
ガーン
OKAY.
YOU WANNA GET GOING?
HUH?
ザワ
ザワ
BUT...
WE HAVE A GAME TOMORROW TOO, YOU KNOW? AND PRACTICE, TOO.
ザワ

Sign: Locker Room Number 1, Sheet: Johnan High School

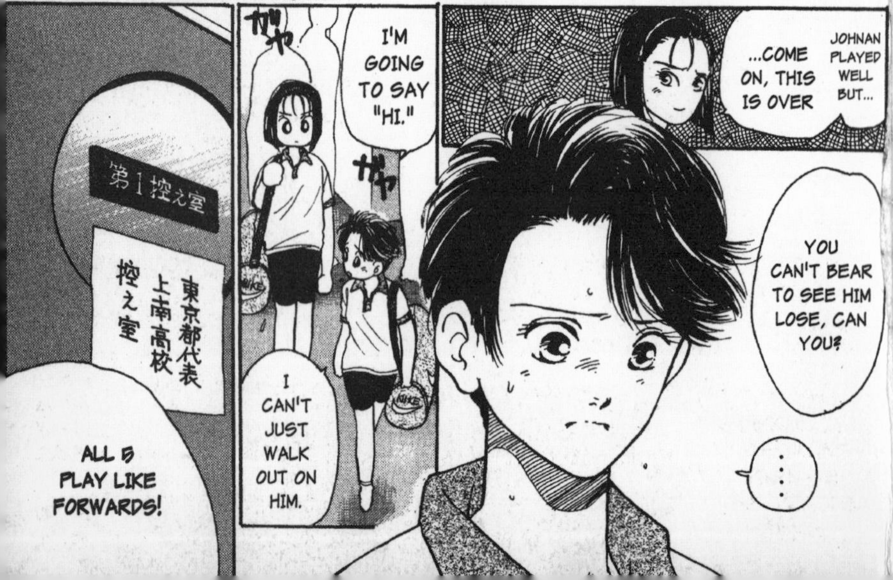
JOHNAN PLAYED WELL BUT...
...COME ON, THIS IS OVER
YOU CAN'T BEAR TO SEE HIM LOSE, CAN YOU?
...
I'M GOING TO SAY "HI."
I CAN'T JUST WALK OUT ON HIM.
第1控え室
東京都代表
上南高校
控え室
ALL 5 PLAY LIKE FORWARDS!

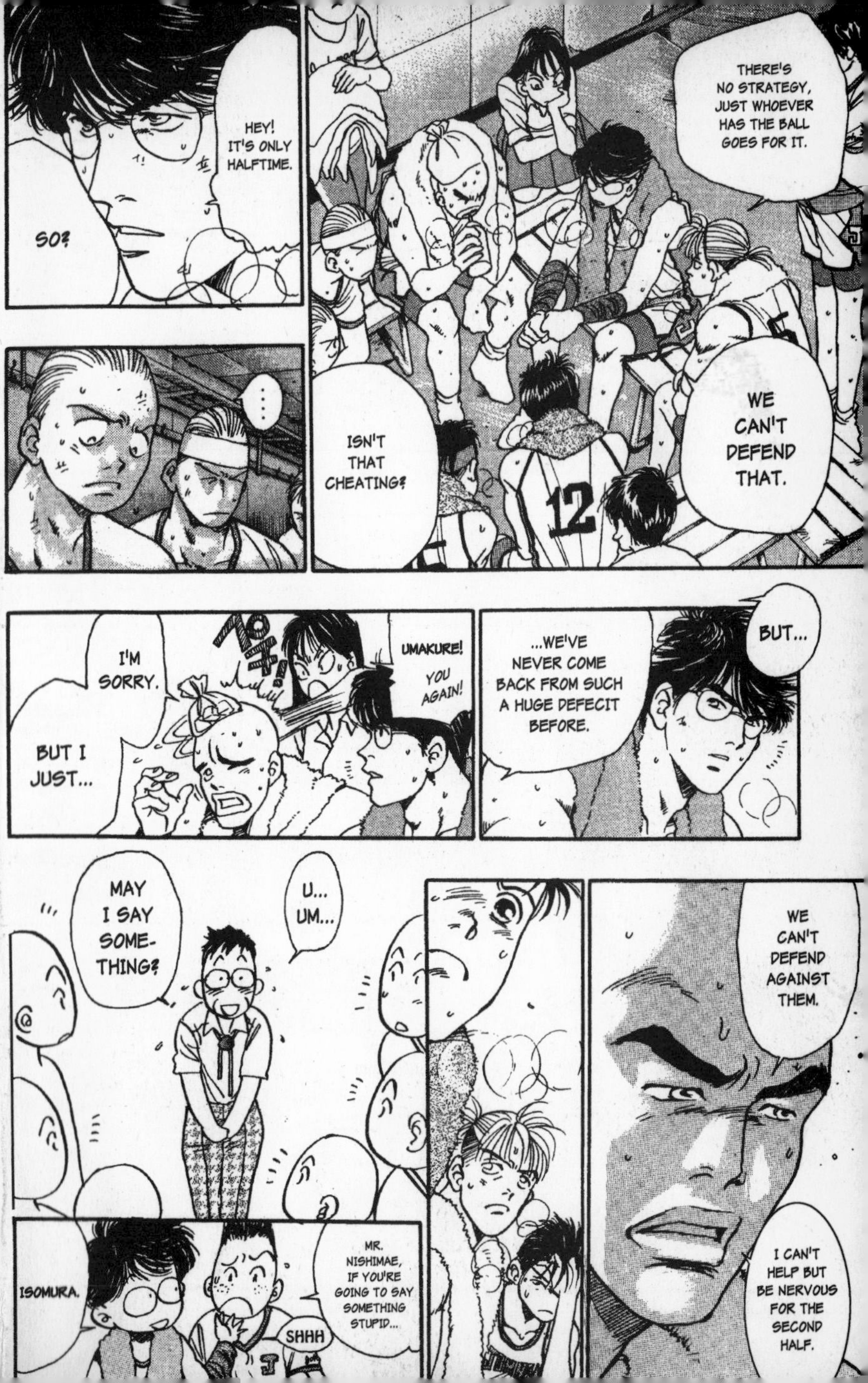
THERE'S NO STRATEGY, JUST WHOEVER HAS THE BALL GOES FOR IT.
WE CAN'T DEFEND THAT.
ISN'T THAT CHEATING?
HEY! IT'S ONLY HALFTIME.
SO?
...
BUT...
...WE'VE NEVER COME BACK FROM SUCH A HUGE DEFECIT BEFORE.
UMAKURE! YOU AGAIN!
I'M SORRY.
BUT I JUST...
WE CAN'T DEFEND AGAINST THEM.
I CAN'T HELP BUT BE NERVOUS FOR THE SECOND HALF.
U... UM...
MAY I SAY SOMETHING?
MR. NISHIMAE, IF YOU'RE GOING TO SAY SOMETHING STUPID...
SHHH
ISOMURA.
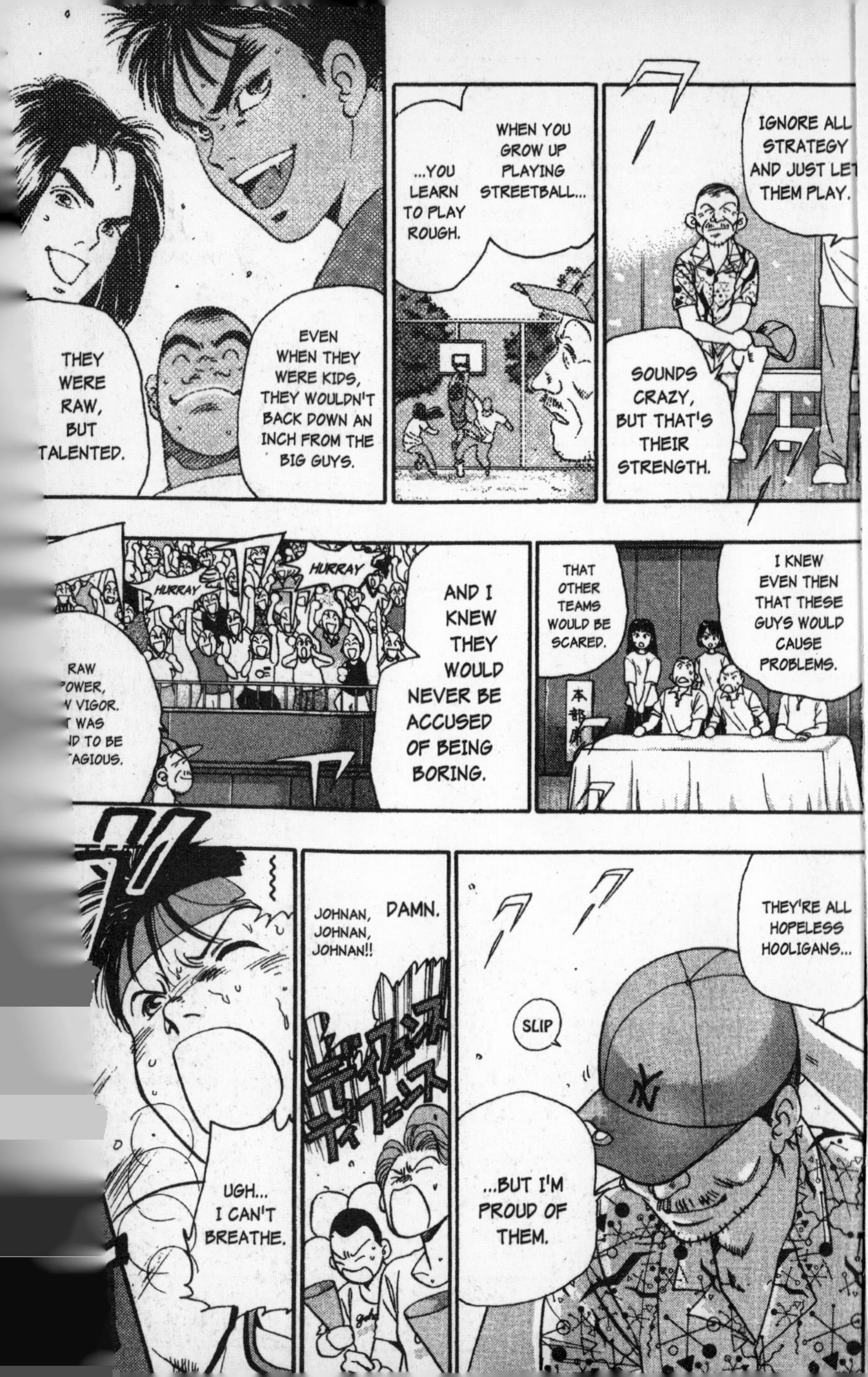
IGNORE ALL STRATEGY AND JUST LET THEM PLAY.
SOUNDS CRAZY, BUT THAT'S THEIR STRENGTH.
WHEN YOU GROW UP PLAYING STREETBALL...
...YOU LEARN TO PLAY ROUGH.
EVEN WHEN THEY WERE KIDS, THEY WOULDN'T BACK DOWN AN INCH FROM THE BIG GUYS.
THEY WERE RAW, BUT TALENTED.
I KNEW EVEN THEN THAT THESE GUYS WOULD CAUSE PROBLEMS.
THAT OTHER TEAMS WOULD BE SCARED.
AND I KNEW THEY WOULD NEVER BE ACCUSED OF BEING BORING.
HURRAY
HURRAY
RAW POWER,
THEY'RE ALL HOPELESS HOOLIGANS...
SLIP
...BUT I'M PROUD OF THEM.
DAMN.
JOHNAN, JOHNAN, JOHNAN!!
UGH... I CAN'T BREATHE.

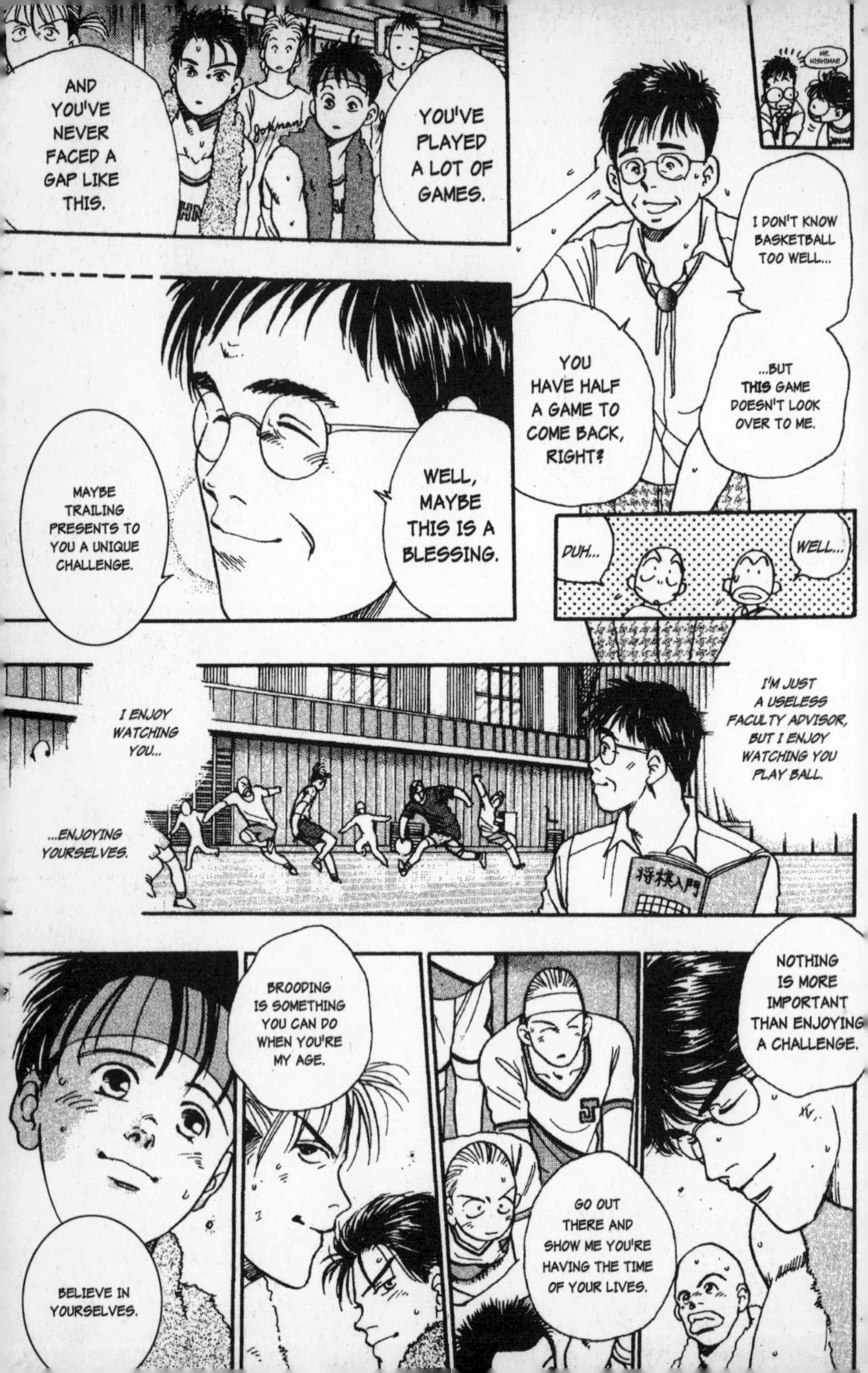
MR. NISHIMAE
I DON'T KNOW BASKETBALL TOO WELL...
...BUT THIS GAME DOESN'T LOOK OVER TO ME.
YOU HAVE HALF A GAME TO COME BACK, RIGHT?
WELL...
DUH...
YOU'VE PLAYED A LOT OF GAMES.
AND YOU'VE NEVER FACED A GAP LIKE THIS.
WELL, MAYBE THIS IS A BLESSING.
MAYBE TRAILING PRESENTS TO YOU A UNIQUE CHALLENGE.
I'M JUST A USELESS FACULTY ADVISOR, BUT I ENJOY WATCHING YOU PLAY BALL.
I ENJOY WATCHING YOU...
...ENJOYING YOURSELVES.
NOTHING IS MORE IMPORTANT THAN ENJOYING A CHALLENGE.
GO OUT THERE AND SHOW ME YOU'RE HAVING THE TIME OF YOUR LIVES.
BROODING IS SOMETHING YOU CAN DO WHEN YOU'RE MY AGE.
BELIEVE IN YOURSELVES.

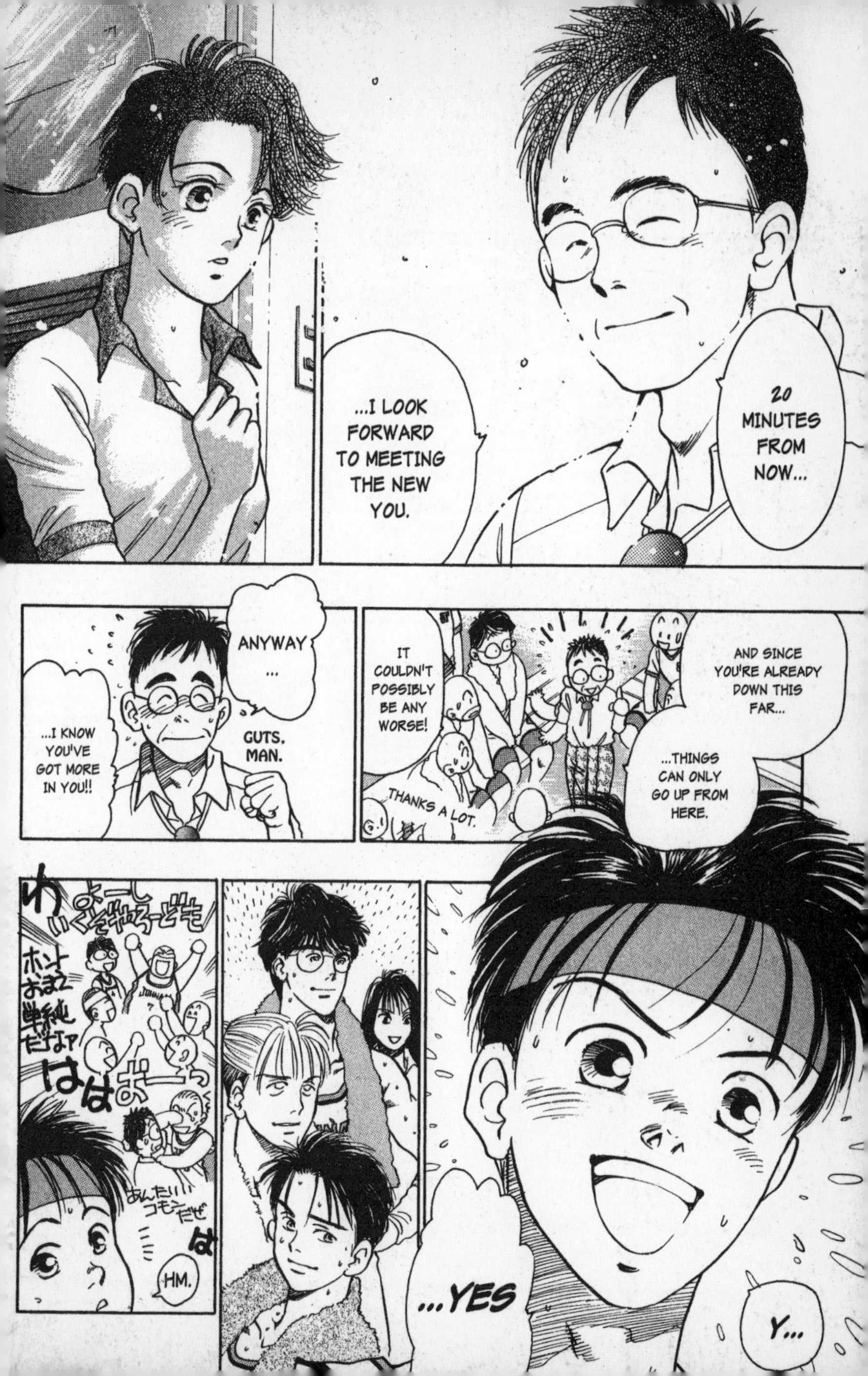
20 MINUTES FROM NOW...
...I LOOK FORWARD TO MEETING THE NEW YOU.
AND SINCE YOU'RE ALREADY DOWN THIS FAR...
...THINGS CAN ONLY GO UP FROM HERE.
IT COULDN'T POSSIBLY BE ANY WORSE!
THANKS A LOT.
ANYWAY ...
GUTS, MAN.
...I KNOW YOU'VE GOT MORE IN YOU!!
Y...
...YES
わ
よーし いくぞやろーども
ホント おまえ 単純だなァ
ははおーっ
あんたりコモンだぜ
な
HM.

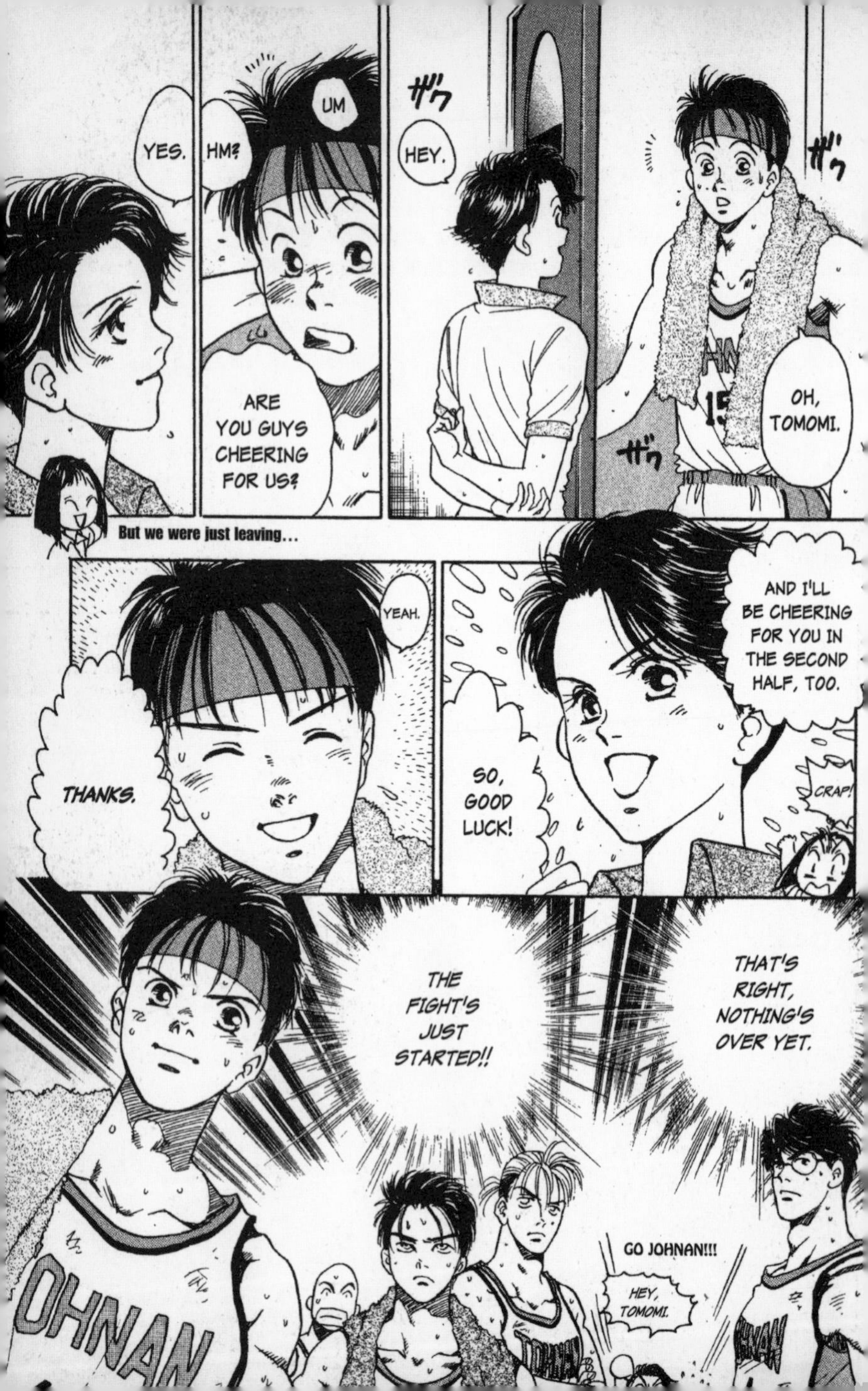

ザワ
OH, TOMOMI.
ザワ
ザワ
HEY.
UM
HM?
ARE YOU GUYS CHEERING FOR US?
YES.
But we were just leaving...
AND I'LL BE CHEERING FOR YOU IN THE SECOND HALF, TOO.
SO, GOOD LUCK!
CRAP!
YEAH.
THANKS.
THAT'S RIGHT, NOTHING'S OVER YET.
THE FIGHT'S JUST STARTED!!
GO JOHNAN!!!
HEY, TOMOMI.

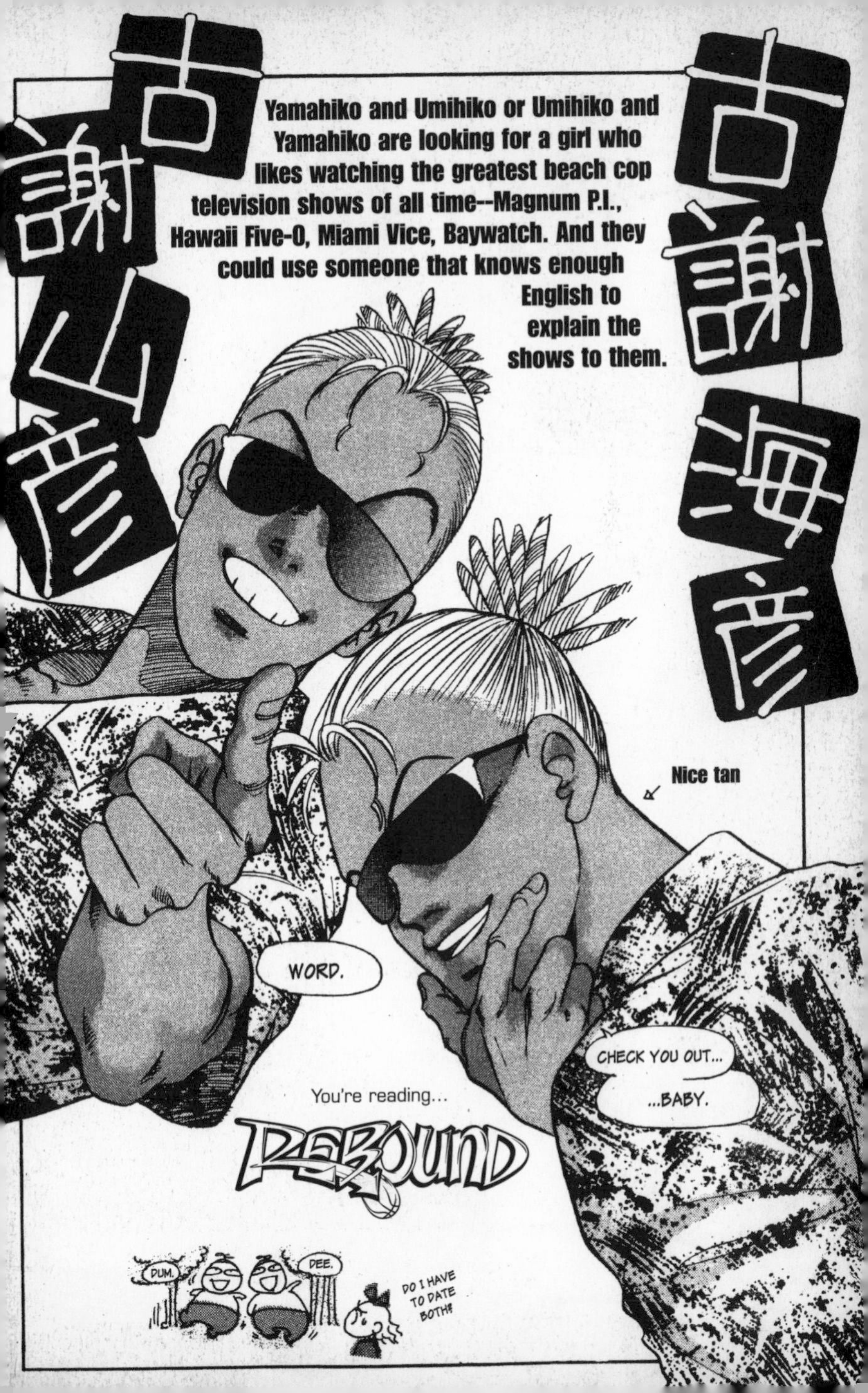
古謝海彦
古謝山彦
Yamahiko and Umihiko or Umihiko and Yamahiko are looking for a girl who likes watching the greatest beach cop television shows of all time--Magnum P.I., Hawaii Five-O, Miami Vice, Baywatch. And they could use someone that knows enough English to explain the shows to them.
Nice tan
WORD.
CHECK YOU OUT...
...BABY.
You're reading...
REBOUND
DUM.
DEE.
DO I HAVE TO DATE BOTH?

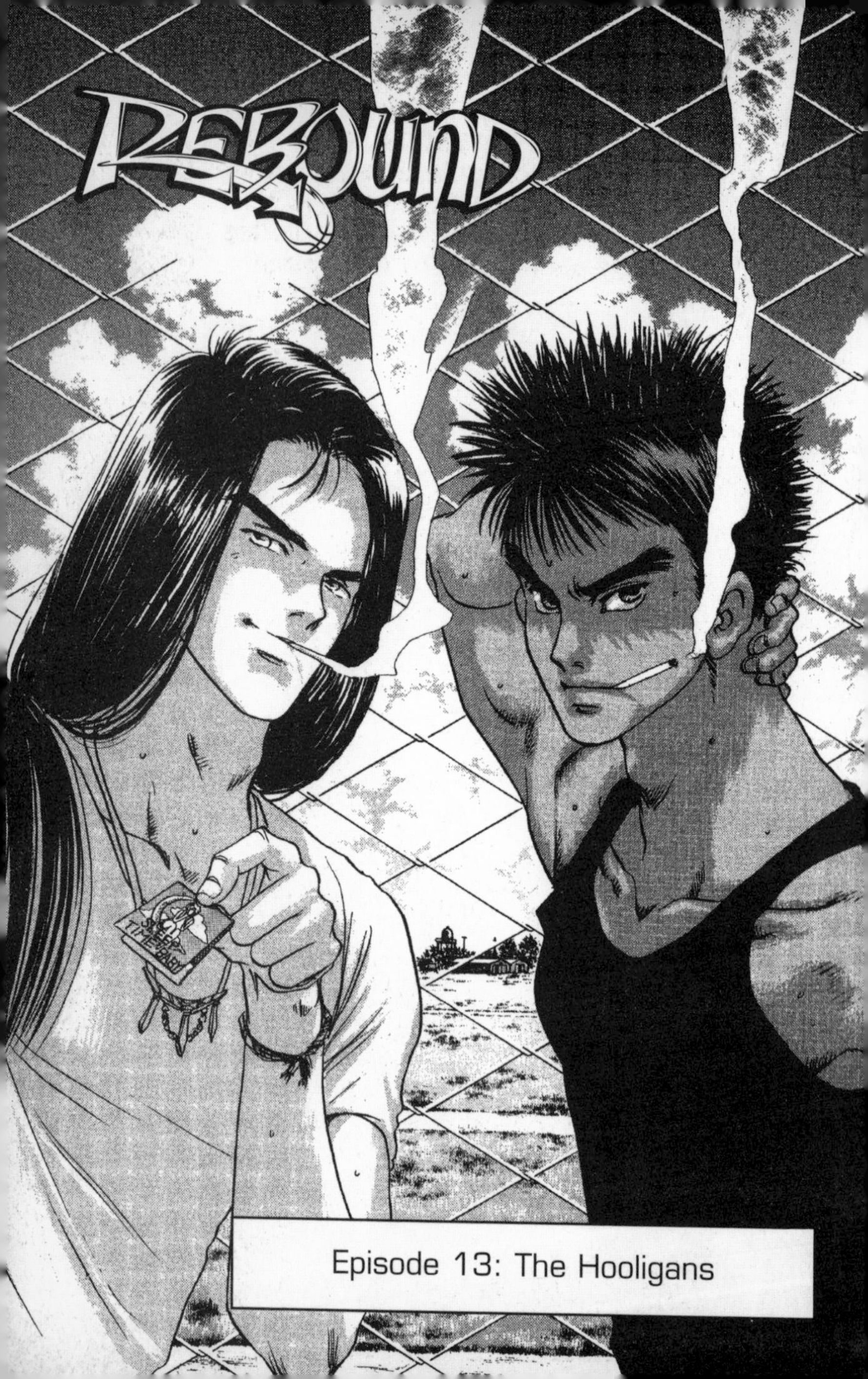
REBOUND
Episode 13: The Hooligans

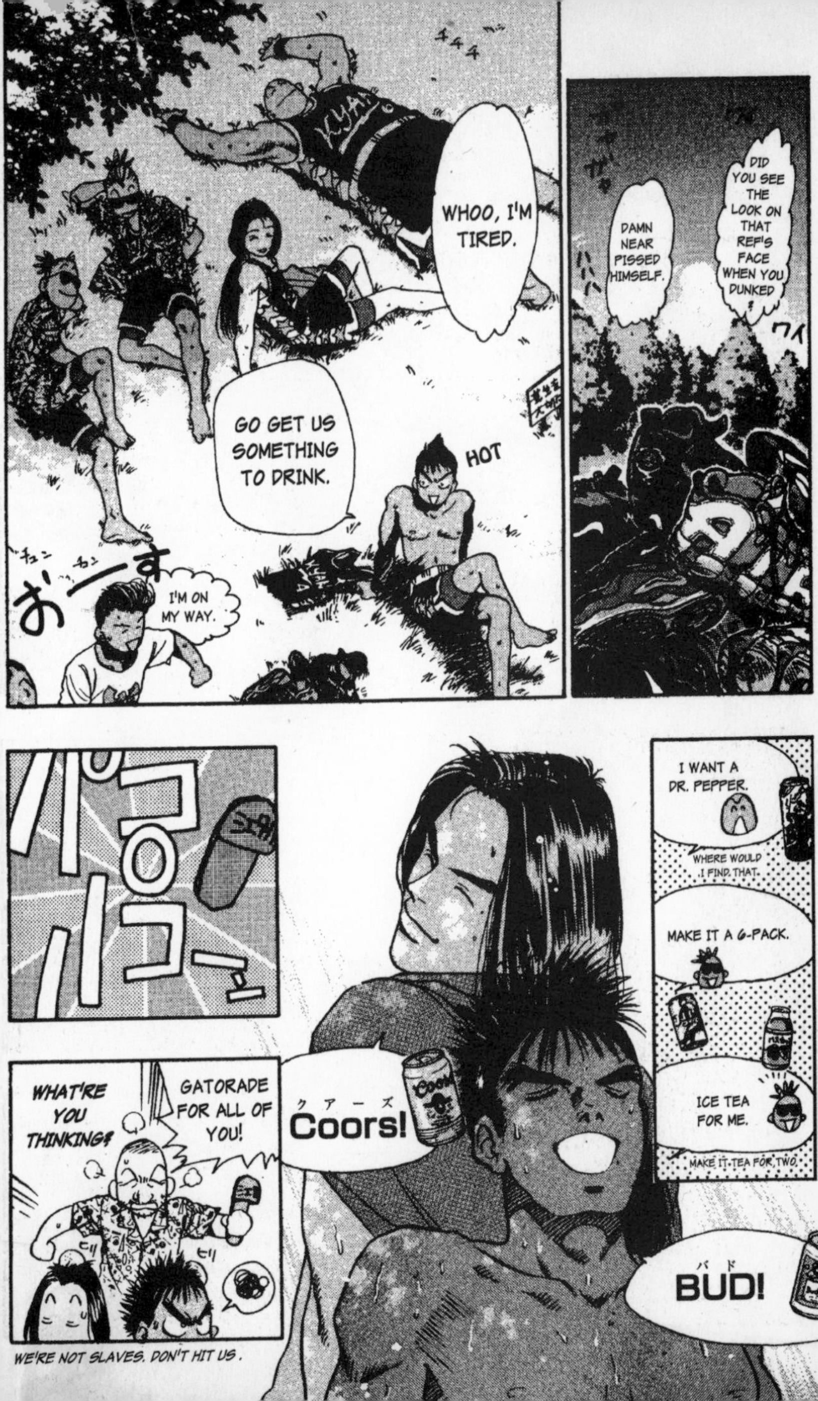
DID YOU SEE THE LOOK ON THAT REF'S FACE WHEN YOU DUNKED?
DAMN NEAR PISSED HIMSELF.
ワイ
WHOO, I'M TIRED.
GO GET US SOMETHING TO DRINK.
HOT
おーす
I'M ON MY WAY.
I WANT A DR. PEPPER.
WHERE WOULD I FIND THAT.
MAKE IT A 6-PACK.
ICE TEA FOR ME.
MAKE IT TEA FOR TWO.
クアーズ
Coors!
バド
BUD!
GATORADE FOR ALL OF YOU!
WHAT'RE YOU THINKING?
WE'RE NOT SLAVES. DON'T HIT US.

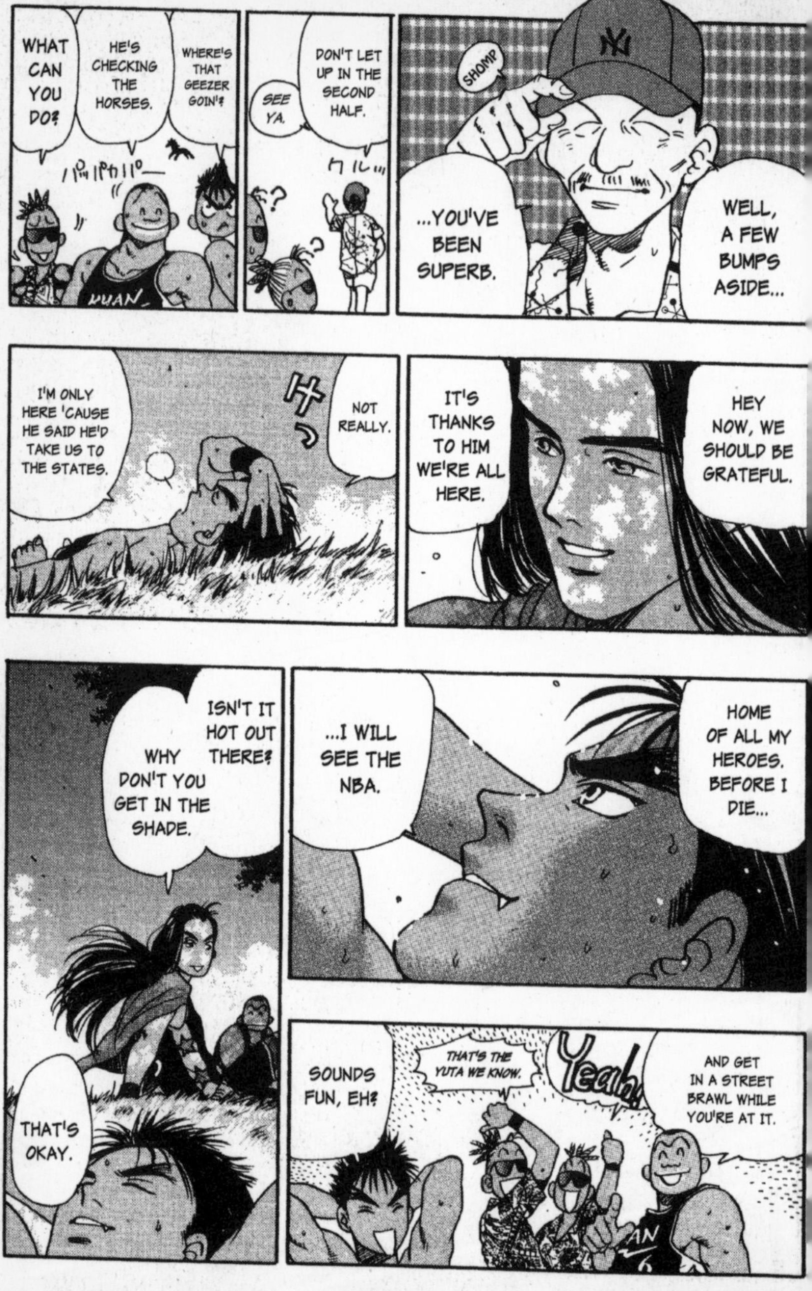
WELL, A FEW BUMPS ASIDE...
...YOU'VE BEEN SUPERB.
SHOMP
DON'T LET UP IN THE SECOND HALF.
SEE YA.
WHERE'S THAT GEEZER GOIN'?
HE'S CHECKING THE HORSES.
WHAT CAN YOU DO?
HEY NOW, WE SHOULD BE GRATEFUL.
IT'S THANKS TO HIM WE'RE ALL HERE.
NOT REALLY.
I'M ONLY HERE 'CAUSE HE SAID HE'D TAKE US TO THE STATES.
HOME OF ALL MY HEROES. BEFORE I DIE...
...I WILL SEE THE NBA.
AND GET IN A STREET BRAWL WHILE YOU'RE AT IT.
Yeah!
THAT'S THE YUTA WE KNOW.
SOUNDS FUN, EH?
ISN'T IT HOT OUT THERE?
WHY DON'T YOU GET IN THE SHADE.
THAT'S OKAY.

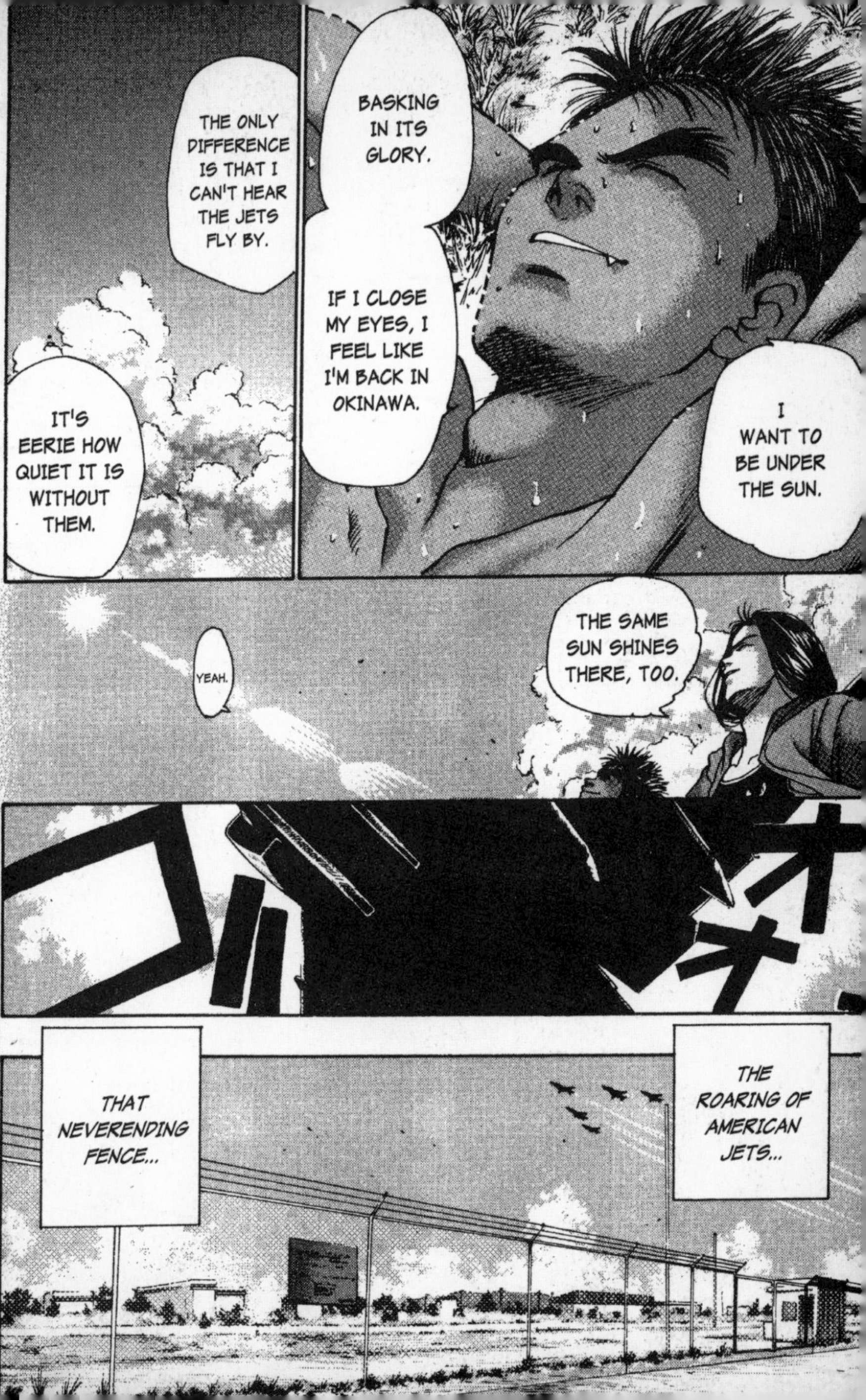
I WANT TO BE UNDER THE SUN.
BASKING IN ITS GLORY.
IF I CLOSE MY EYES, I FEEL LIKE I'M BACK IN OKINAWA.
THE ONLY DIFFERENCE IS THAT I CAN'T HEAR THE JETS FLY BY.
IT'S EERIE HOW QUIET IT IS WITHOUT THEM.
THE SAME SUN SHINES THERE, TOO.
YEAH.
ゴォォ
THE ROARING OF AMERICAN JETS...
THAT NEVERENDING FENCE...

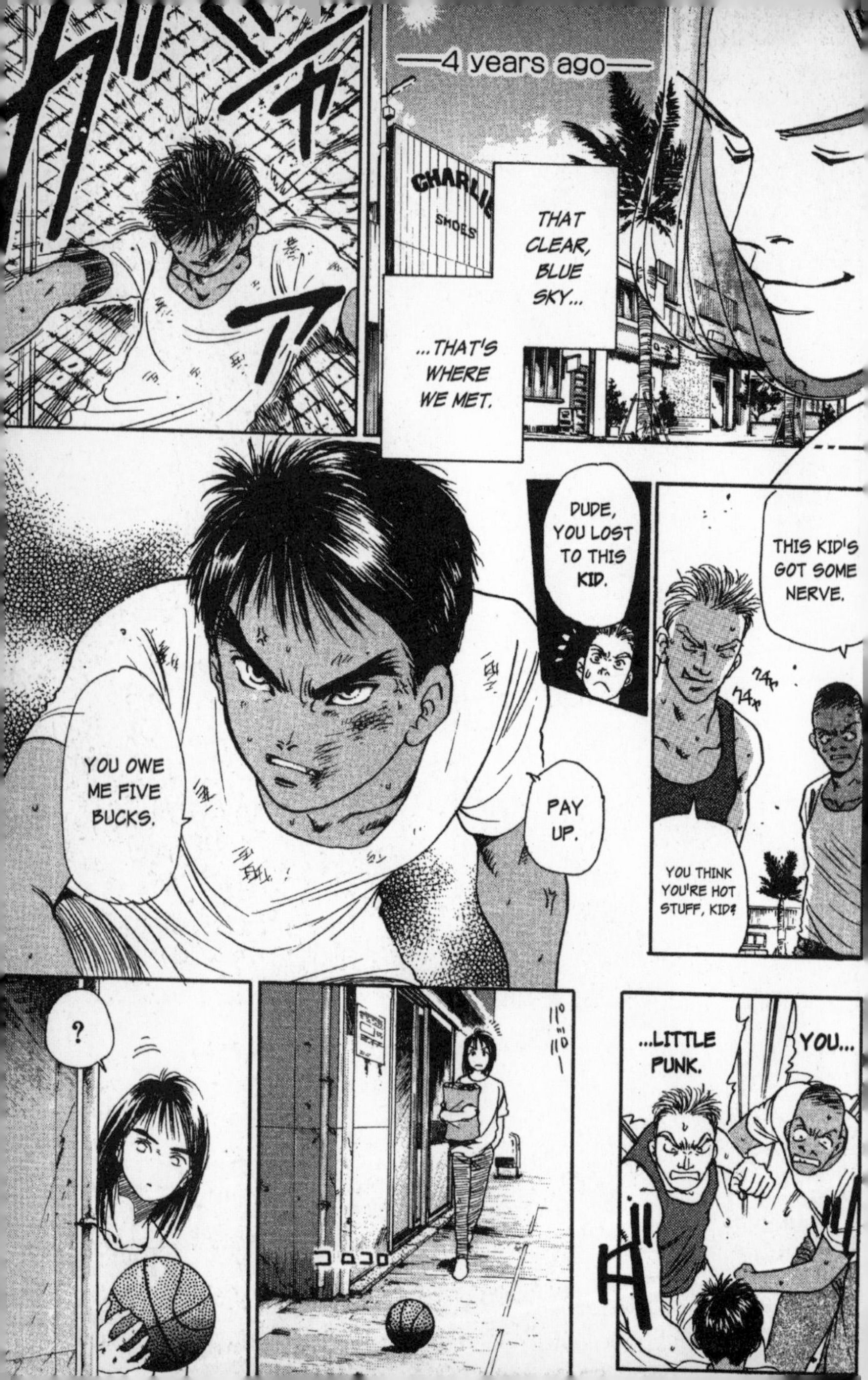
—4 years ago—
THAT CLEAR, BLUE SKY...
...THAT'S WHERE WE MET.
THIS KID'S GOT SOME NERVE.
YOU THINK YOU'RE HOT STUFF, KID?
DUDE, YOU LOST TO THIS KID.
PAY UP.
YOU OWE ME FIVE BUCKS.
YOU...
...LITTLE PUNK.
?

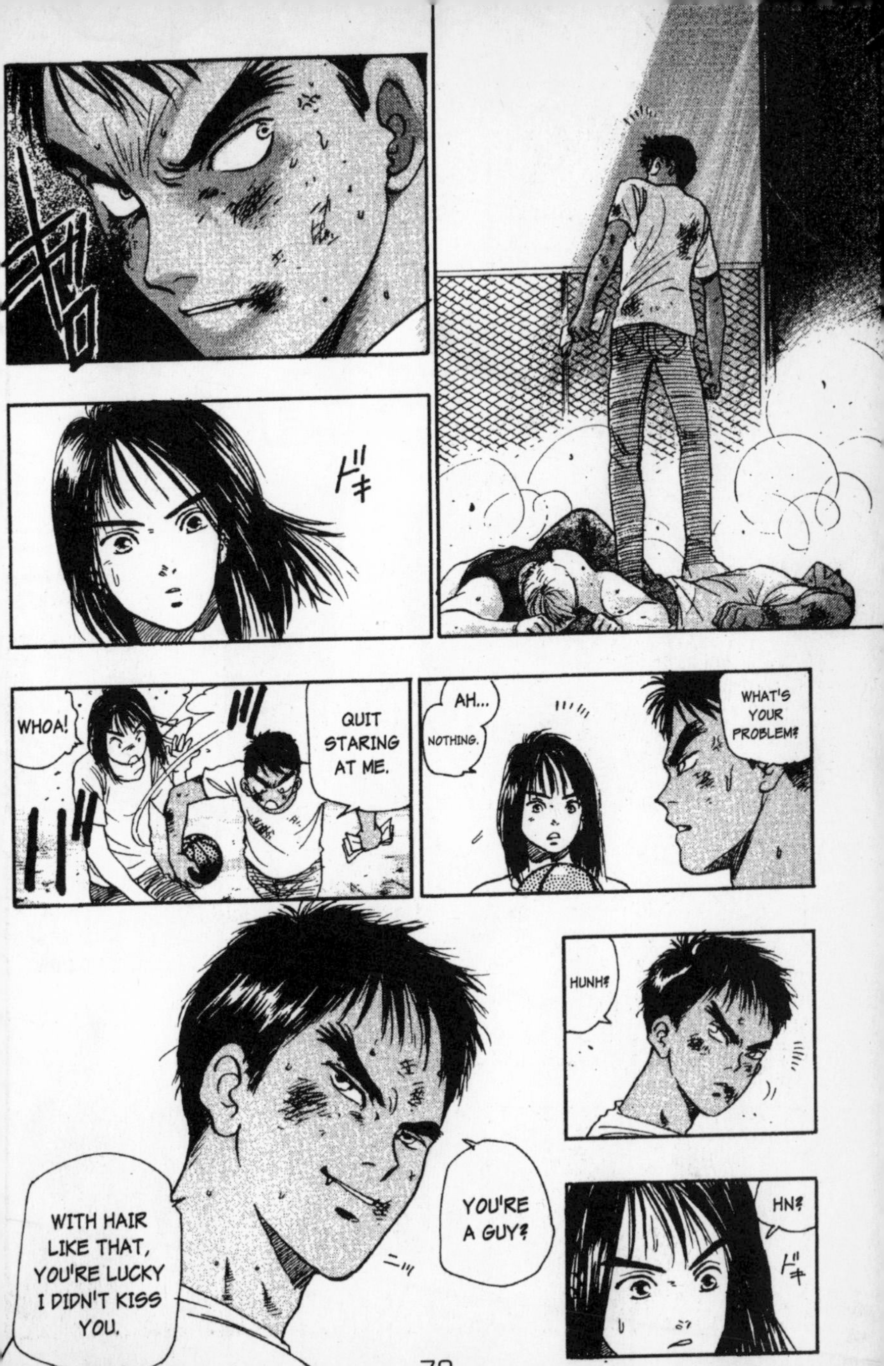
WHAT'S YOUR PROBLEM?
AH...
NOTHING.
QUIT STARING AT ME.
WHOA!
HUNH?
HN?
YOU'RE A GUY?
WITH HAIR LIKE THAT, YOU'RE LUCKY I DIDN'T KISS YOU.

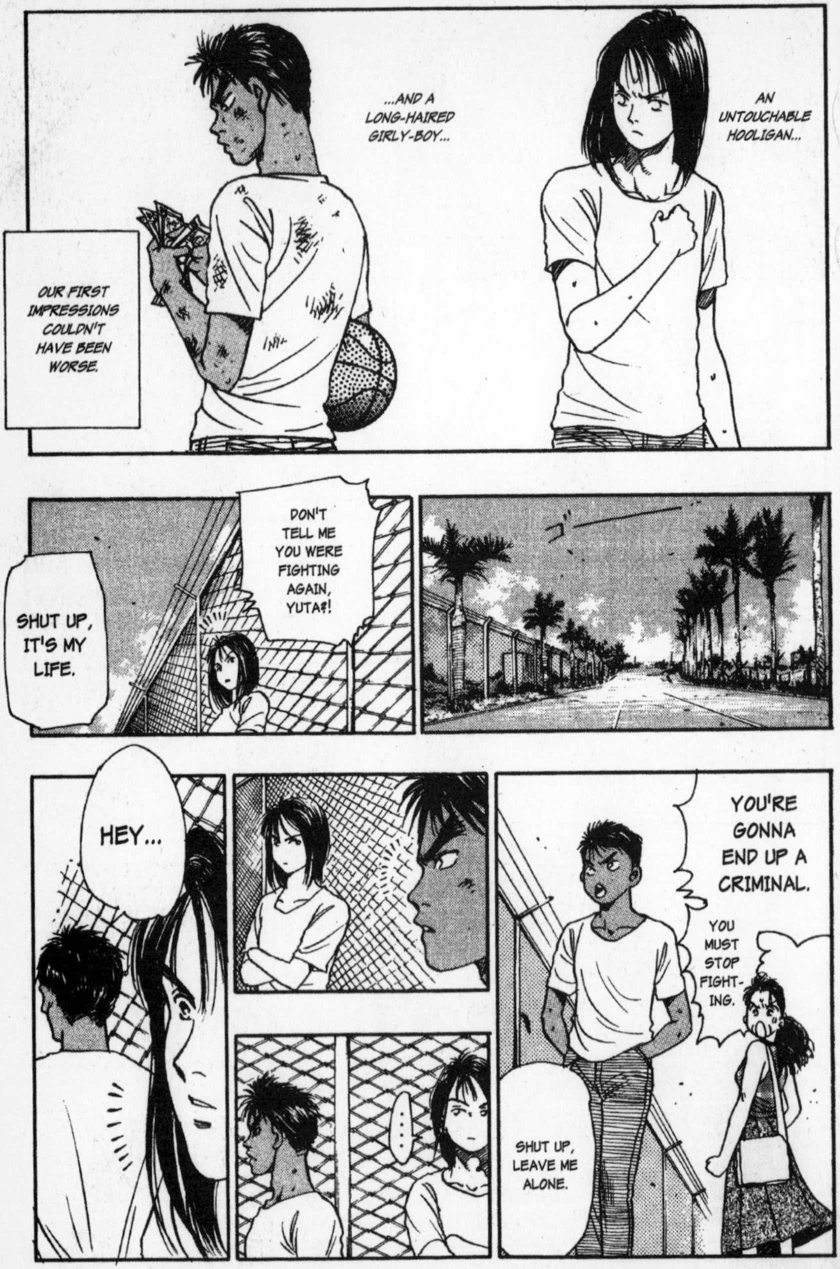
AN UNTOUCHABLE HOOLIGAN...
...AND A LONG-HAIRED GIRLY-BOY...
OUR FIRST IMPRESSIONS COULDN'T HAVE BEEN WORSE.
DON'T TELL ME YOU WERE FIGHTING AGAIN, YUTA?!
SHUT UP, IT'S MY LIFE.
YOU'RE GONNA END UP A CRIMINAL.
YOU MUST STOP FIGHT-ING.
SHUT UP, LEAVE ME ALONE.
...
HEY...

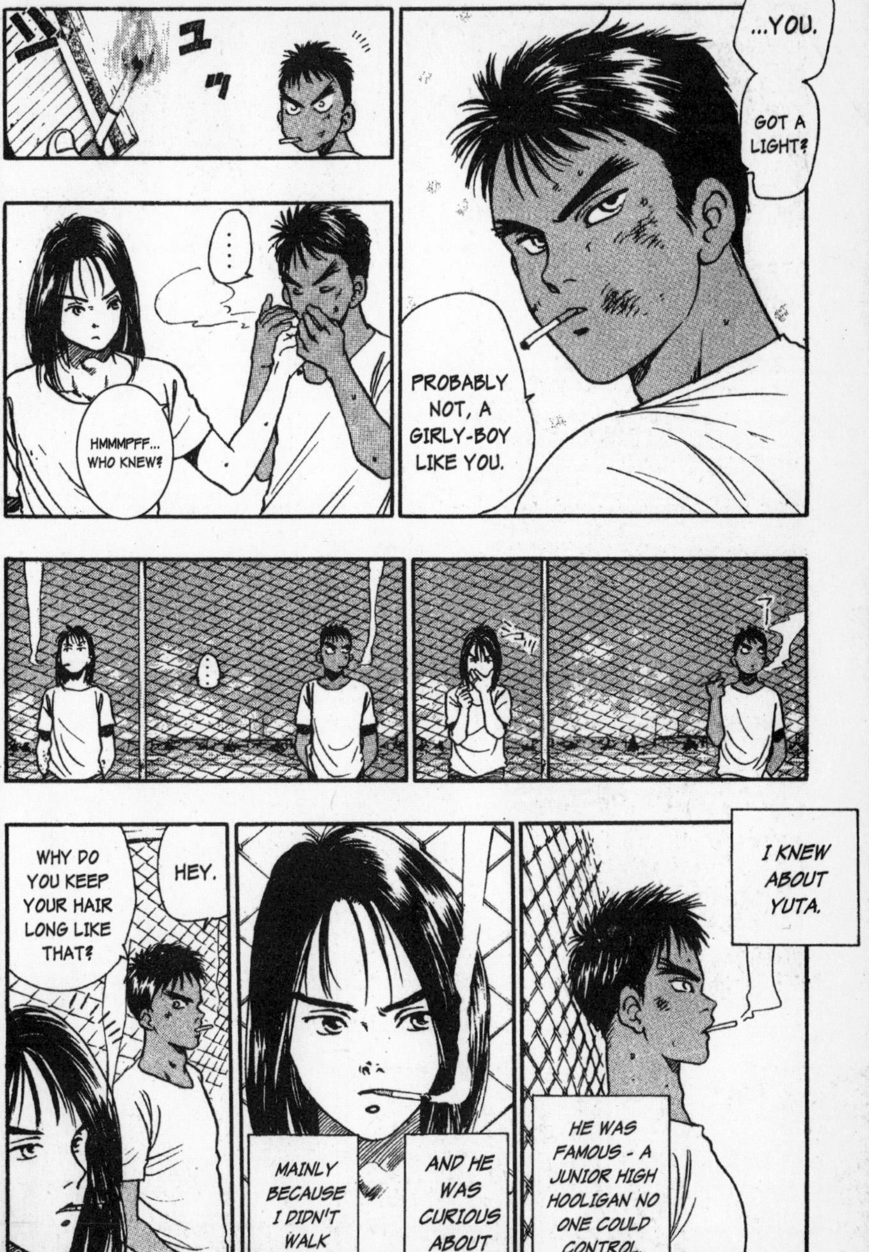
...YOU.
GOT A LIGHT?
PROBABLY NOT, A GIRLY-BOY LIKE YOU.
HMMMPFF... WHO KNEW?
I KNEW ABOUT YUTA.
HE WAS FAMOUS - A JUNIOR HIGH HOOLIGAN NO ONE COULD CONTROL.
AND HE WAS CURIOUS ABOUT ME.
MAINLY BECAUSE I DIDN'T WALK AWAY.
HEY.
WHY DO YOU KEEP YOUR HAIR LONG LIKE THAT?

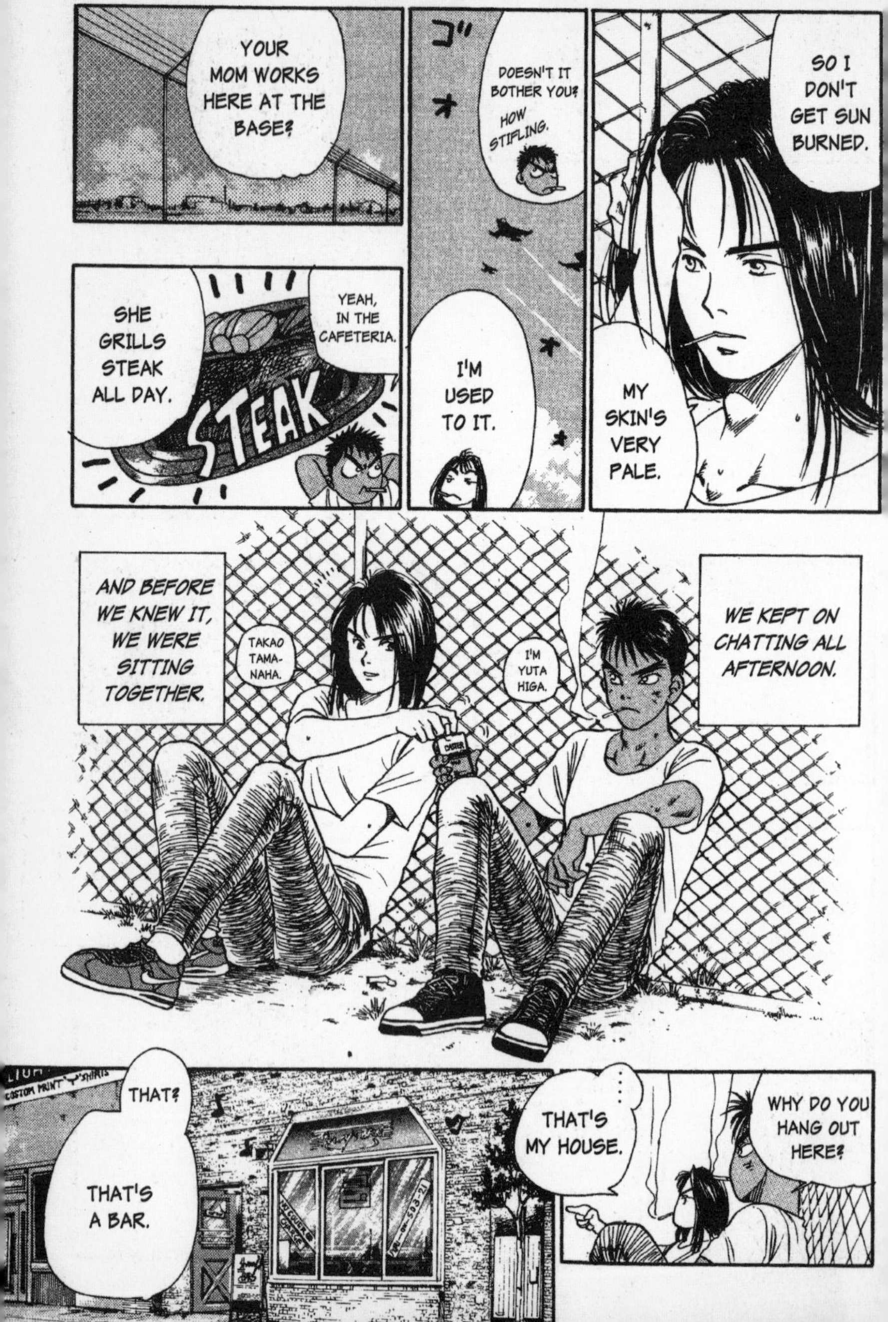
SO I DON'T GET SUN BURNED.
MY SKIN'S VERY PALE.
DOESN'T IT BOTHER YOU?
HOW STIFLING.
I'M USED TO IT.
YOUR MOM WORKS HERE AT THE BASE?
YEAH, IN THE CAFETERIA.
SHE GRILLS STEAK ALL DAY.
STEAK
WE KEPT ON CHATTING ALL AFTERNOON.
I'M YUTA HIGA.
TAKAO TAMANAHA.
AND BEFORE WE KNEW IT, WE WERE SITTING TOGETHER.
WHY DO YOU HANG OUT HERE?
THAT'S MY HOUSE.
THAT?
THAT'S A BAR.

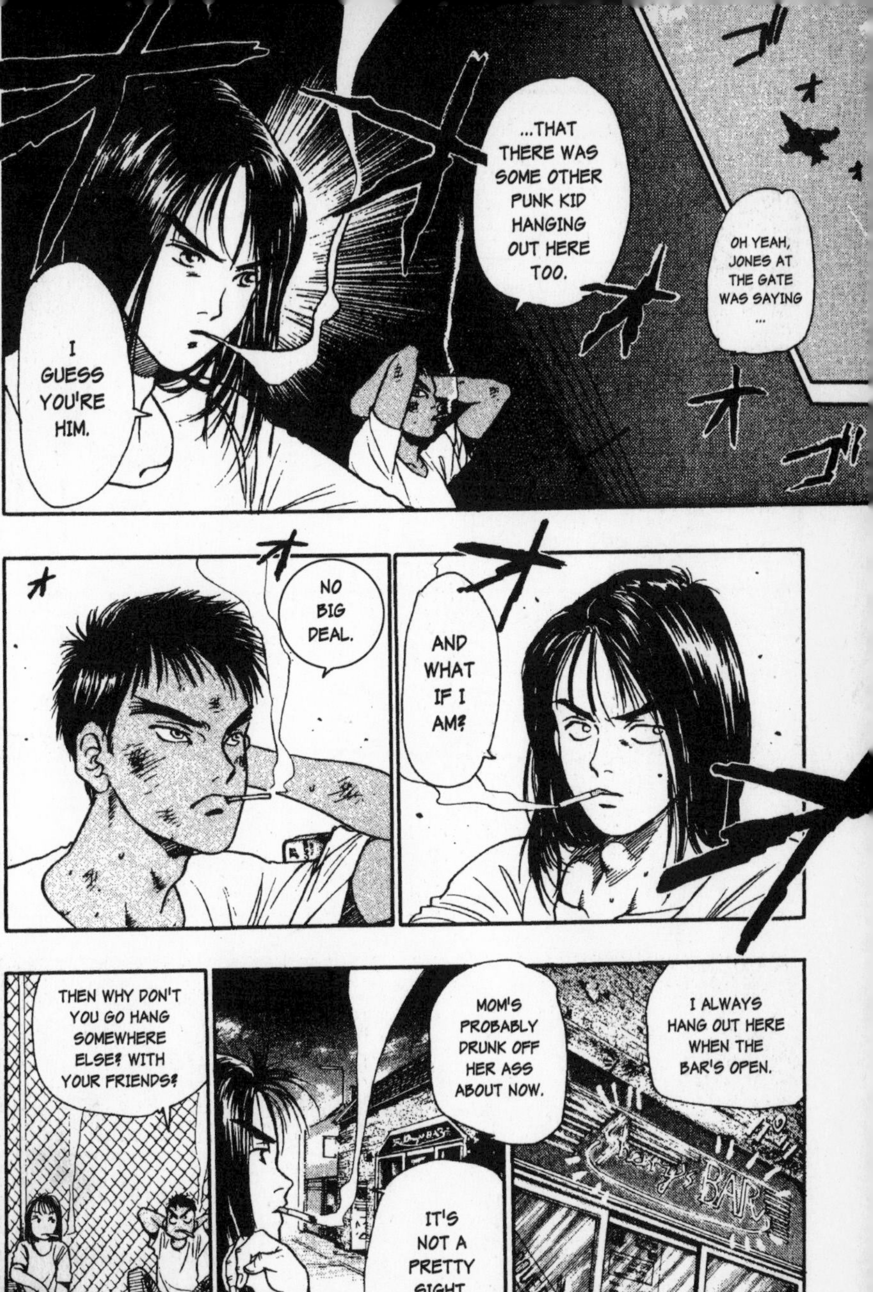
OH YEAH, JONES AT THE GATE WAS SAYING ...
...THAT THERE WAS SOME OTHER PUNK KID HANGING OUT HERE TOO.
I GUESS YOU'RE HIM.
AND WHAT IF I AM?
NO BIG DEAL.
I ALWAYS HANG OUT HERE WHEN THE BAR'S OPEN.
MOM'S PROBABLY DRUNK OFF HER ASS ABOUT NOW.
IT'S NOT A PRETTY SIGHT.
THEN WHY DON'T YOU GO HANG SOMEWHERE ELSE? WITH YOUR FRIENDS?

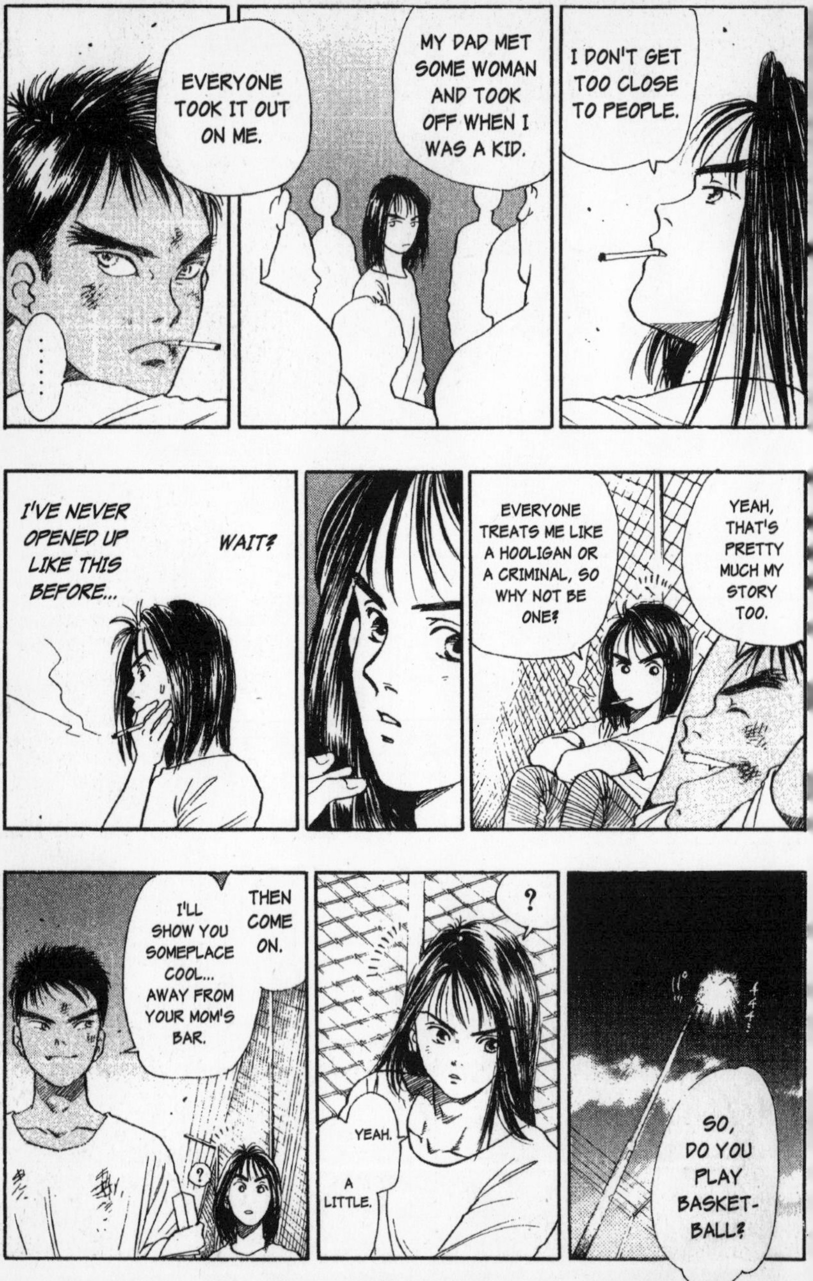
I DON'T GET TOO CLOSE TO PEOPLE.
MY DAD MET SOME WOMAN AND TOOK OFF WHEN I WAS A KID.
EVERYONE TOOK IT OUT ON ME.
......
YEAH, THAT'S PRETTY MUCH MY STORY TOO.
EVERYONE TREATS ME LIKE A HOOLIGAN OR A CRIMINAL, SO WHY NOT BE ONE?
WAIT?
I'VE NEVER OPENED UP LIKE THIS BEFORE...
SO, DO YOU PLAY BASKET-BALL?
?
YEAH.
A LITTLE.
THEN COME ON.
I'LL SHOW YOU SOMEPLACE COOL... AWAY FROM YOUR MOM'S BAR.
?

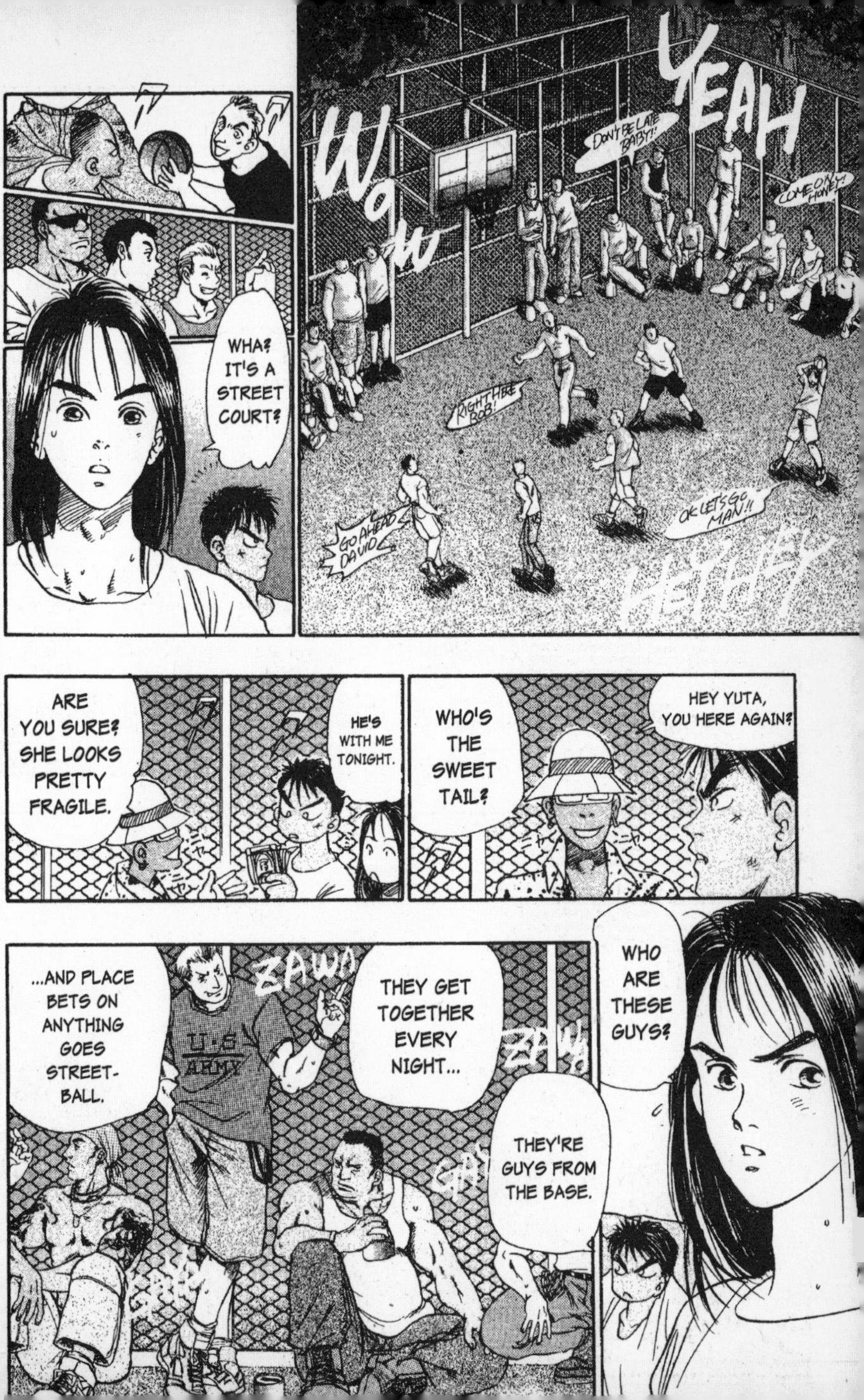
Wow
YEAH
DON'T BE LATE BABY!!
COME ON HONEY!
RIGHT HERE BOB!
OK LET'S GO MAN!!
GO AHEAD DAVID
WHA? IT'S A STREET COURT?
HEY YUTA, YOU HERE AGAIN?
WHO'S THE SWEET TAIL?
HE'S WITH ME TONIGHT.
ARE YOU SURE? SHE LOOKS PRETTY FRAGILE.
WHO ARE THESE GUYS?
THEY'RE GUYS FROM THE BASE.
ZAWA
THEY GET TOGETHER EVERY NIGHT...
ZAWA
...AND PLACE BETS ON ANYTHING GOES STREET-BALL.

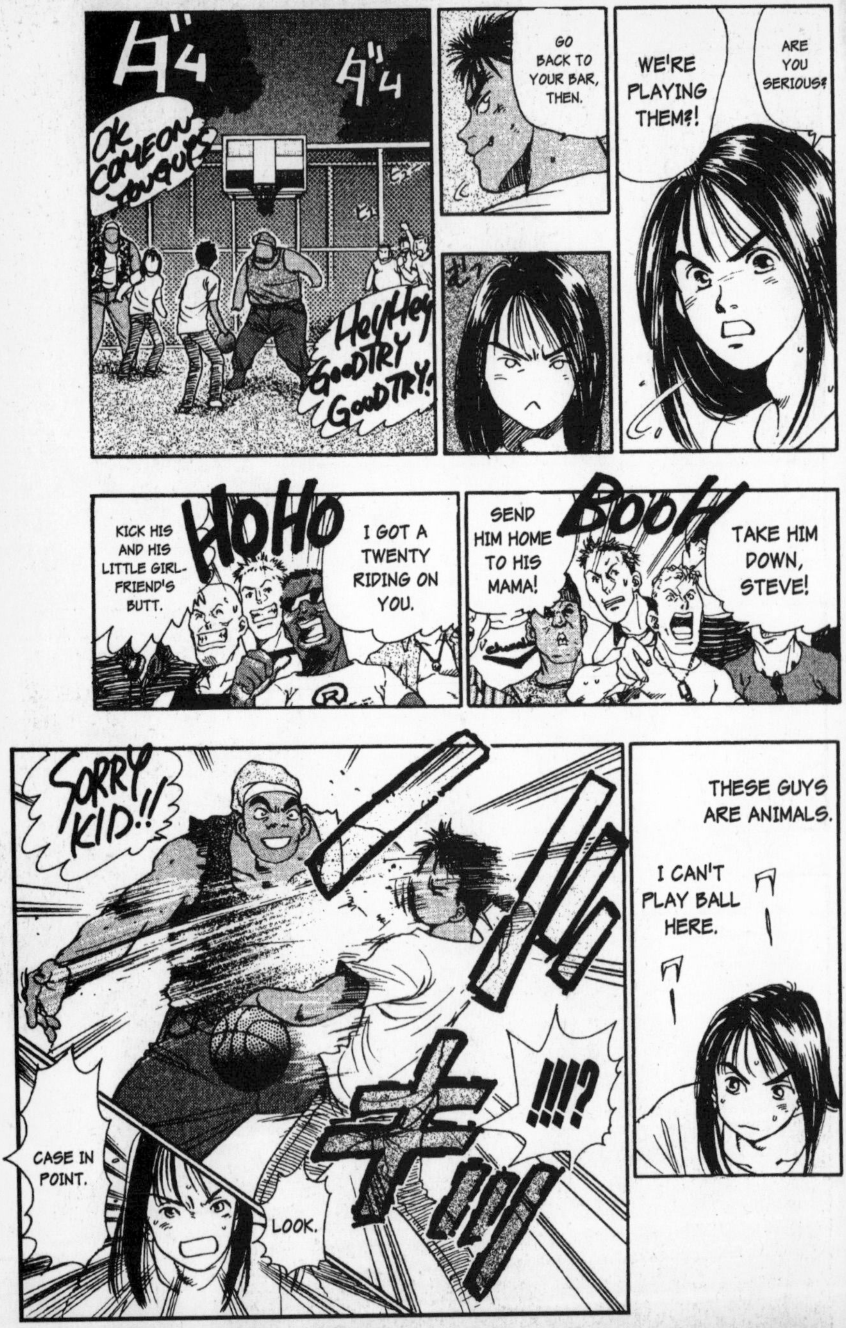
ARE YOU SERIOUS?
WE'RE PLAYING THEM?!
GO BACK TO YOUR BAR, THEN.
ダム
ダム
OK COME ON YOU GUYS
HEY HEY GOOD TRY GOOD TRY!
TAKE HIM DOWN, STEVE!
BOOH
SEND HIM HOME TO HIS MAMA!
I GOT A TWENTY RIDING ON YOU.
HOHO
KICK HIS AND HIS LITTLE GIRL-FRIEND'S BUTT.
THESE GUYS ARE ANIMALS.
I CAN'T PLAY BALL HERE.
SORRY KID!!
!!!?
LOOK.
CASE IN POINT.

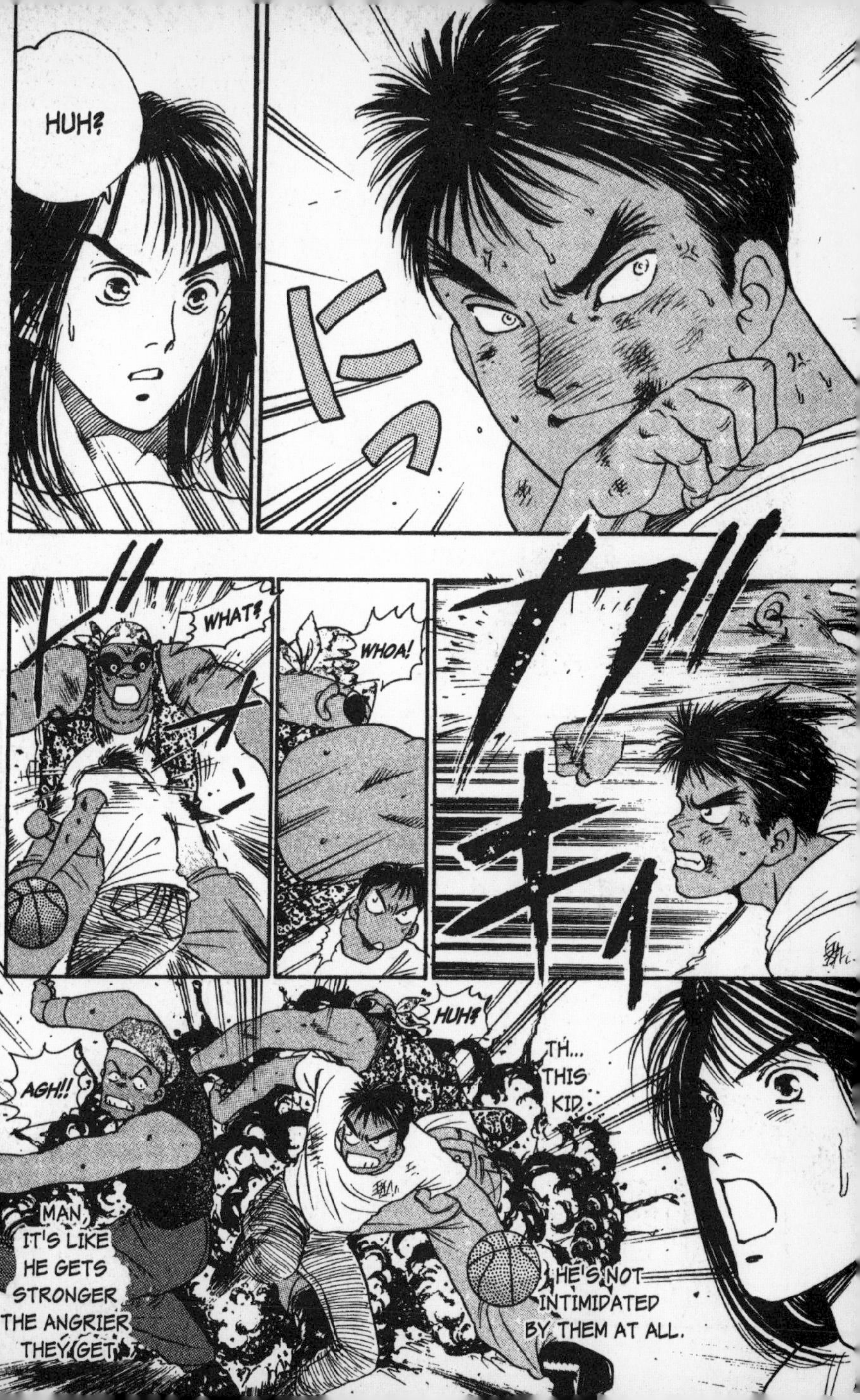
HUH?
WHOA!
WHAT?
TH... THIS KID.
HE'S NOT INTIMIDATED BY THEM AT ALL.
HUH?
AGH!!
MAN, IT'S LIKE HE GETS STRONGER THE ANGRIER THEY GET

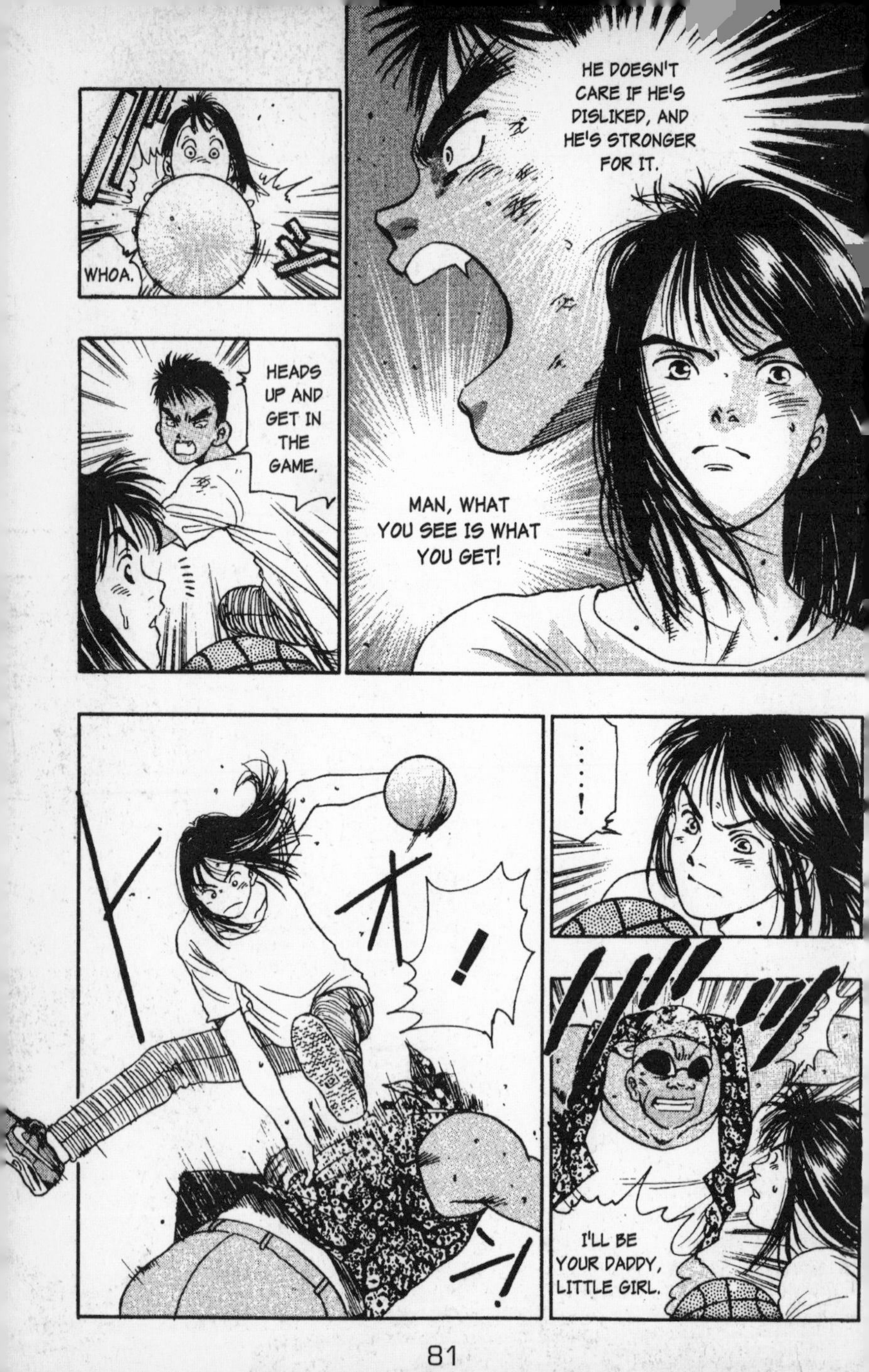
HE DOESN'T CARE IF HE'S DISLIKED, AND HE'S STRONGER FOR IT.
MAN, WHAT YOU SEE IS WHAT YOU GET!
WHOA.
HEADS UP AND GET IN THE GAME.
......!
I'LL BE YOUR DADDY, LITTLE GIRL.
!
!

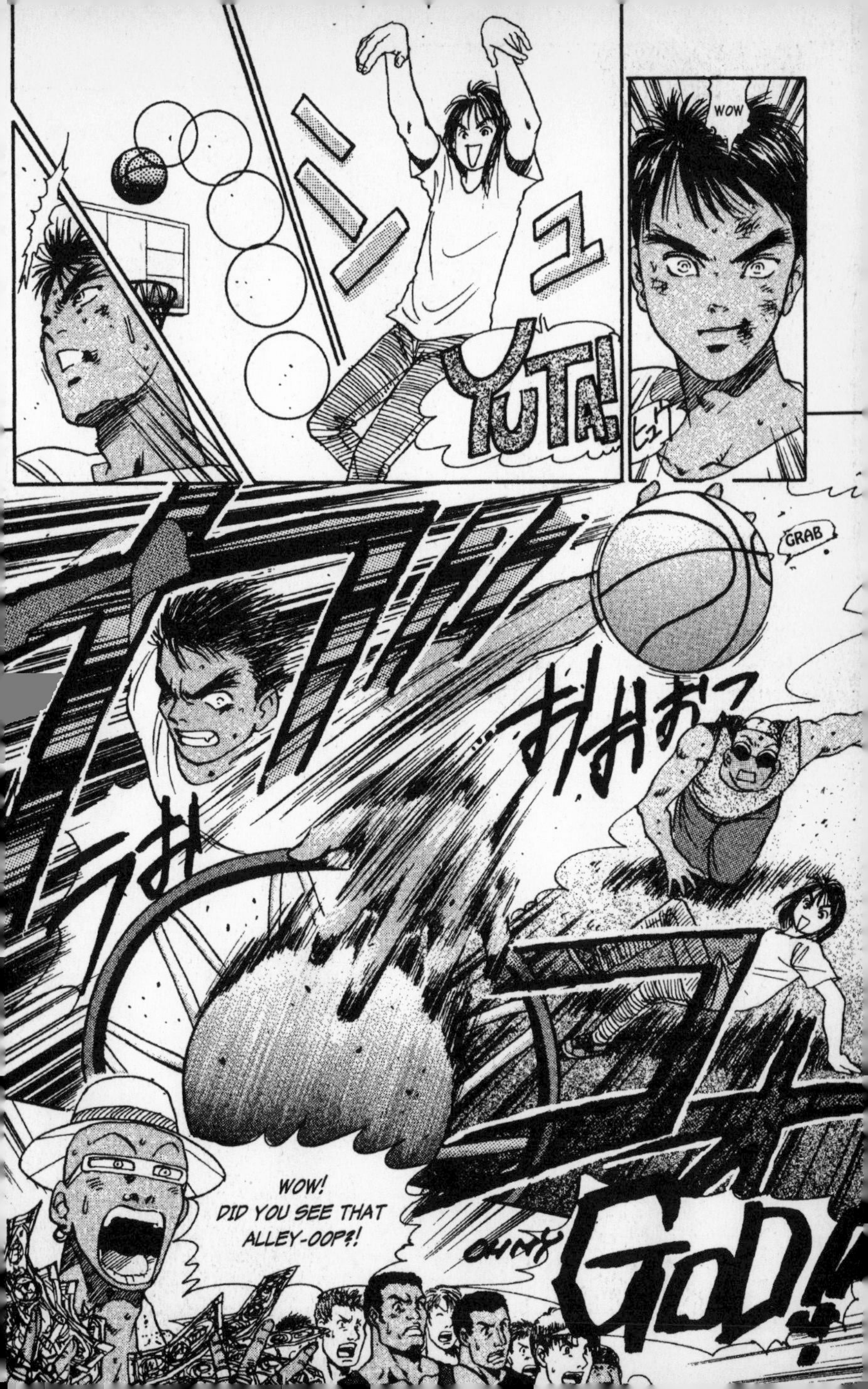
WOW
YUTA!
GRAB
おおおっ
WOW!
DID YOU SEE THAT
ALLEY-OOP?!

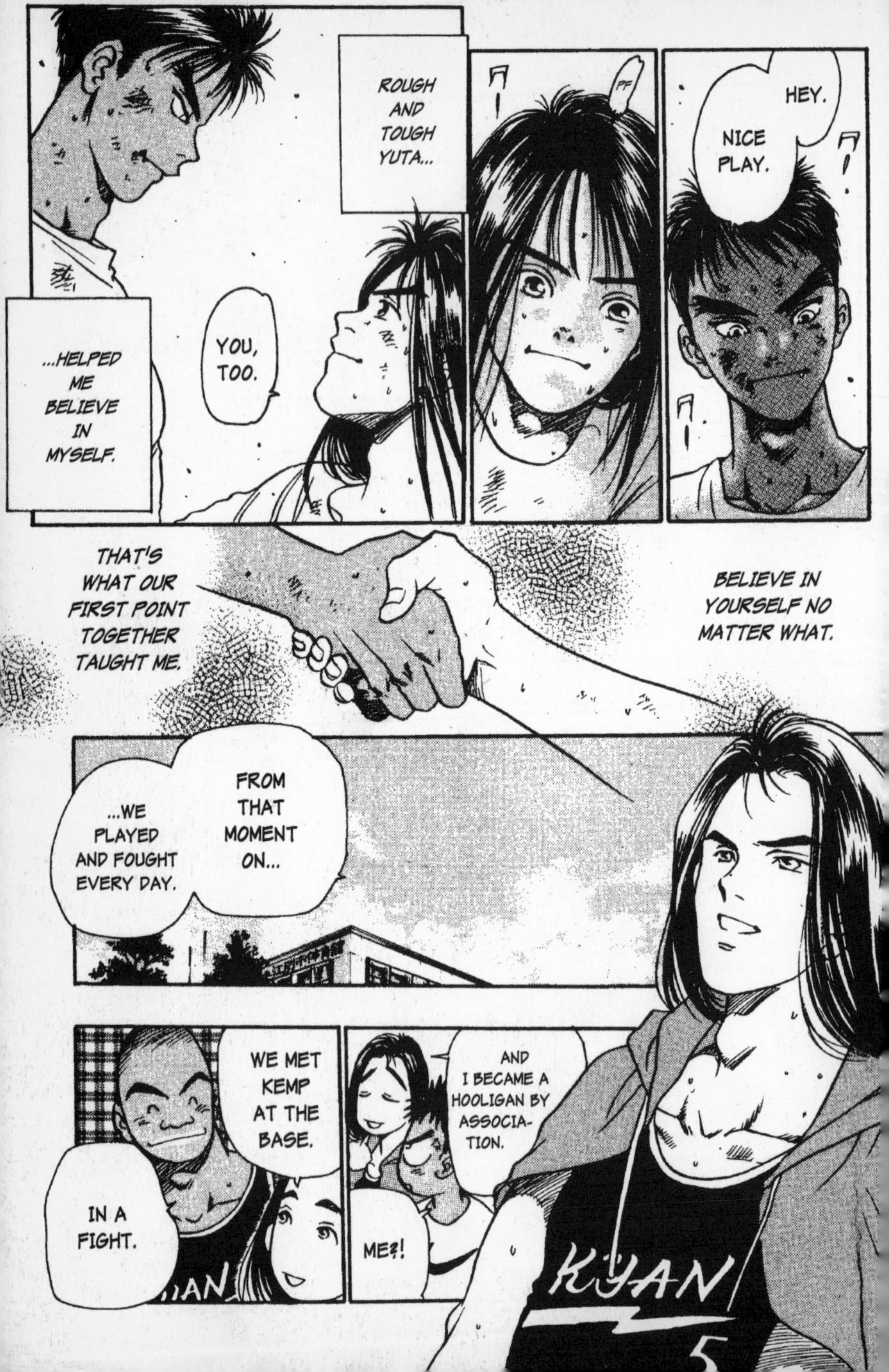
HEY. NICE PLAY.
PF
ROUGH AND TOUGH YUTA...
YOU, TOO.
...HELPED ME BELIEVE IN MYSELF.
BELIEVE IN YOURSELF NO MATTER WHAT.
THAT'S WHAT OUR FIRST POINT TOGETHER TAUGHT ME.
FROM THAT MOMENT ON...
...WE PLAYED AND FOUGHT EVERY DAY.
KYAN
5
AND I BECAME A HOOLIGAN BY ASSOCIATION.
ME?!
WE MET KEMP AT THE BASE.
IN A FIGHT.

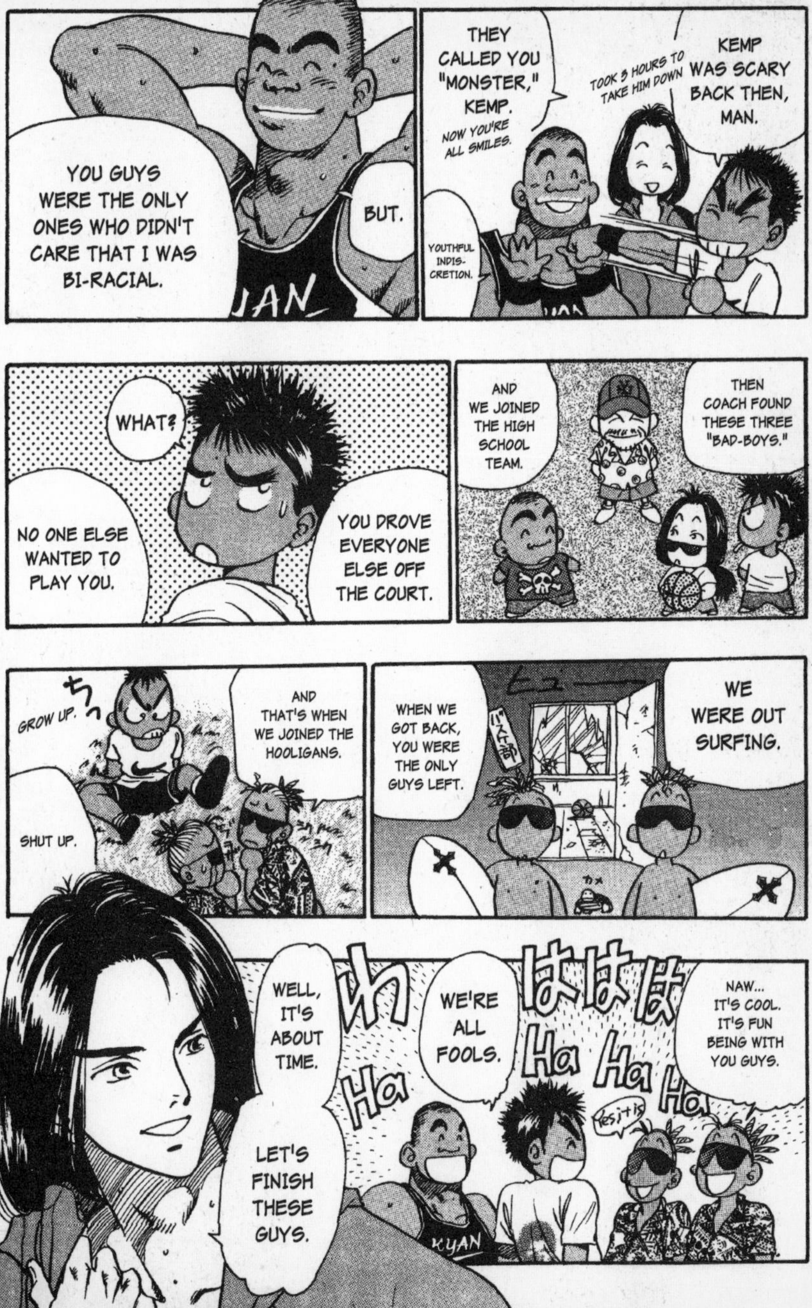
KEMP WAS SCARY BACK THEN, MAN.
TOOK 3 HOURS TO TAKE HIM DOWN
THEY CALLED YOU "MONSTER," KEMP.
NOW YOU'RE ALL SMILES.
YOUTHFUL INDIS-CRETION.
BUT.
YOU GUYS WERE THE ONLY ONES WHO DIDN'T CARE THAT I WAS BI-RACIAL.
THEN COACH FOUND THESE THREE "BAD-BOYS."
AND WE JOINED THE HIGH SCHOOL TEAM.
WHAT?
YOU DROVE EVERYONE ELSE OFF THE COURT.
NO ONE ELSE WANTED TO PLAY YOU.
WE WERE OUT SURFING.
WHEN WE GOT BACK, YOU WERE THE ONLY GUYS LEFT.
AND THAT'S WHEN WE JOINED THE HOOLIGANS.
GROW UP.
SHUT UP.
NAW... IT'S COOL. IT'S FUN BEING WITH YOU GUYS.
ははは
Ha Ha Ha
Yes it is
WE'RE ALL FOOLS.
わ
Ha
WELL, IT'S ABOUT TIME.
LET'S FINISH THESE GUYS.

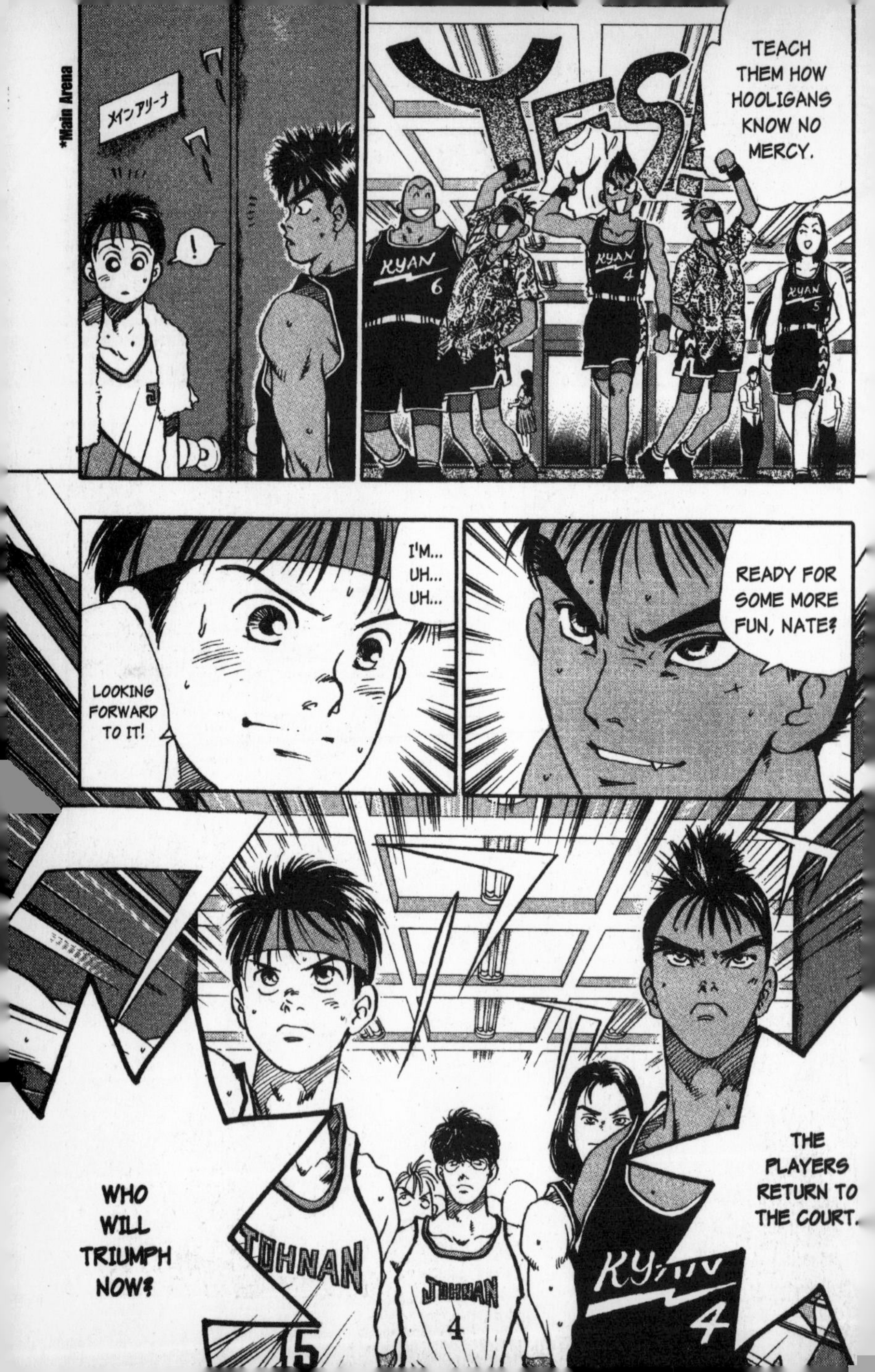
YES!
TEACH THEM HOW HOOLIGANS KNOW NO MERCY.
KYAN 6
KYAN 4
KYAN 5
メインアリーナ
*Main Arena
!
READY FOR SOME MORE FUN, NATE?
I'M... UH... UH...
LOOKING FORWARD TO IT!
THE PLAYERS RETURN TO THE COURT.
WHO WILL TRIUMPH NOW?
TOHNAN
15
TOHNAN
4
4

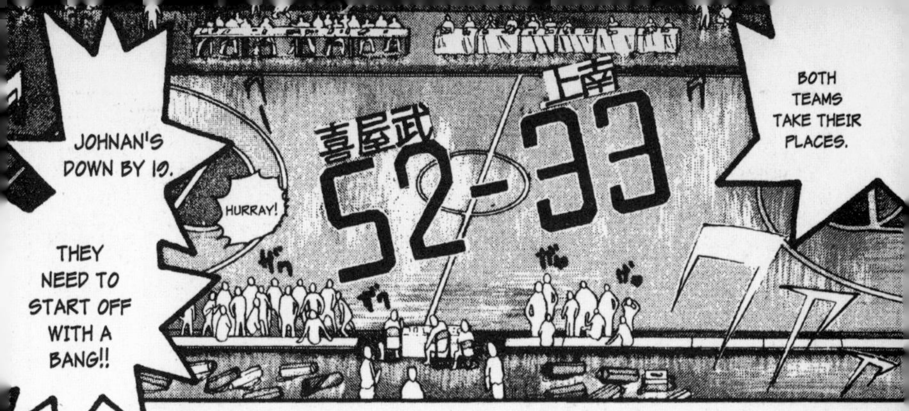
BOTH TEAMS TAKE THEIR PLACES.
上南
喜屋武
52-33
JOHNAN'S DOWN BY 19.
HURRAY!
THEY NEED TO START OFF WITH A BANG!!

You're reading…

REBOUND

Episode 14: In the Bag

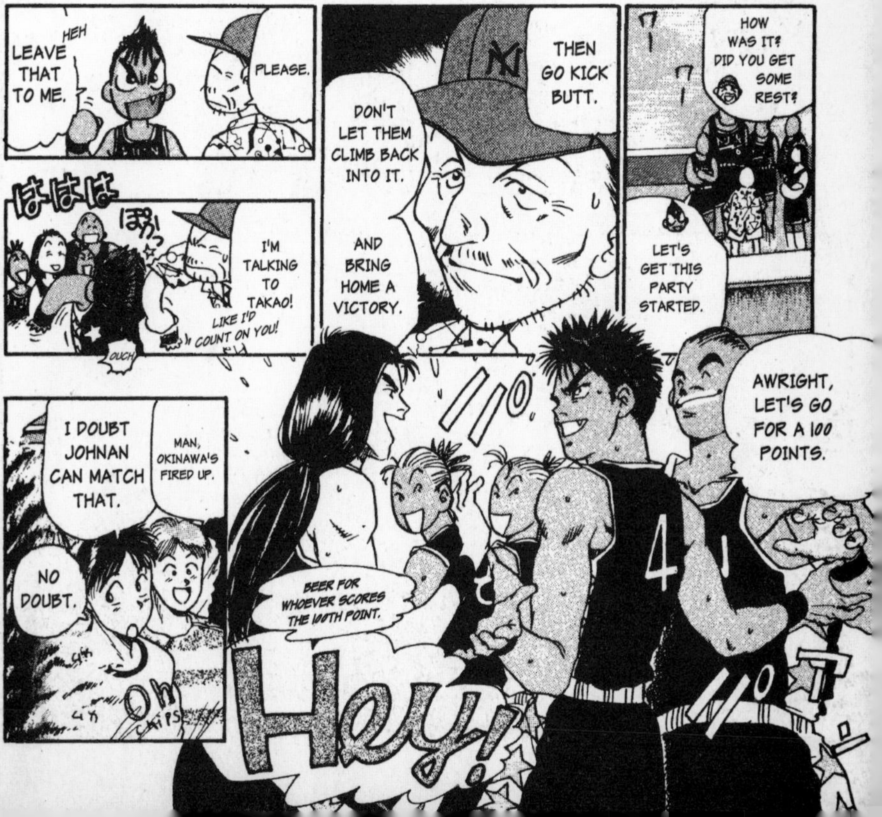
HOW WAS IT? DID YOU GET SOME REST?
LET'S GET THIS PARTY STARTED.
THEN GO KICK BUTT.
DON'T LET THEM CLIMB BACK INTO IT.
AND BRING HOME A VICTORY.
PLEASE.
HEH
LEAVE THAT TO ME.
ははは
ぽかっ
I'M TALKING TO TAKAO!
LIKE I'D COUNT ON YOU!
OUCH
AWRIGHT, LET'S GO FOR A 100 POINTS.
BEER FOR WHOEVER SCORES THE 100TH POINT.
Hey!
MAN, OKINAWA'S FIRED UP.
I DOUBT JOHNAN CAN MATCH THAT.
NO DOUBT.
Oh
CHIPS

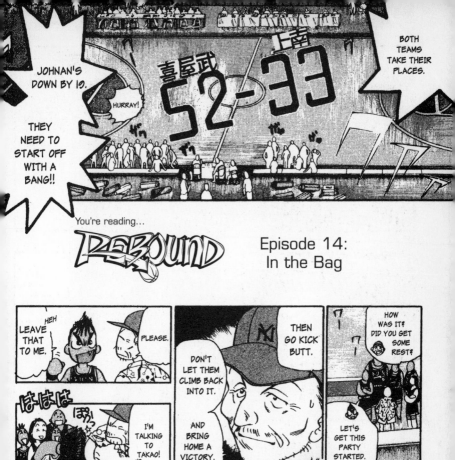

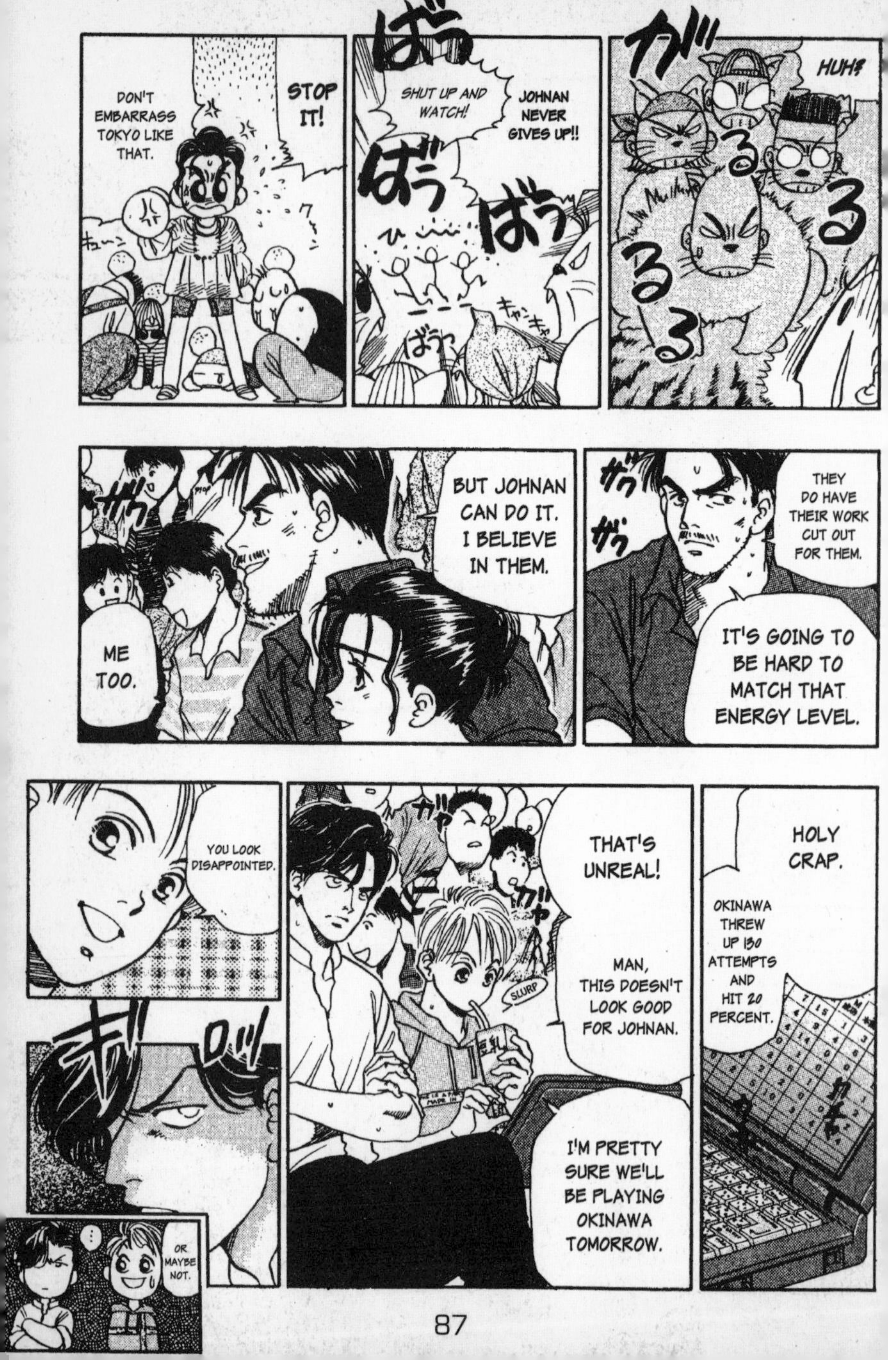
HUH!?
SHUT UP AND WATCH!
JOHNAN NEVER GIVES UP!!
STOP IT!
DON'T EMBARRASS TOKYO LIKE THAT.
THEY DO HAVE THEIR WORK CUT OUT FOR THEM.
IT'S GOING TO BE HARD TO MATCH THAT ENERGY LEVEL.
BUT JOHNAN CAN DO IT. I BELIEVE IN THEM.
ME TOO.
HOLY CRAP.
OKINAWA THREW UP 130 ATTEMPTS AND HIT 20 PERCENT.
THAT'S UNREAL!
MAN, THIS DOESN'T LOOK GOOD FOR JOHNAN.
SLURP
I'M PRETTY SURE WE'LL BE PLAYING OKINAWA TOMORROW.
YOU LOOK DISAPPOINTED.
OR MAYBE NOT.

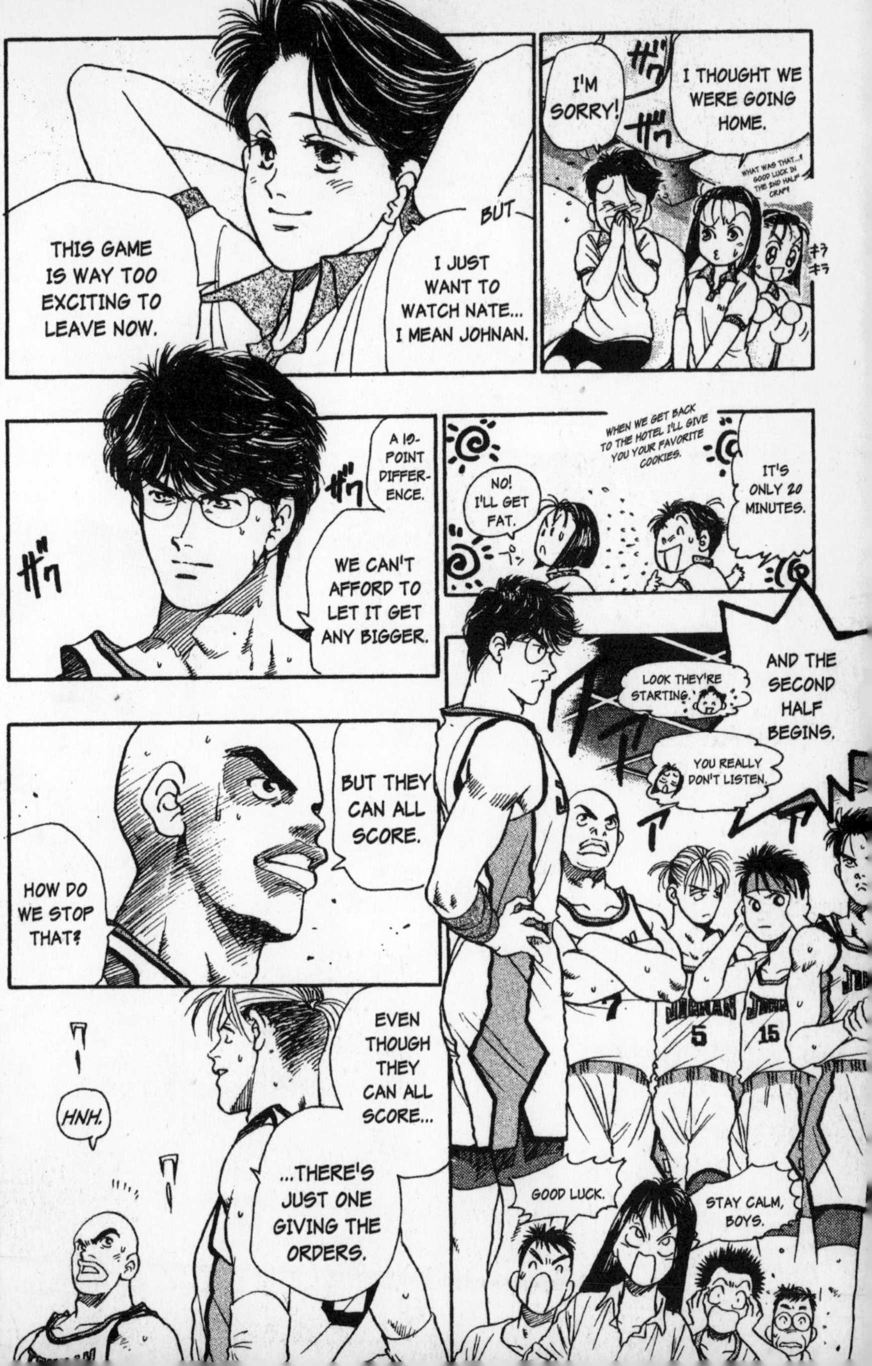
I THOUGHT WE WERE GOING HOME.
I'M SORRY!
WHAT WAS THAT...? GOOD LUCK IN THE 2ND HALF! CRAP!
BUT
I JUST WANT TO WATCH NATE... I MEAN JOHNAN.
THIS GAME IS WAY TOO EXCITING TO LEAVE NOW.
IT'S ONLY 20 MINUTES.
WHEN WE GET BACK TO THE HOTEL I'LL GIVE YOU YOUR FAVORITE COOKIES.
NO! I'LL GET FAT.
A 10-POINT DIFFERENCE.
WE CAN'T AFFORD TO LET IT GET ANY BIGGER.
AND THE SECOND HALF BEGINS.
LOOK THEY'RE STARTING.
YOU REALLY DON'T LISTEN.
STAY CALM, BOYS.
GOOD LUCK.
BUT THEY CAN ALL SCORE.
HOW DO WE STOP THAT?
EVEN THOUGH THEY CAN ALL SCORE...
...THERE'S JUST ONE GIVING THE ORDERS.
HNH.

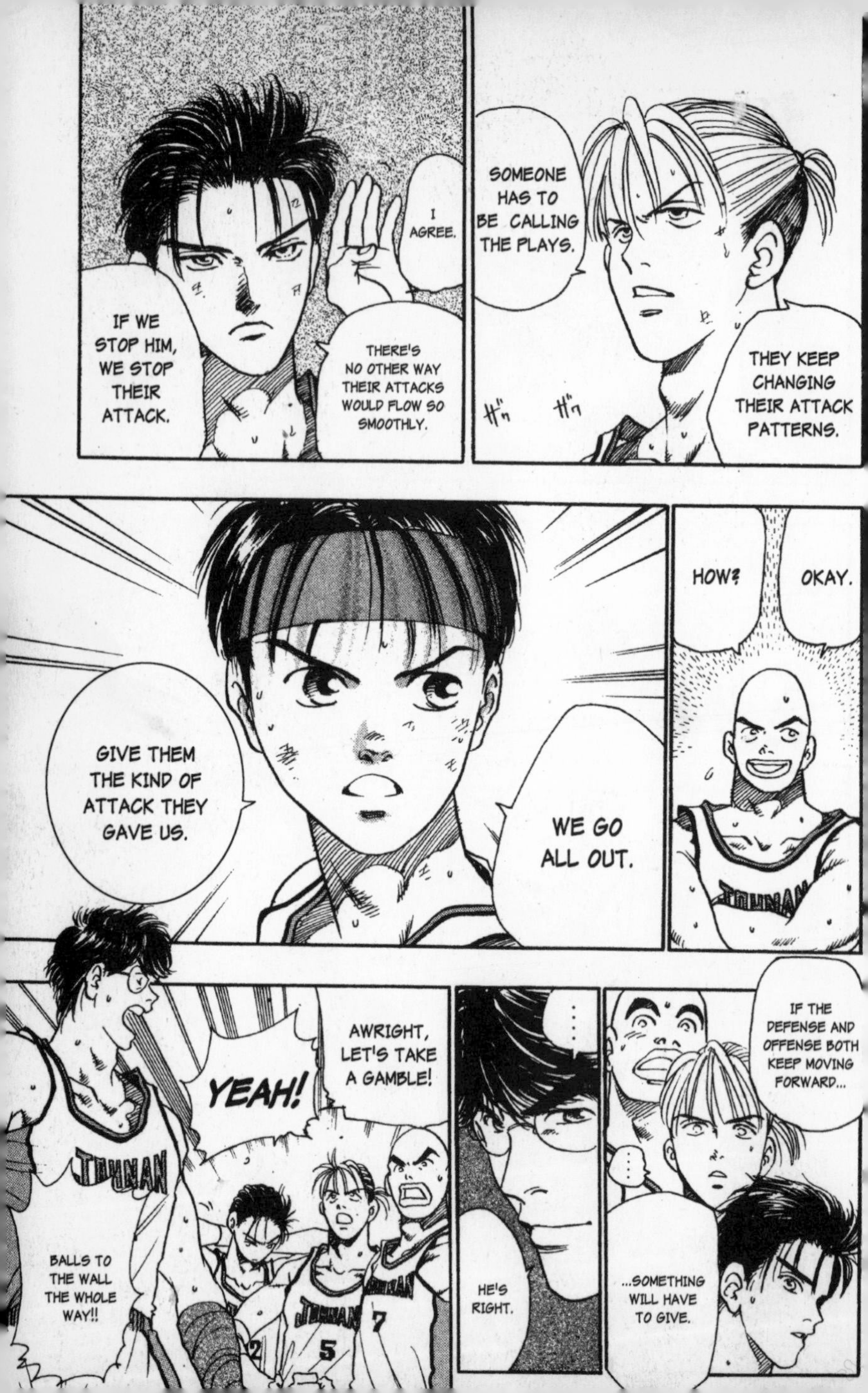
SOMEONE HAS TO BE CALLING THE PLAYS.
THEY KEEP CHANGING THEIR ATTACK PATTERNS.
I AGREE.
THERE'S NO OTHER WAY THEIR ATTACKS WOULD FLOW SO SMOOTHLY.
IF WE STOP HIM, WE STOP THEIR ATTACK.
OKAY.
HOW?
WE GO ALL OUT.
GIVE THEM THE KIND OF ATTACK THEY GAVE US.
IF THE DEFENSE AND OFFENSE BOTH KEEP MOVING FORWARD...
...SOMETHING WILL HAVE TO GIVE.
HE'S RIGHT.
AWRIGHT, LET'S TAKE A GAMBLE!
YEAH!
BALLS TO THE WALL THE WHOLE WAY!!

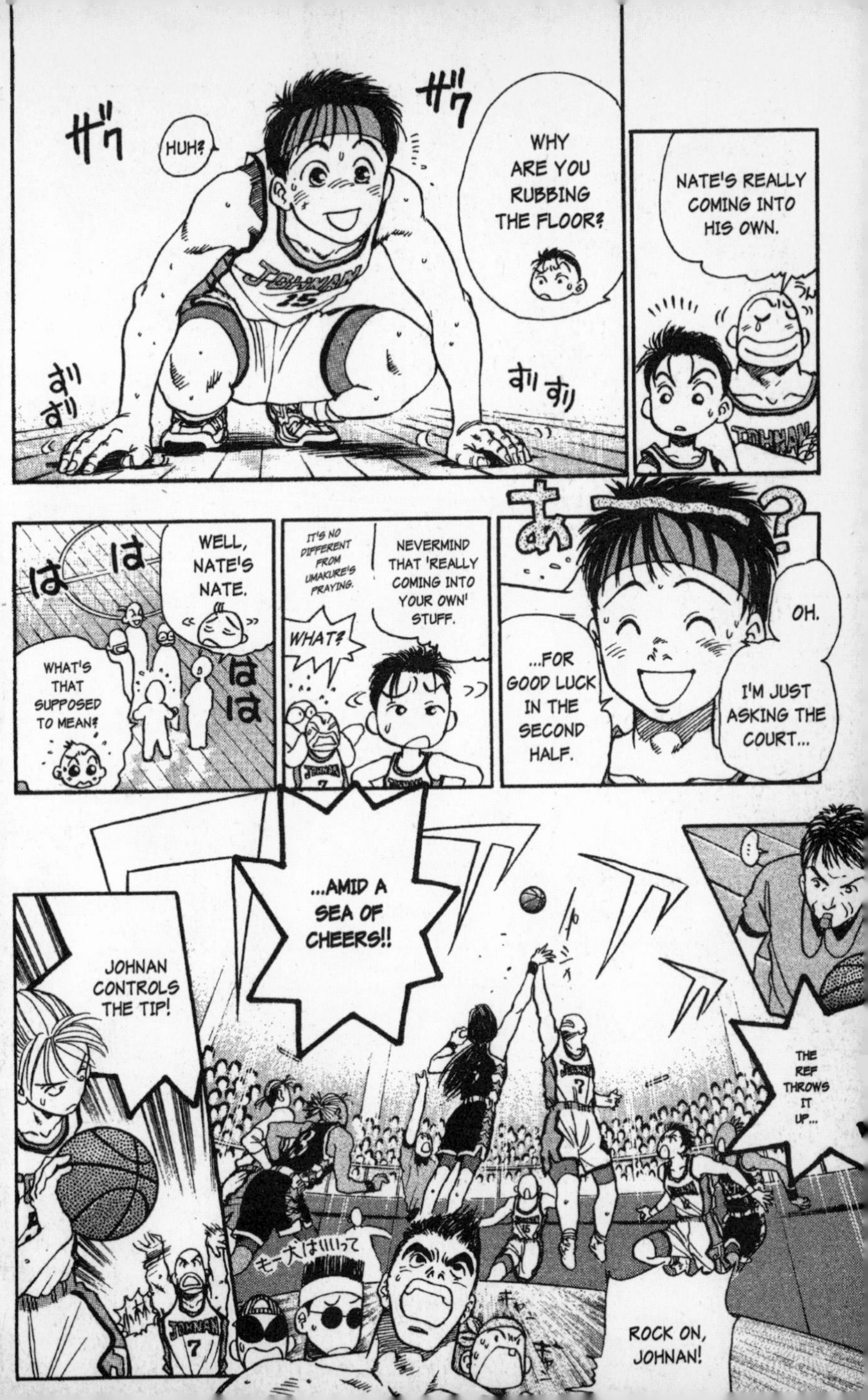
NATE'S REALLY COMING INTO HIS OWN.
ザワ
WHY ARE YOU RUBBING THE FLOOR?
ザワ
HUH?
ずりずり
ずりずり
あ
?
OH.
I'M JUST ASKING THE COURT...
...FOR GOOD LUCK IN THE SECOND HALF.
NEVERMIND THAT 'REALLY COMING INTO YOUR OWN' STUFF.
IT'S NO DIFFERENT FROM UMAKURE'S PRAYING.
WHAT?
WELL, NATE'S NATE.
はは
はは
WHAT'S THAT SUPPOSED TO MEAN?
THE REF THROWS IT UP...
...AMID A SEA OF CHEERS!!
JOHNAN CONTROLS THE TIP!
ROCK ON, JOHNAN!

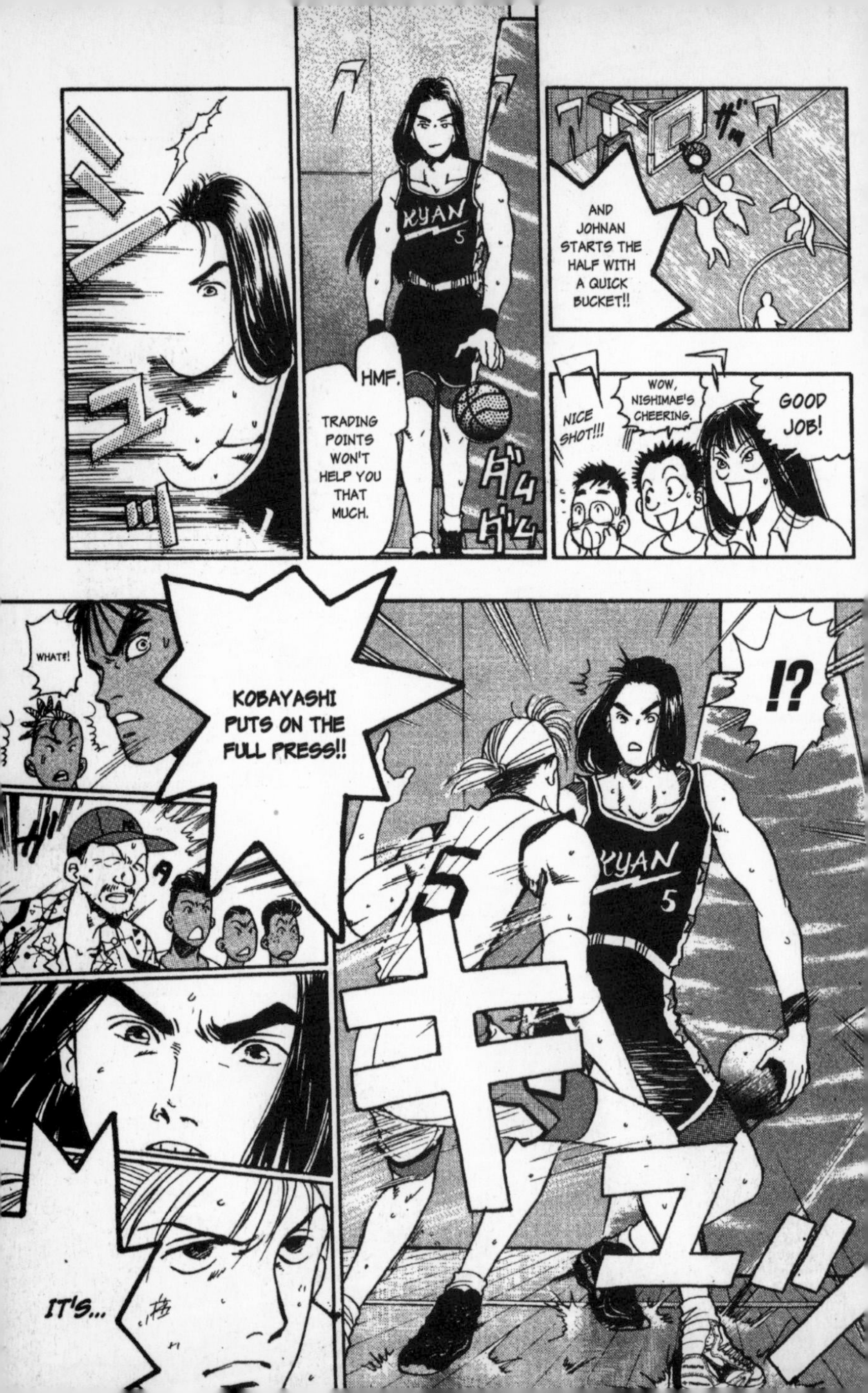
AND JOHNAN STARTS THE HALF WITH A QUICK BUCKET!!
GOOD JOB!
WOW, NISHIMAE'S CHEERING.
NICE SHOT!!!
HMF.
TRADING POINTS WON'T HELP YOU THAT MUCH.
!?
KOBAYASHI PUTS ON THE FULL PRESS!!
WHAT?!
IT'S...

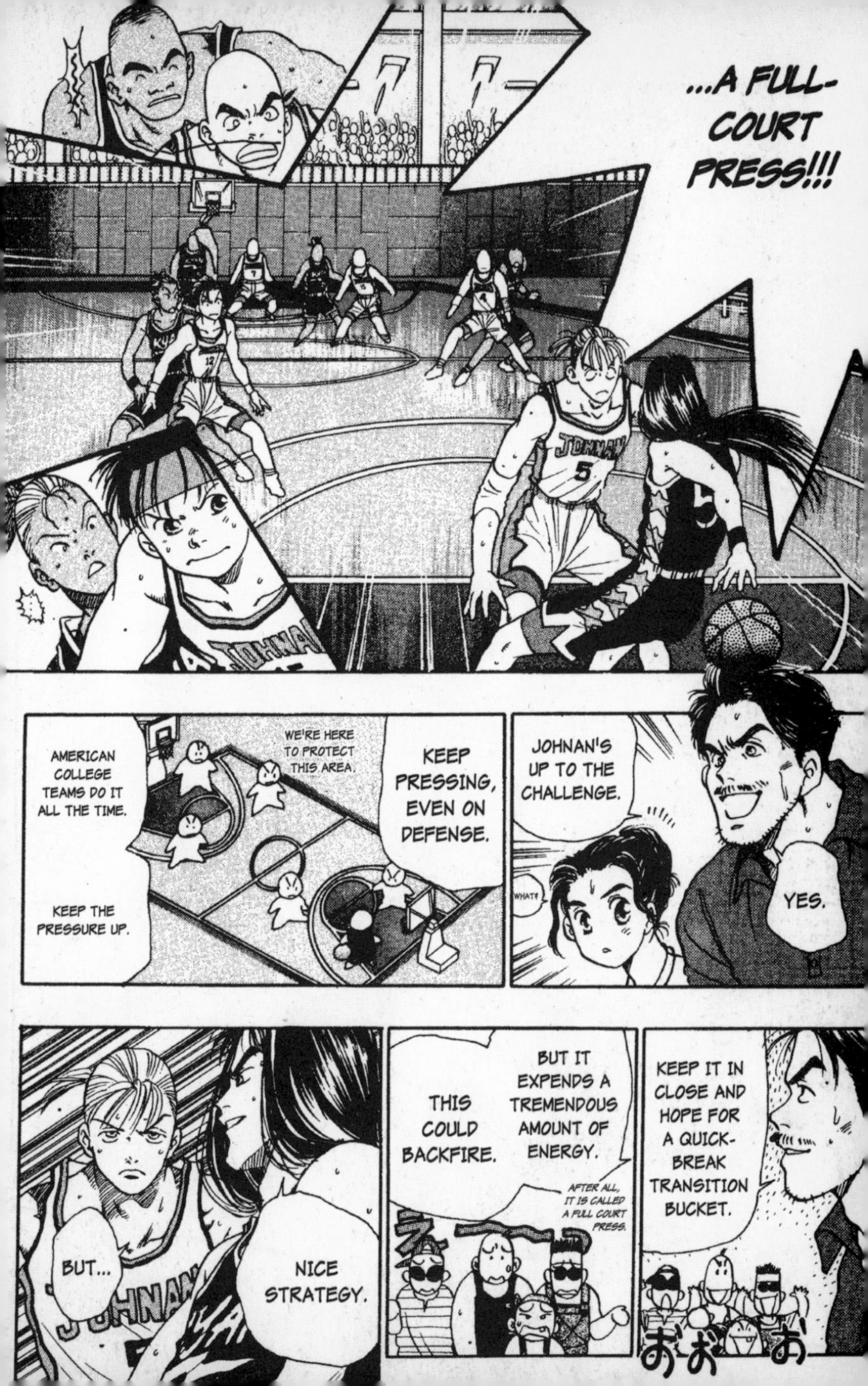
...A FULL-COURT PRESS!!!
JOHNAN'S UP TO THE CHALLENGE.
WHAT?
YES.
KEEP PRESSING, EVEN ON DEFENSE.
WE'RE HERE TO PROTECT THIS AREA.
AMERICAN COLLEGE TEAMS DO IT ALL THE TIME.
KEEP THE PRESSURE UP.
KEEP IT IN CLOSE AND HOPE FOR A QUICK-BREAK TRANSITION BUCKET.
BUT IT EXPENDS A TREMENDOUS AMOUNT OF ENERGY.
THIS COULD BACKFIRE.
AFTER ALL, IT IS CALLED A FULL COURT PRESS.
NICE STRATEGY.
BUT...

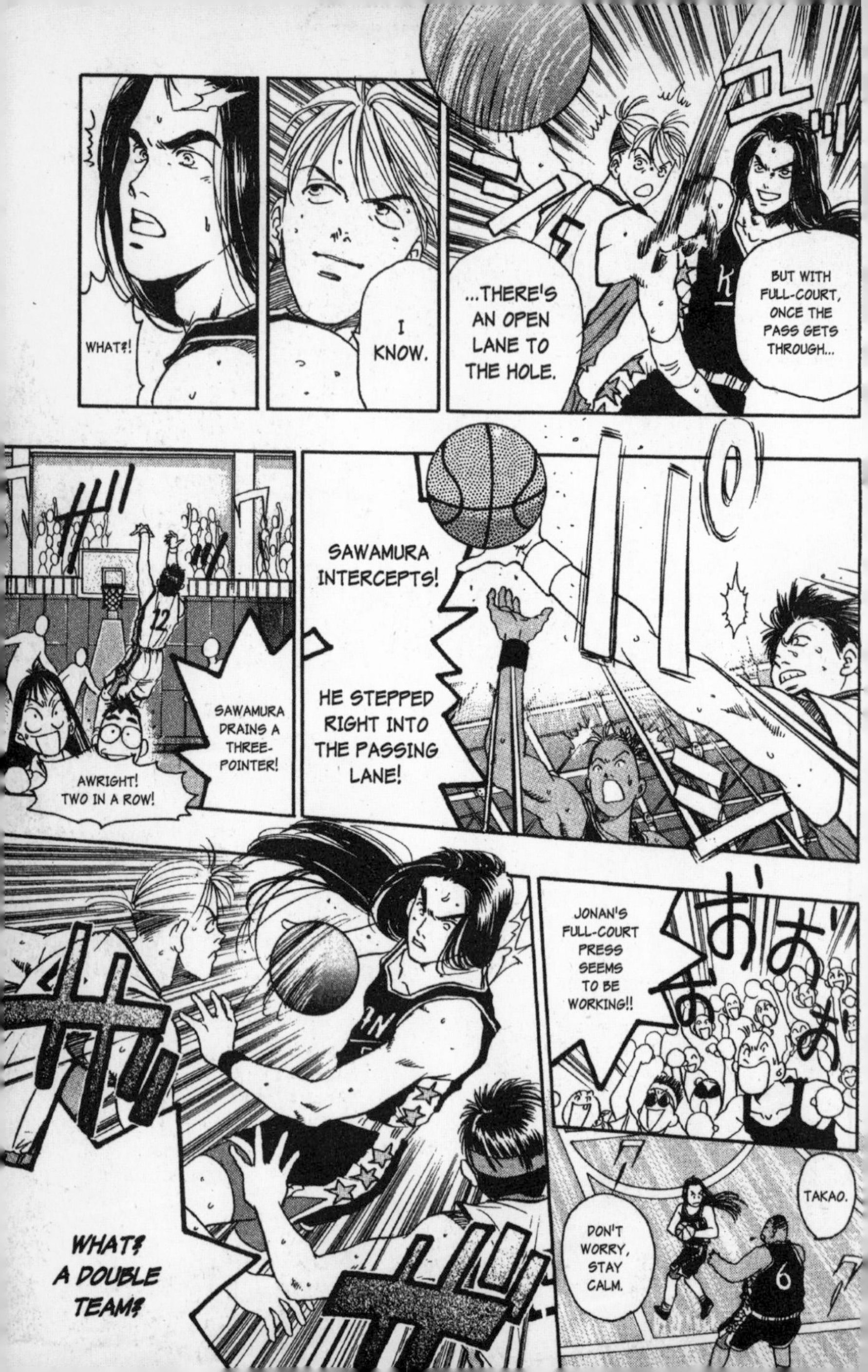
BUT WITH FULL-COURT, ONCE THE PASS GETS THROUGH...
...THERE'S AN OPEN LANE TO THE HOLE.
I KNOW.
WHAT?!
SAWAMURA INTERCEPTS!
HE STEPPED RIGHT INTO THE PASSING LANE!
SAWAMURA DRAINS A THREE-POINTER!
AWRIGHT! TWO IN A ROW!
JONAN'S FULL-COURT PRESS SEEMS TO BE WORKING!!
TAKAO.
DON'T WORRY, STAY CALM.
WHAT? A DOUBLE TEAM?

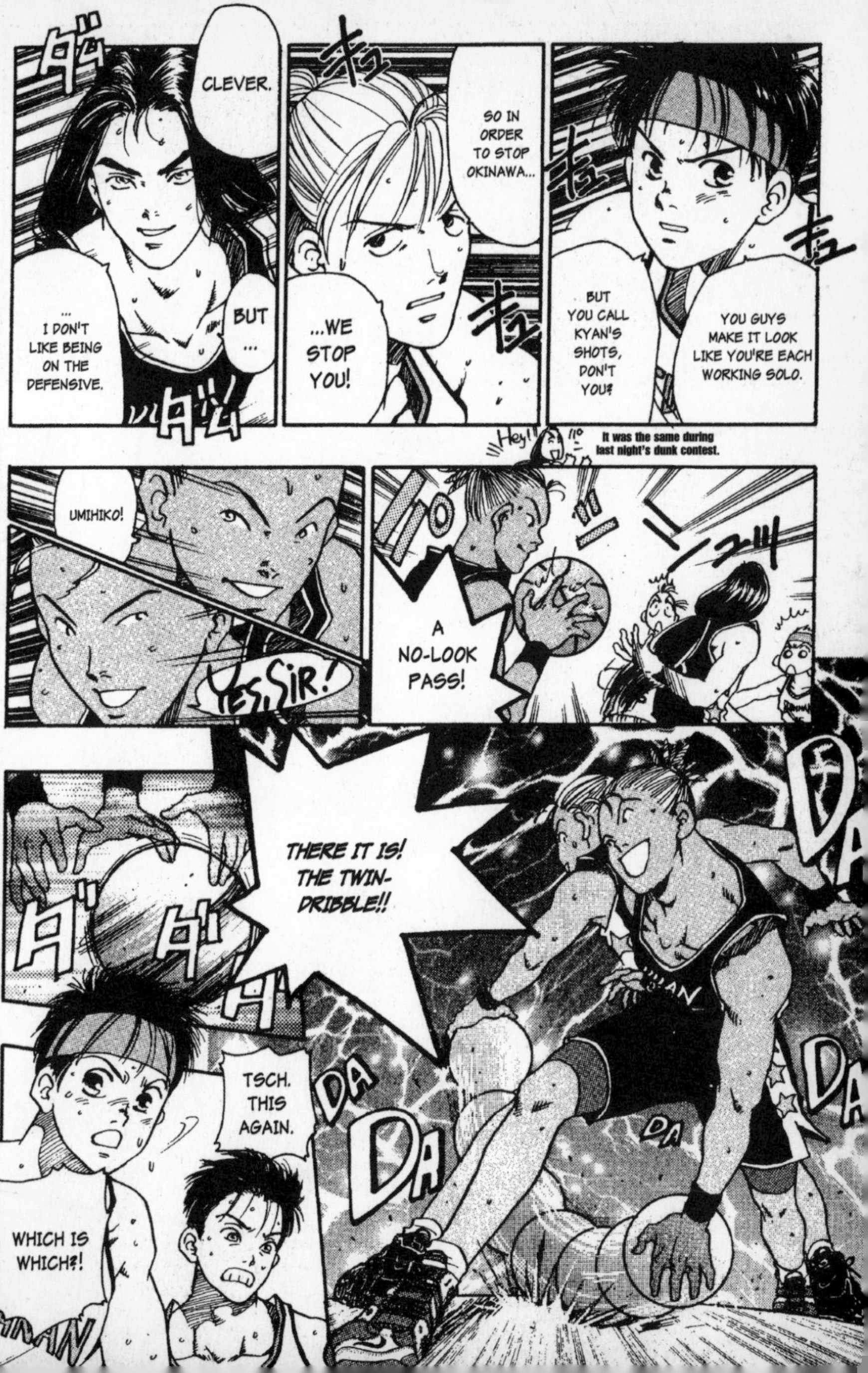
YOU GUYS MAKE IT LOOK LIKE YOU'RE EACH WORKING SOLO.
BUT YOU CALL KYAN'S SHOTS, DON'T YOU?
SO IN ORDER TO STOP OKINAWA...
...WE STOP YOU!
CLEVER.
BUT ...
... I DON'T LIKE BEING ON THE DEFENSIVE.
Hey!!
It was the same during last night's dunk contest.
A NO-LOOK PASS!
UMIHIKO!
YES SIR!
THERE IT IS! THE TWIN-DRIBBLE!!
DA
DA
DA
DA
DA
TSCH. THIS AGAIN.
WHICH IS WHICH?!

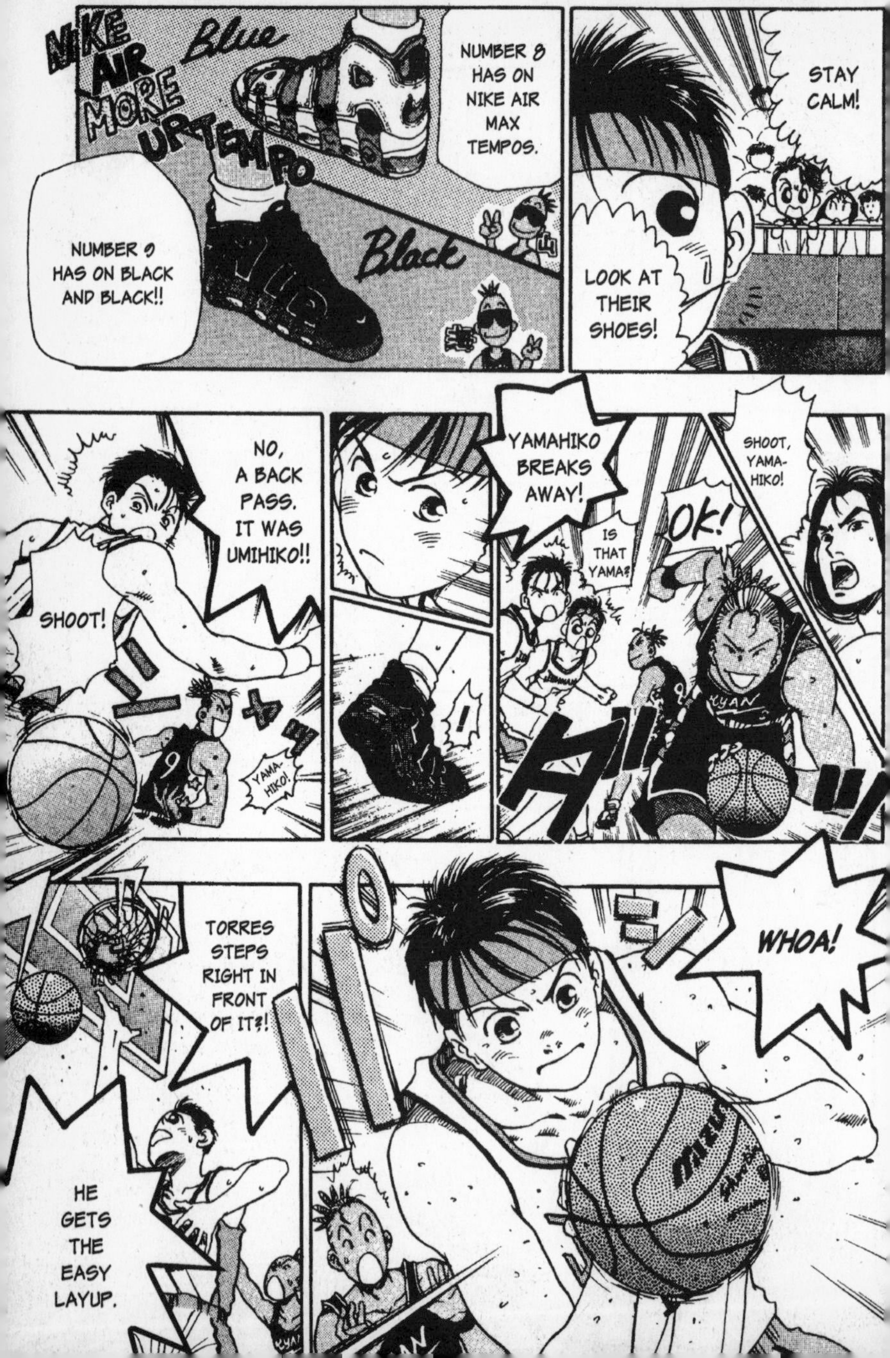
STAY CALM!
LOOK AT THEIR SHOES!
NUMBER 8 HAS ON NIKE AIR MAX TEMPOS.
NIKE AIR MORE UPTEMPO
Blue
Black
NUMBER 9 HAS ON BLACK AND BLACK!!
SHOOT, YAMAHIKO!
OK!
IS THAT YAMA?
YAMAHIKO BREAKS AWAY!
NO, A BACK PASS. IT WAS UMIHIKO!!
SHOOT!
YAMAHIKO!
WHOA!
TORRES STEPS RIGHT IN FRONT OF IT?!
HE GETS THE EASY LAYUP.

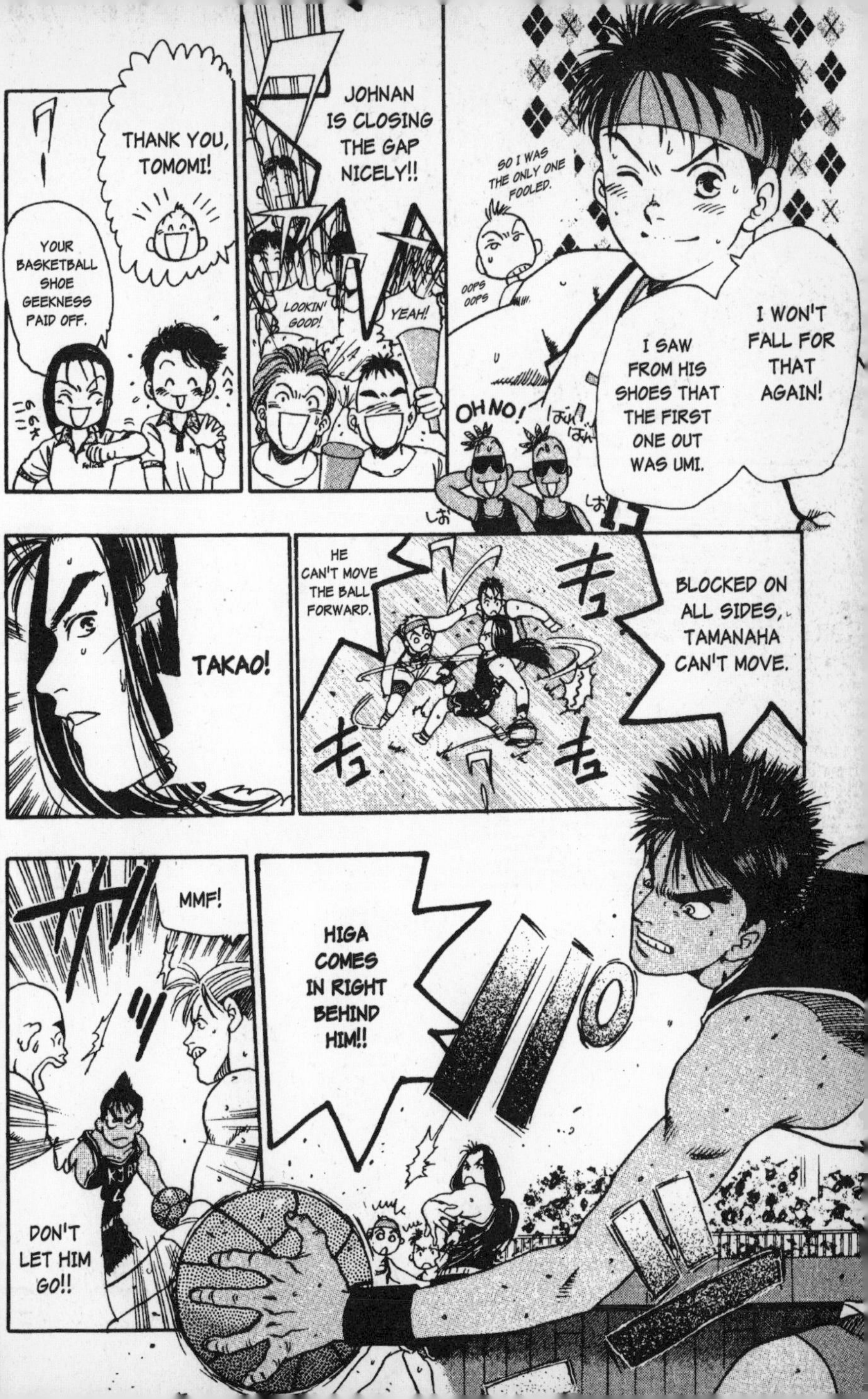
I WON'T FALL FOR THAT AGAIN!
I SAW FROM HIS SHOES THAT THE FIRST ONE OUT WAS UMI.
SO I WAS THE ONLY ONE FOOLED.
OOPS OOPS
OH NO!
JOHNAN IS CLOSING THE GAP NICELY!!
YEAH!
LOOKIN' GOOD!
THANK YOU, TOMOMI!
YOUR BASKETBALL SHOE GEEKNESS PAID OFF.
BLOCKED ON ALL SIDES, TAMANAHA CAN'T MOVE.
HE CAN'T MOVE THE BALL FORWARD.
TAKAO!
HIGA COMES IN RIGHT BEHIND HIM!!
MMF!
DON'T LET HIM GO!!

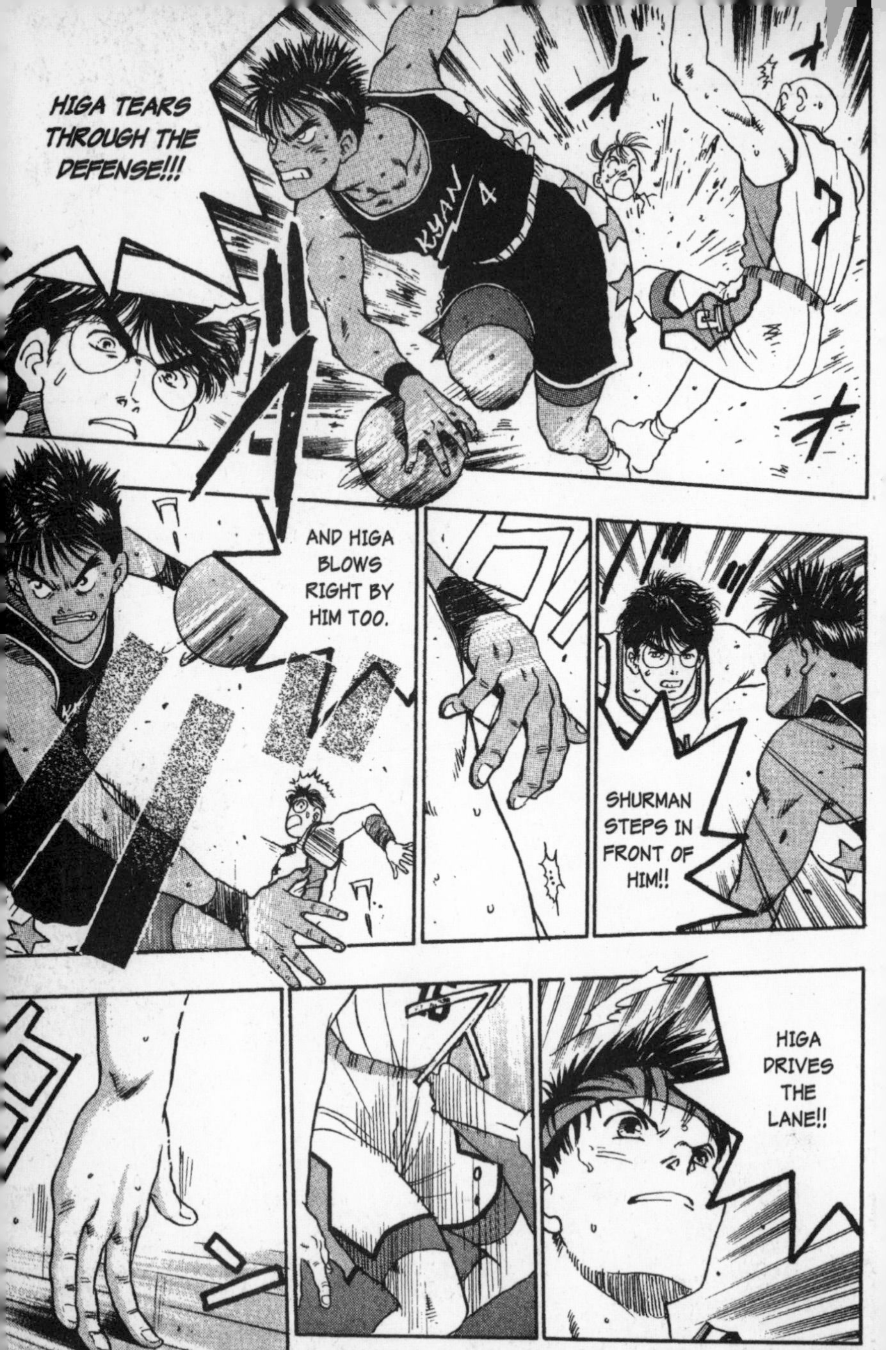
HIGA TEARS THROUGH THE DEFENSE!!!
SHURMAN STEPS IN FRONT OF HIM!!
AND HIGA BLOWS RIGHT BY HIM TOO.
HIGA DRIVES THE LANE!!

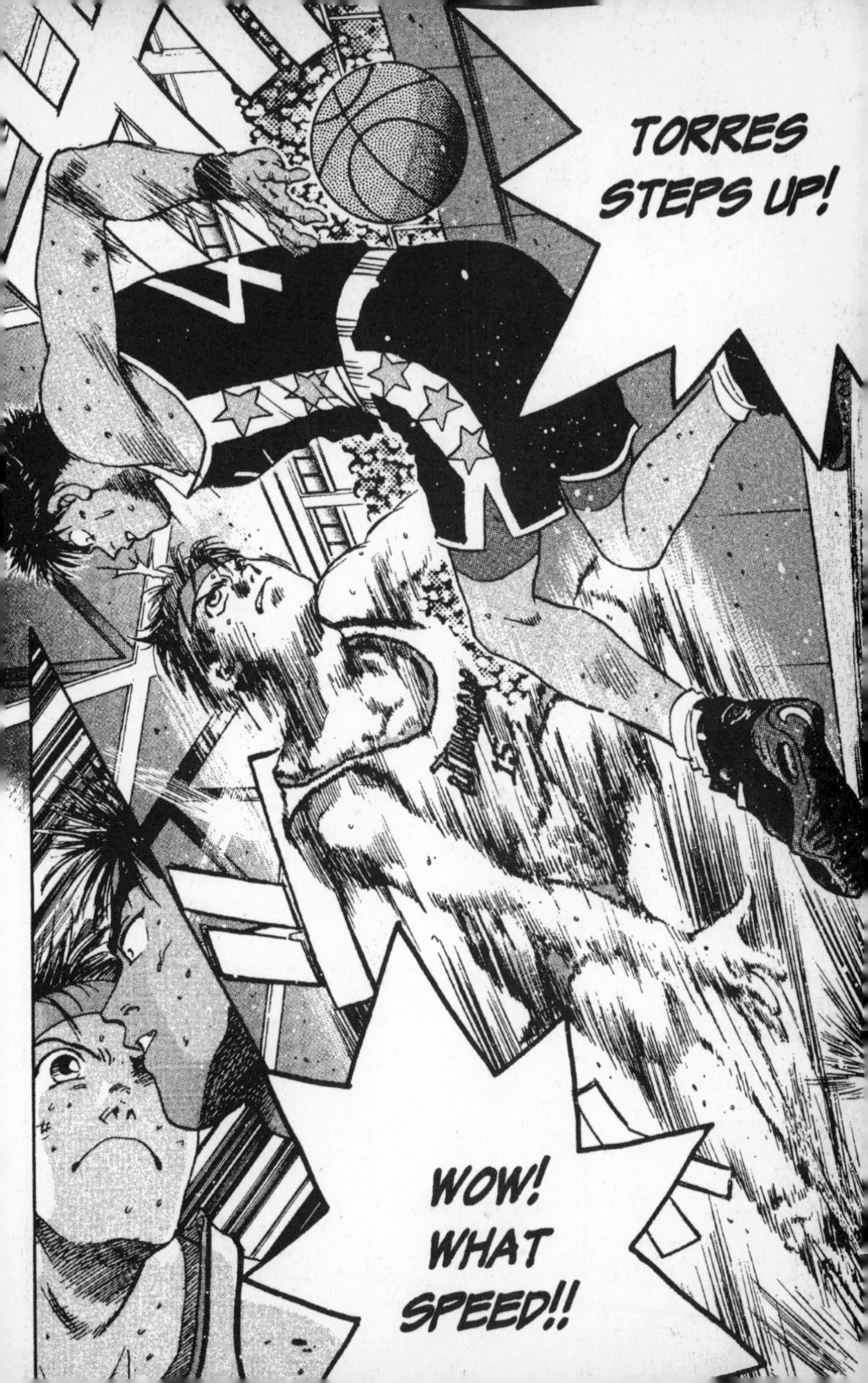
TORRES STEPS UP!
WOW! WHAT SPEED!!

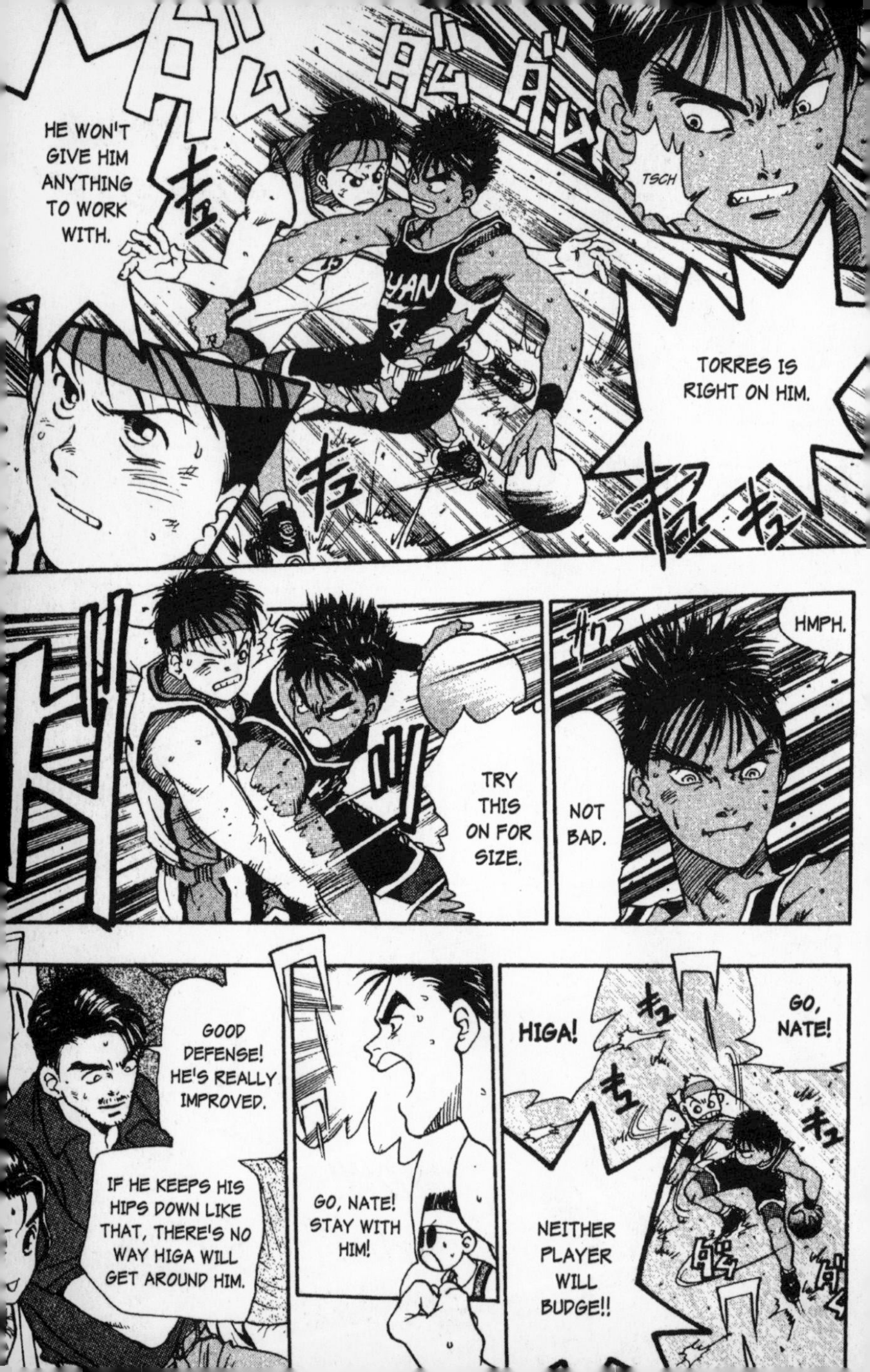
TSCH
TORRES IS RIGHT ON HIM.
HE WON'T GIVE HIM ANYTHING TO WORK WITH.
HMPH.
NOT BAD.
TRY THIS ON FOR SIZE.
GO, NATE!
HIGA!
NEITHER PLAYER WILL BUDGE!!
GO, NATE! STAY WITH HIM!
GOOD DEFENSE! HE'S REALLY IMPROVED.
IF HE KEEPS HIS HIPS DOWN LIKE THAT, THERE'S NO WAY HIGA WILL GET AROUND HIM.

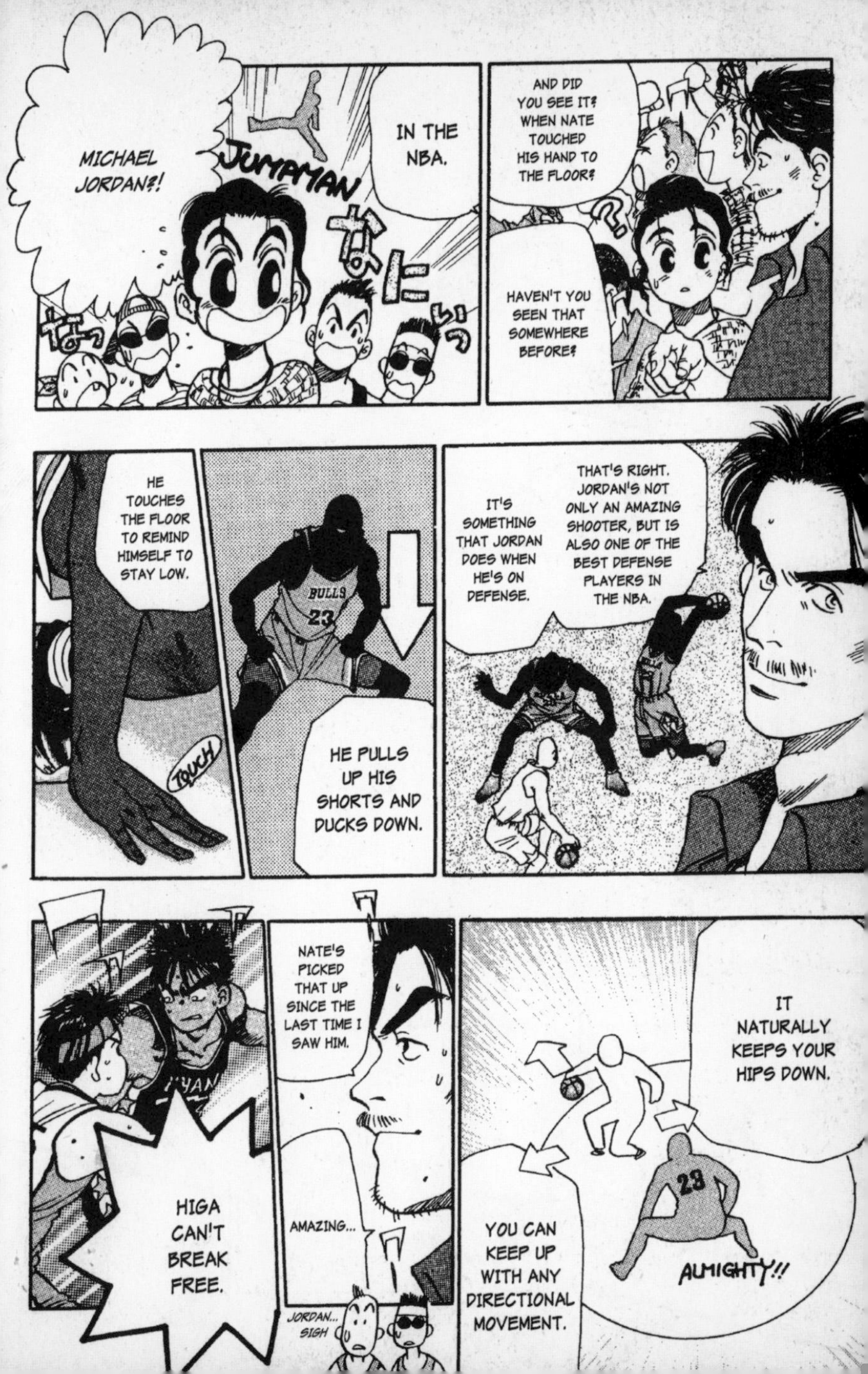
AND DID YOU SEE IT? WHEN NATE TOUCHED HIS HAND TO THE FLOOR?
HAVEN'T YOU SEEN THAT SOMEWHERE BEFORE?
IN THE NBA.
JUMPMAN
なにっ
MICHAEL JORDAN?!
なっ
THAT'S RIGHT. JORDAN'S NOT ONLY AN AMAZING SHOOTER, BUT IS ALSO ONE OF THE BEST DEFENSE PLAYERS IN THE NBA.
IT'S SOMETHING THAT JORDAN DOES WHEN HE'S ON DEFENSE.
BULLS
23
HE PULLS UP HIS SHORTS AND DUCKS DOWN.
HE TOUCHES THE FLOOR TO REMIND HIMSELF TO STAY LOW.
TOUCH
IT NATURALLY KEEPS YOUR HIPS DOWN.
23
YOU CAN KEEP UP WITH ANY DIRECTIONAL MOVEMENT.
ALMIGHTY!!
NATE'S PICKED THAT UP SINCE THE LAST TIME I SAW HIM.
AMAZING...
JORDAN... SIGH
HIGA CAN'T BREAK FREE.

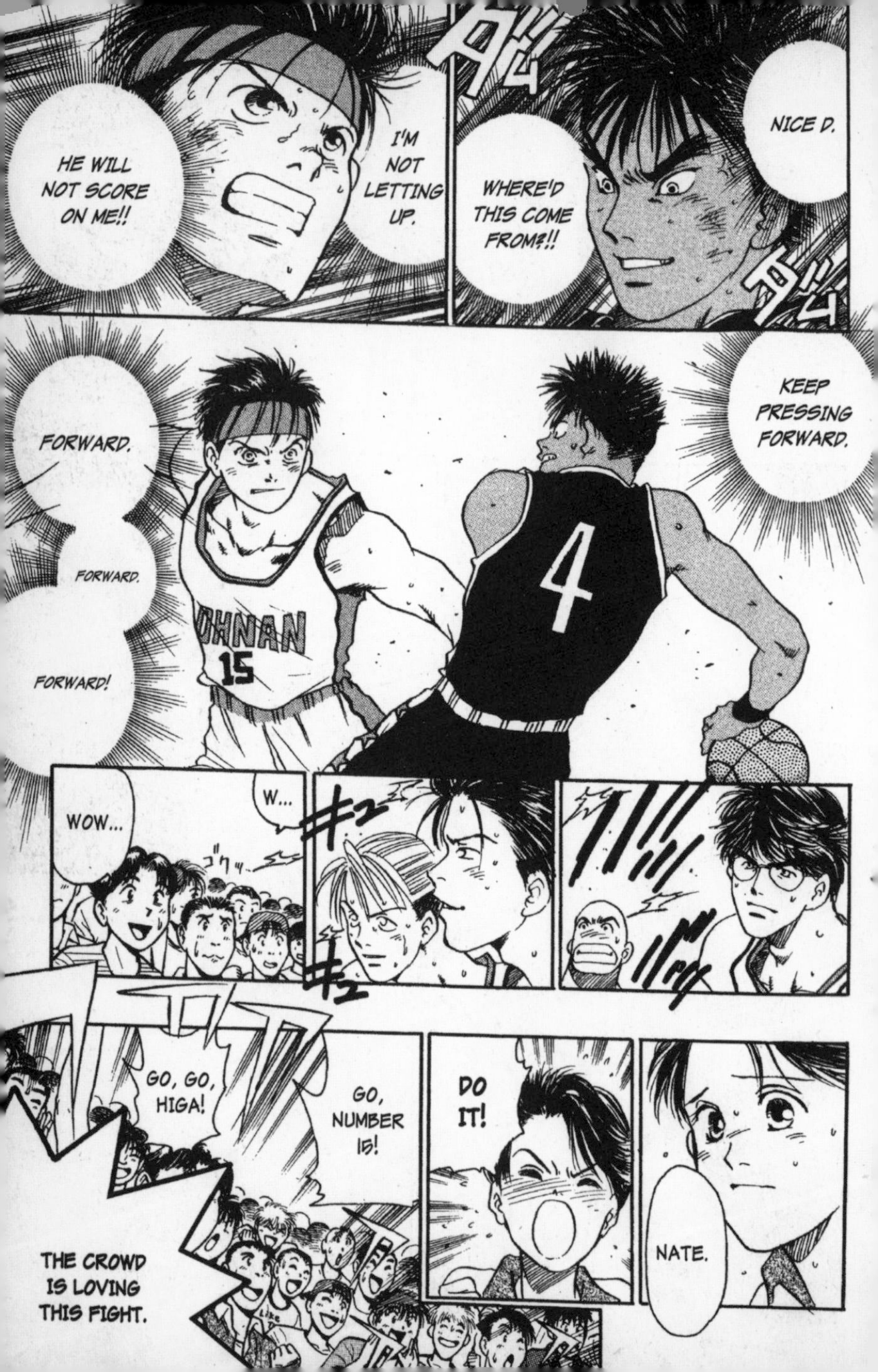
NICE D.
WHERE'D THIS COME FROM?!!
I'M NOT LETTING UP.
HE WILL NOT SCORE ON ME!!
KEEP PRESSING FORWARD.
FORWARD.
FORWARD.
FORWARD!
W...
WOW...
NATE.
DO IT!
GO, NUMBER 15!
GO, GO, HIGA!
THE CROWD IS LOVING THIS FIGHT.

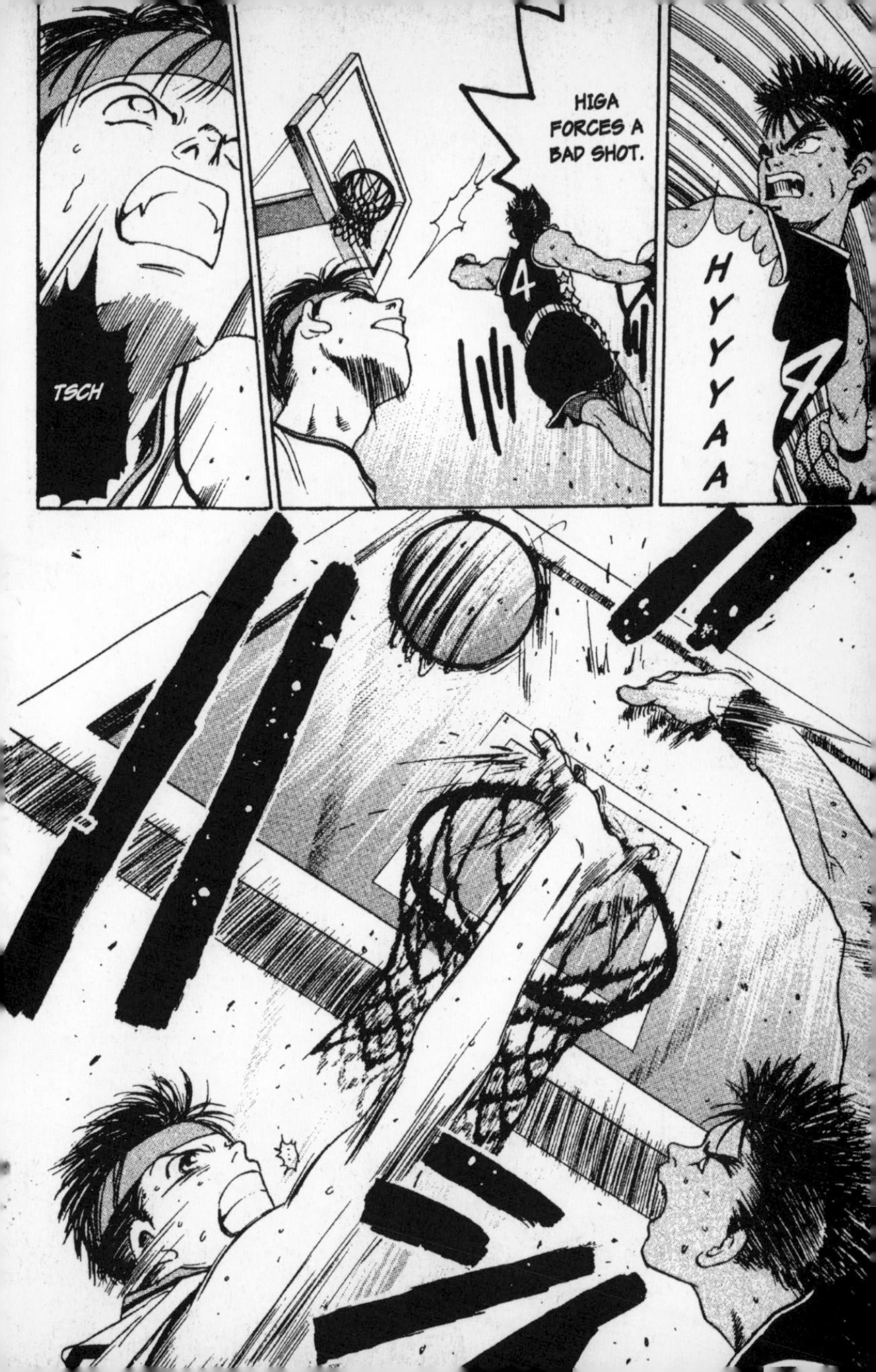
HYYYAA
HIGA FORCES A BAD SHOT.
TSCH

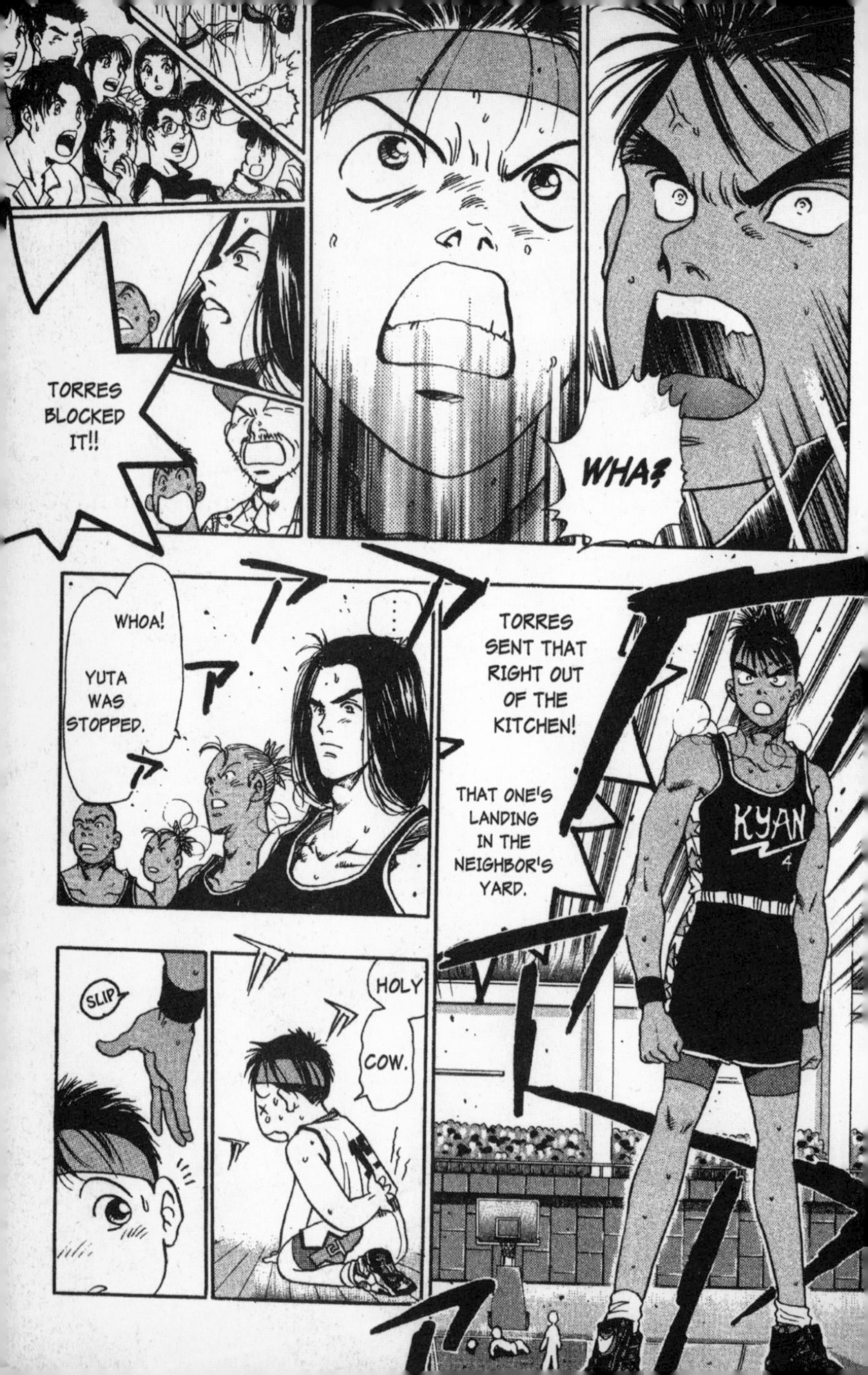
WHA?
TORRES BLOCKED IT!!
TORRES SENT THAT RIGHT OUT OF THE KITCHEN!
THAT ONE'S LANDING IN THE NEIGHBOR'S YARD.
...
WHOA!
YUTA WAS STOPPED.
HOLY
COW.
SLIP

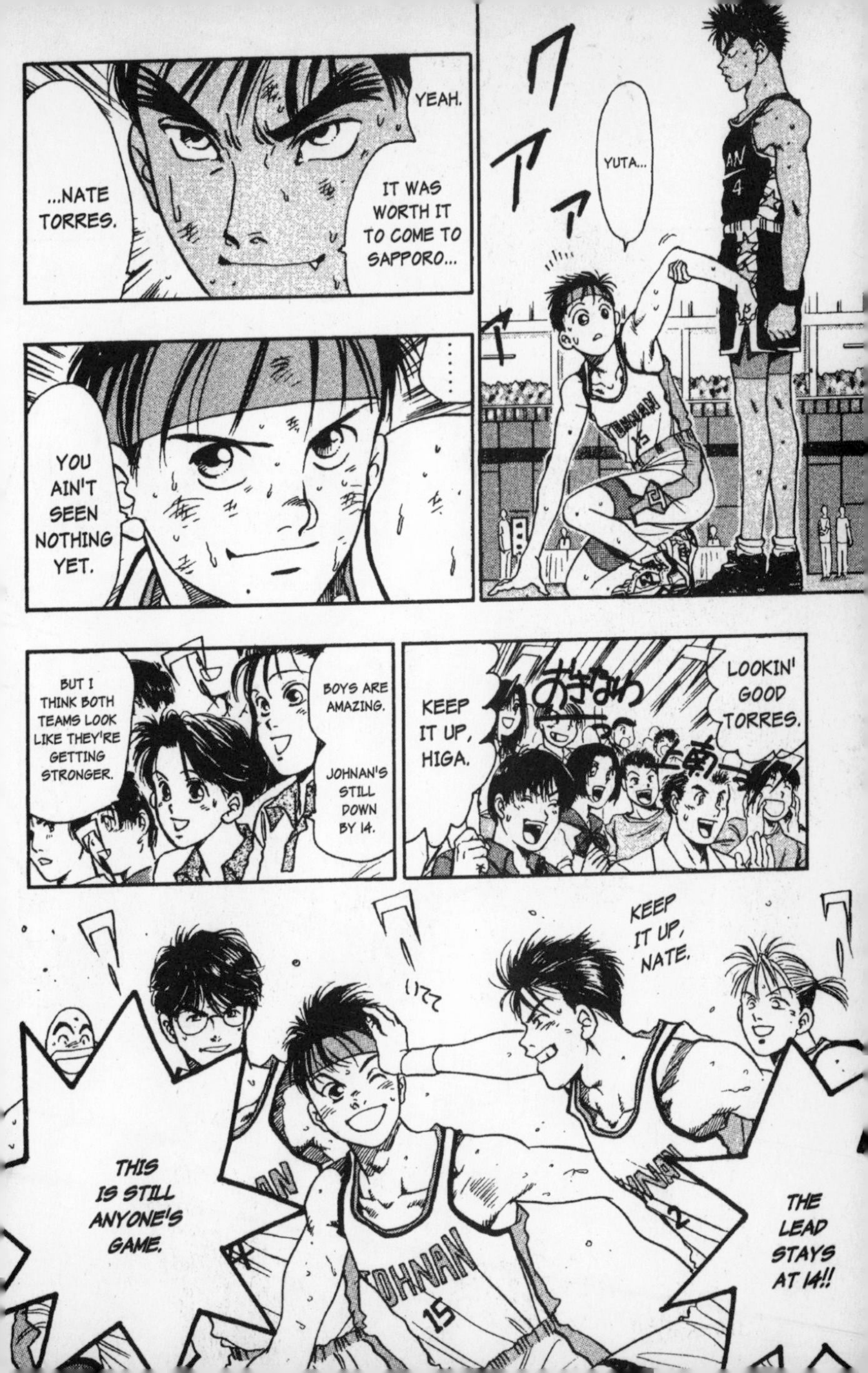
YUTA...
YEAH.
IT WAS WORTH IT TO COME TO SAPPORO...
...NATE TORRES.
......
YOU AIN'T SEEN NOTHING YET.
LOOKIN' GOOD TORRES.
KEEP IT UP, HIGA.
BOYS ARE AMAZING.
JOHNAN'S STILL DOWN BY 14.
BUT I THINK BOTH TEAMS LOOK LIKE THEY'RE GETTING STRONGER.
KEEP IT UP, NATE.
THE LEAD STAYS AT 14!!
THIS IS STILL ANYONE'S GAME.

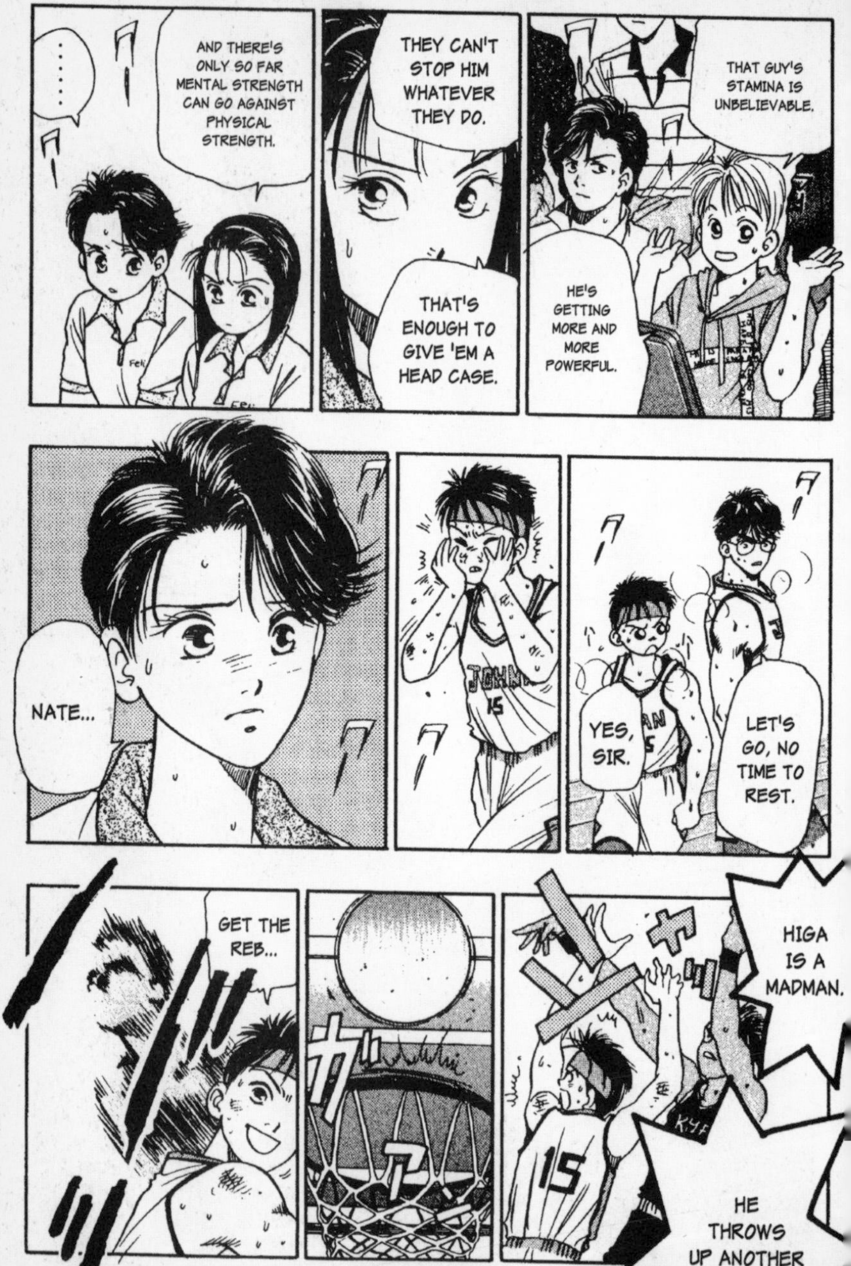
THAT GUY'S STAMINA IS UNBELIEVABLE.
HE'S GETTING MORE AND MORE POWERFUL.
THEY CAN'T STOP HIM WHATEVER THEY DO.
THAT'S ENOUGH TO GIVE 'EM A HEAD CASE.
AND THERE'S ONLY SO FAR MENTAL STRENGTH CAN GO AGAINST PHYSICAL STRENGTH.
......
LET'S GO, NO TIME TO REST.
YES, SIR.
NATE...
HIGA IS A MADMAN.
HE THROWS UP ANOTHER SHOT.
GET THE REB...

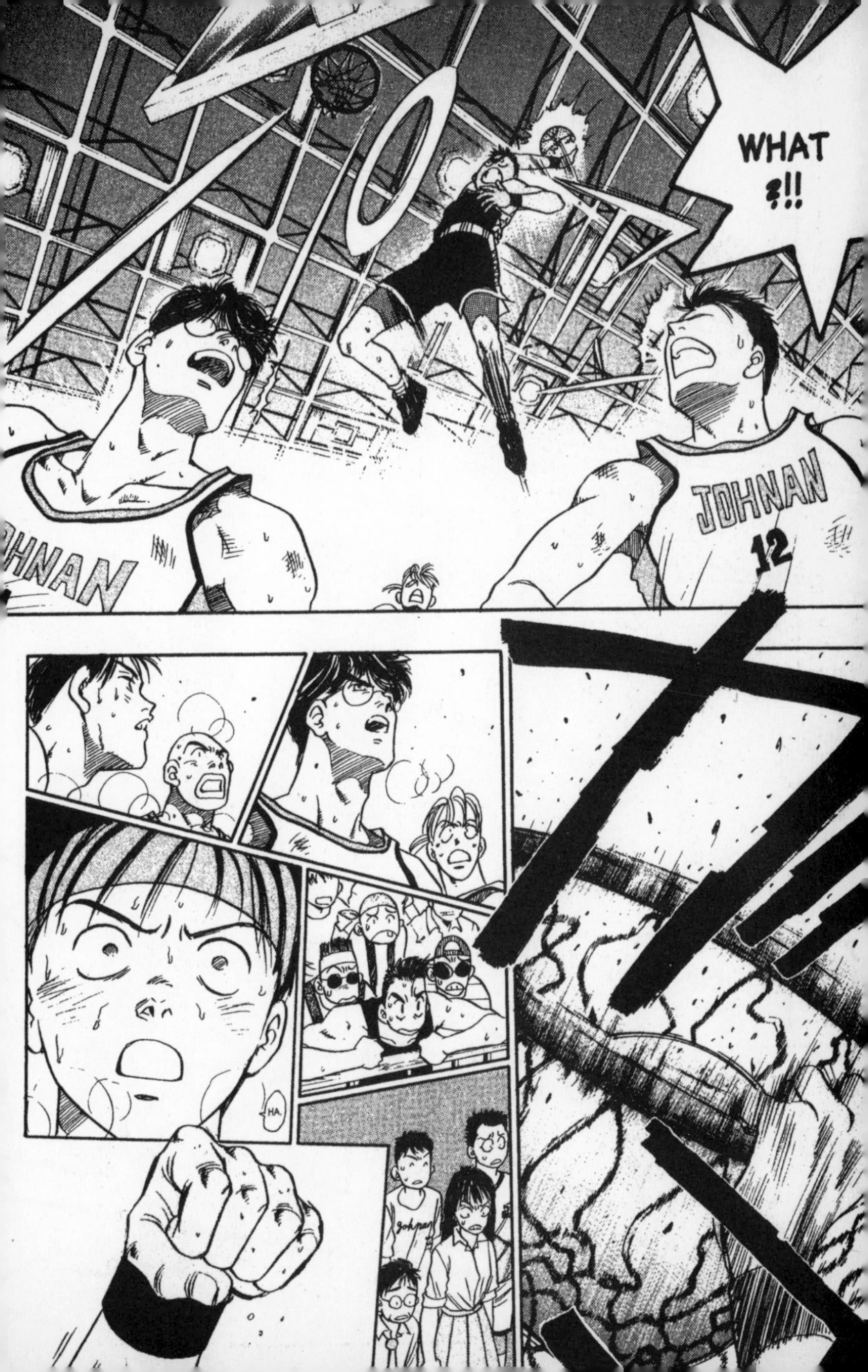
WHAT ?!!
JOHNAN
12
JOHNAN
HA.
gohnan

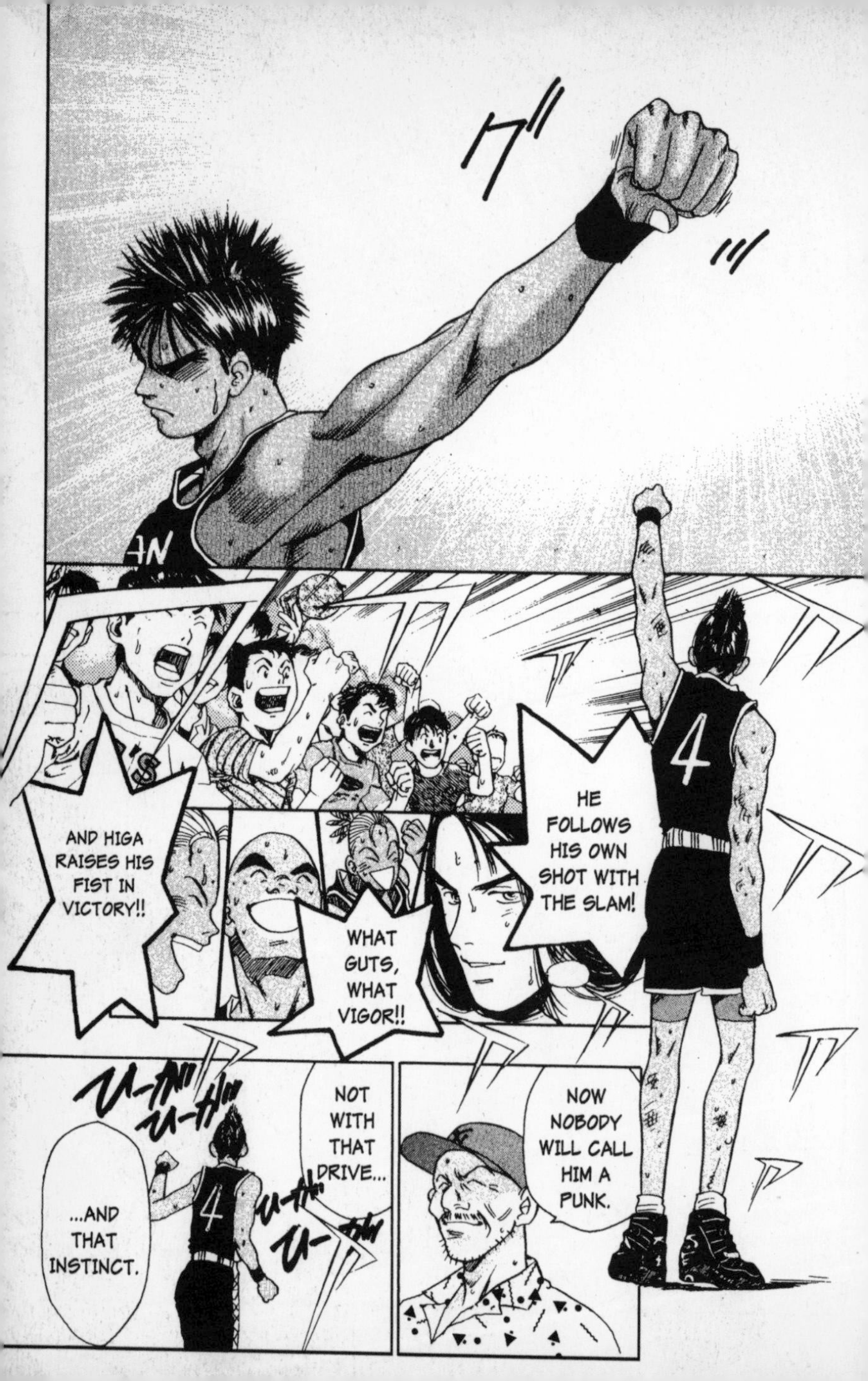
AND HIGA RAISES HIS FIST IN VICTORY!!
HE FOLLOWS HIS OWN SHOT WITH THE SLAM!
WHAT GUTS, WHAT VIGOR!!
NOW NOBODY WILL CALL HIM A PUNK.
NOT WITH THAT DRIVE...
...AND THAT INSTINCT.

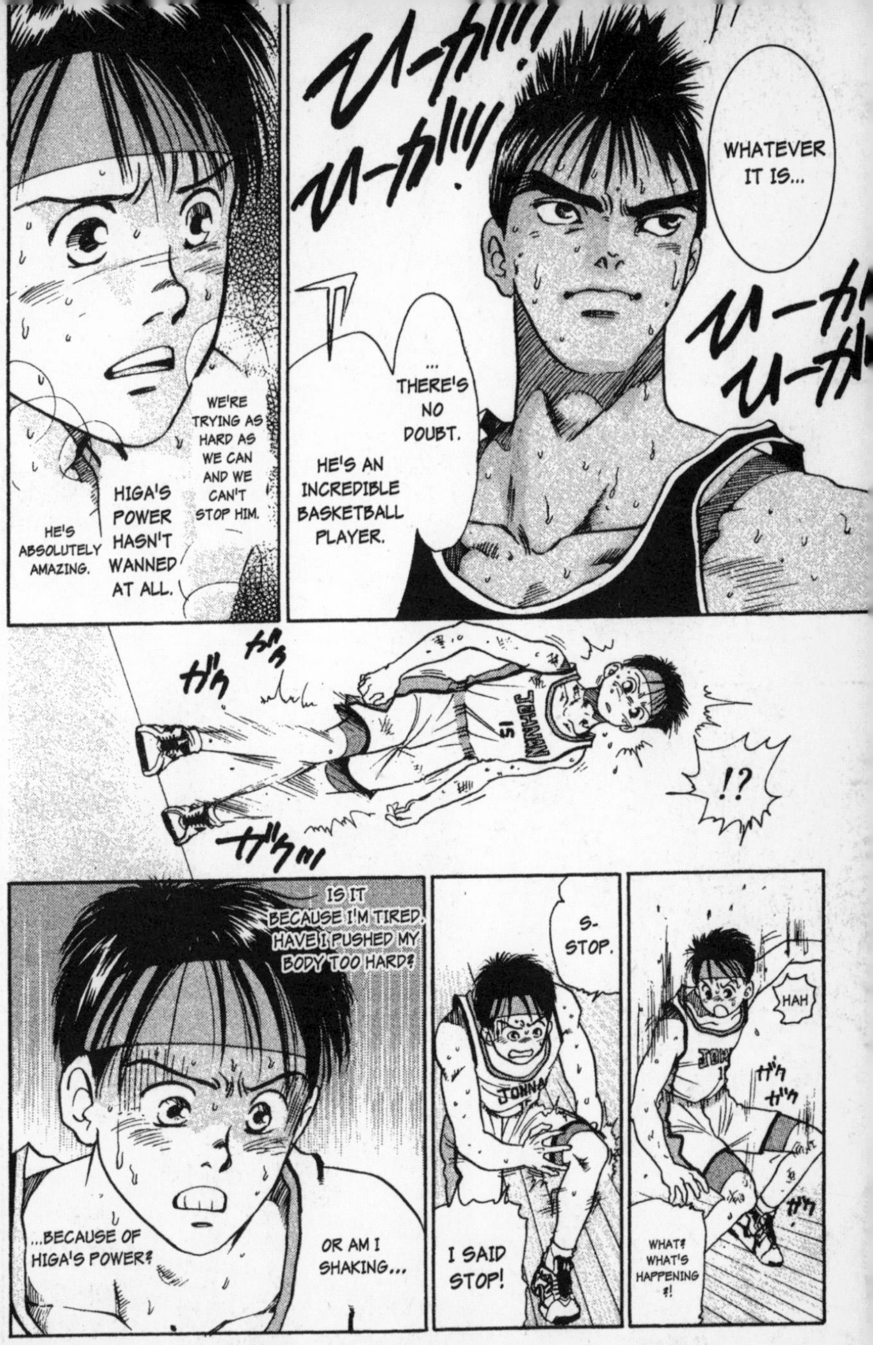
WHATEVER IT IS...
... THERE'S NO DOUBT.
HE'S AN INCREDIBLE BASKETBALL PLAYER.
WE'RE TRYING AS HARD AS WE CAN AND WE CAN'T STOP HIM.
HIGA'S POWER HASN'T WANNED AT ALL.
HE'S ABSOLUTELY AMAZING.
!?
HAH
WHAT? WHAT'S HAPPENING ?!
S- STOP.
I SAID STOP!
IS IT BECAUSE I'M TIRED. HAVE I PUSHED MY BODY TOO HARD?
OR AM I SHAKING...
...BECAUSE OF HIGA'S POWER?

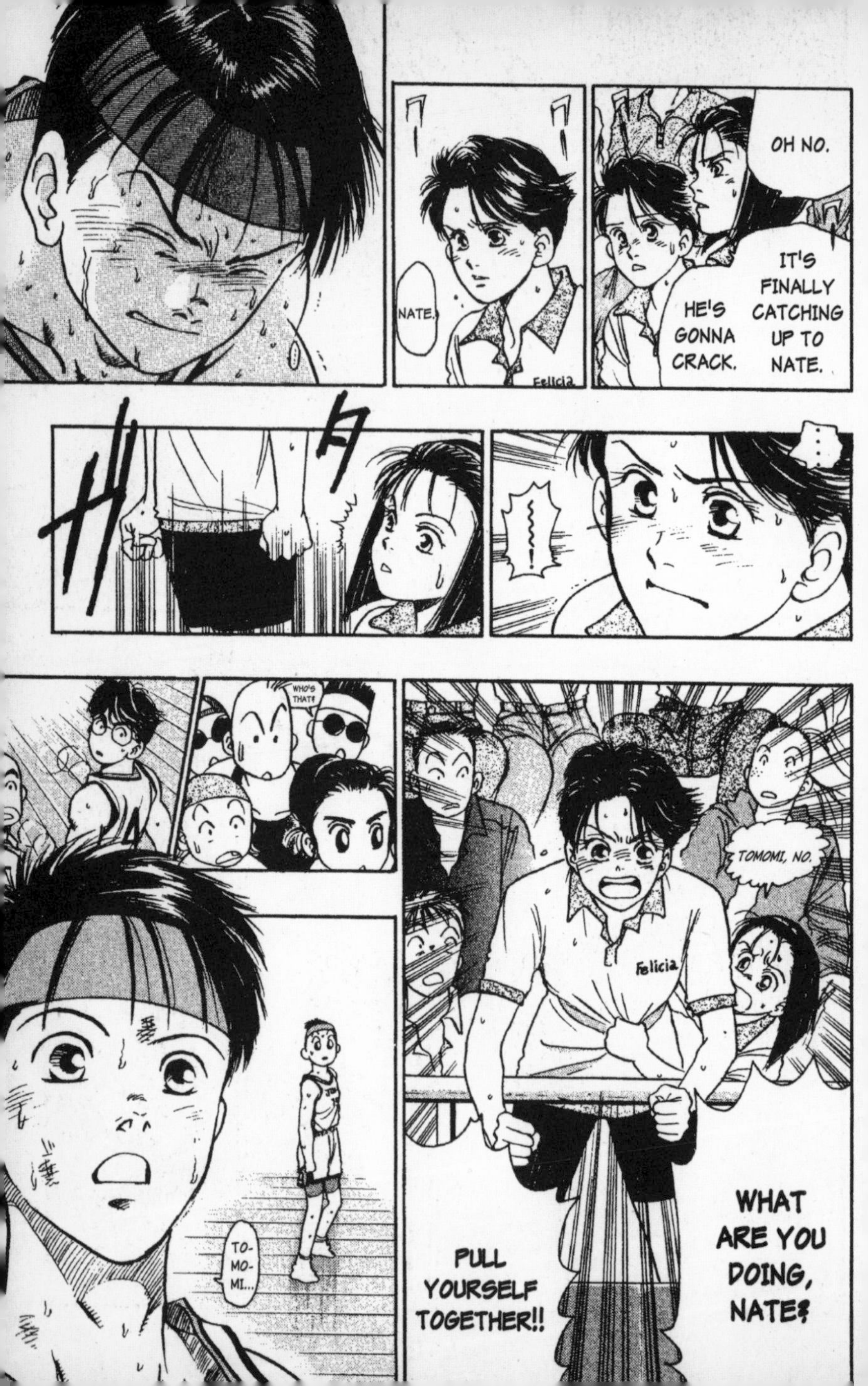
OH NO.
IT'S FINALLY CATCHING UP TO NATE.
HE'S GONNA CRACK.
NATE.
Felicia
TOMOMI, NO.
Felicia
WHAT ARE YOU DOING, NATE?
PULL YOURSELF TOGETHER!!
WHO'S THAT?
TO-MO-MI...

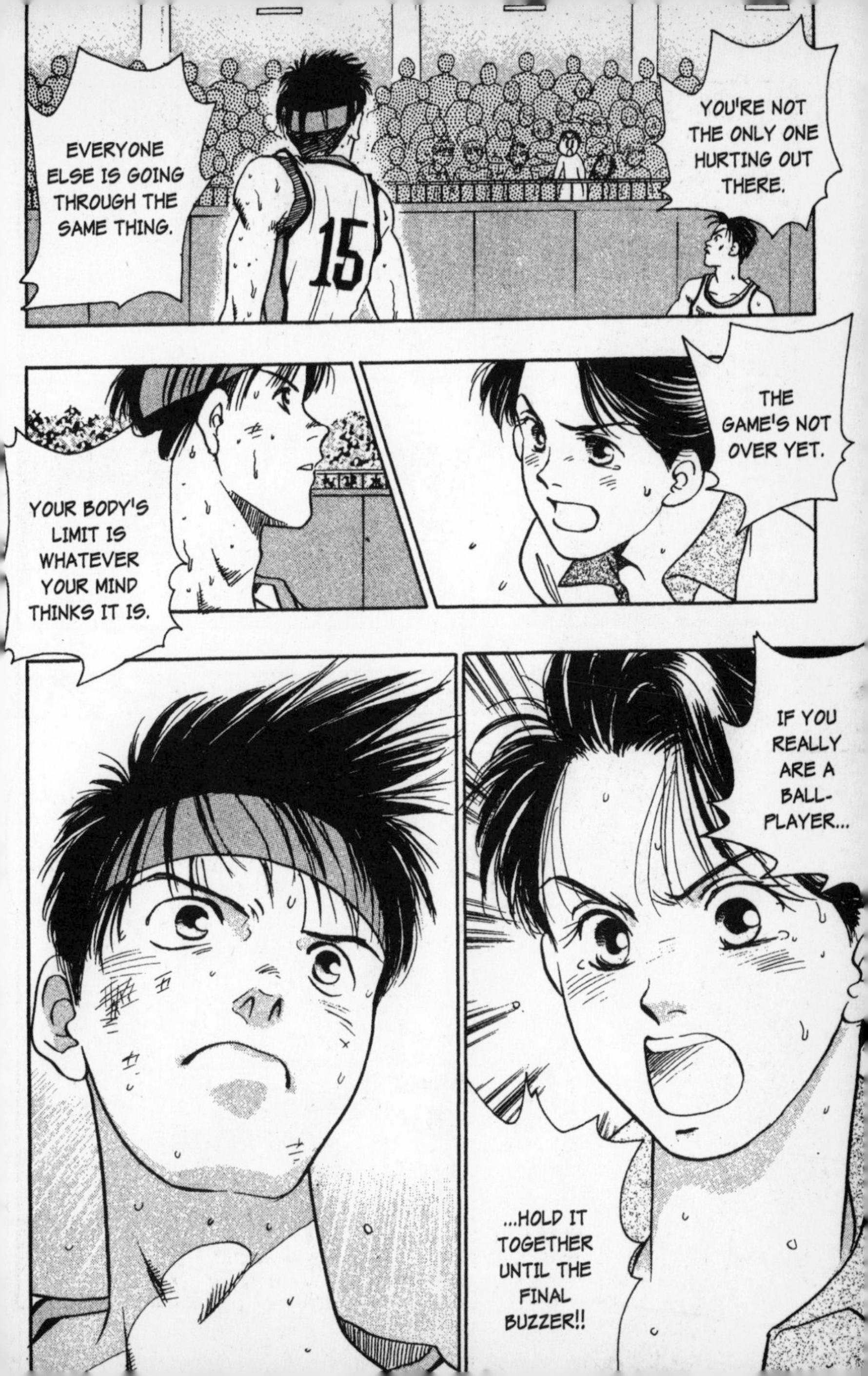
YOU'RE NOT THE ONLY ONE HURTING OUT THERE.
EVERYONE ELSE IS GOING THROUGH THE SAME THING.
THE GAME'S NOT OVER YET.
YOUR BODY'S LIMIT IS WHATEVER YOUR MIND THINKS IT IS.
IF YOU REALLY ARE A BALL-PLAYER...
...HOLD IT TOGETHER UNTIL THE FINAL BUZZER!!

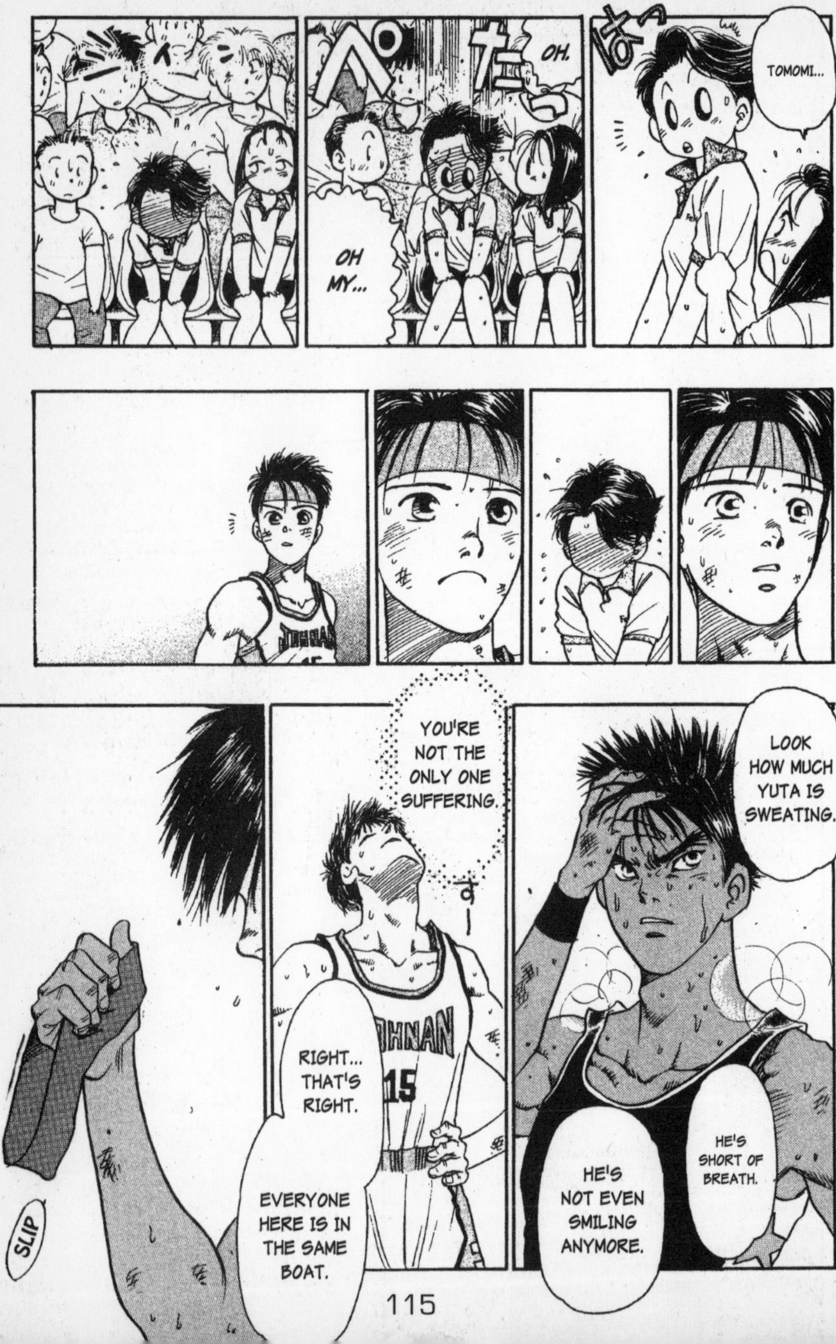
TOMOMI...
OH.
OH MY...
LOOK HOW MUCH YUTA IS SWEATING.
HE'S SHORT OF BREATH.
HE'S NOT EVEN SMILING ANYMORE.
YOU'RE NOT THE ONLY ONE SUFFERING.
RIGHT... THAT'S RIGHT.
EVERYONE HERE IS IN THE SAME BOAT.
SLIP

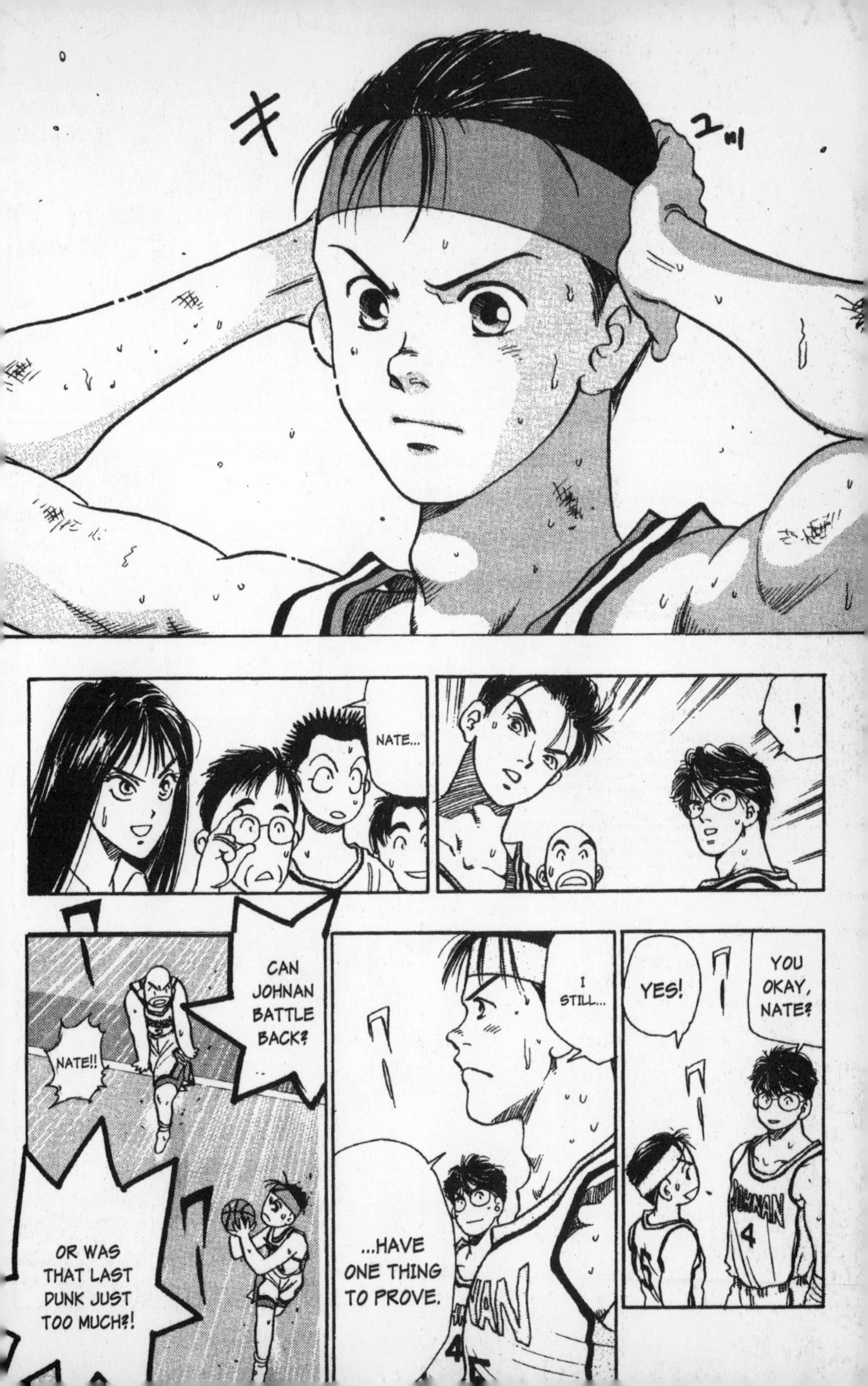
キ
!
NATE...
YOU OKAY, NATE?
YES!
I STILL...
...HAVE ONE THING TO PROVE.
CAN JOHNAN BATTLE BACK?
NATE!!
OR WAS THAT LAST DUNK JUST TOO MUCH?!

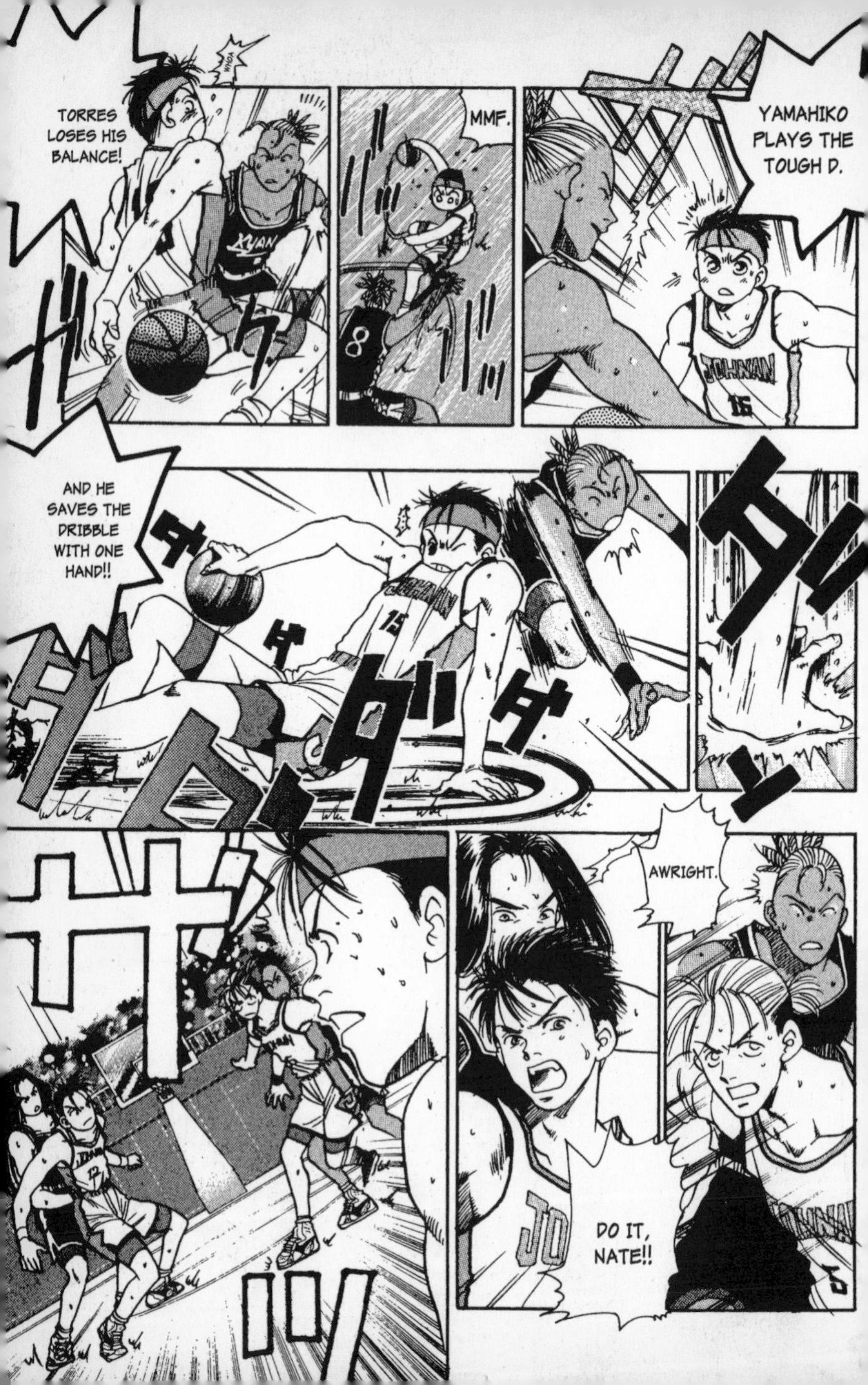
YAMAHIKO PLAYS THE TOUGH D.
MMF.
WHOA
TORRES LOSES HIS BALANCE!
AND HE SAVES THE DRIBBLE WITH ONE HAND!!
AWRIGHT.
DO IT, NATE!!

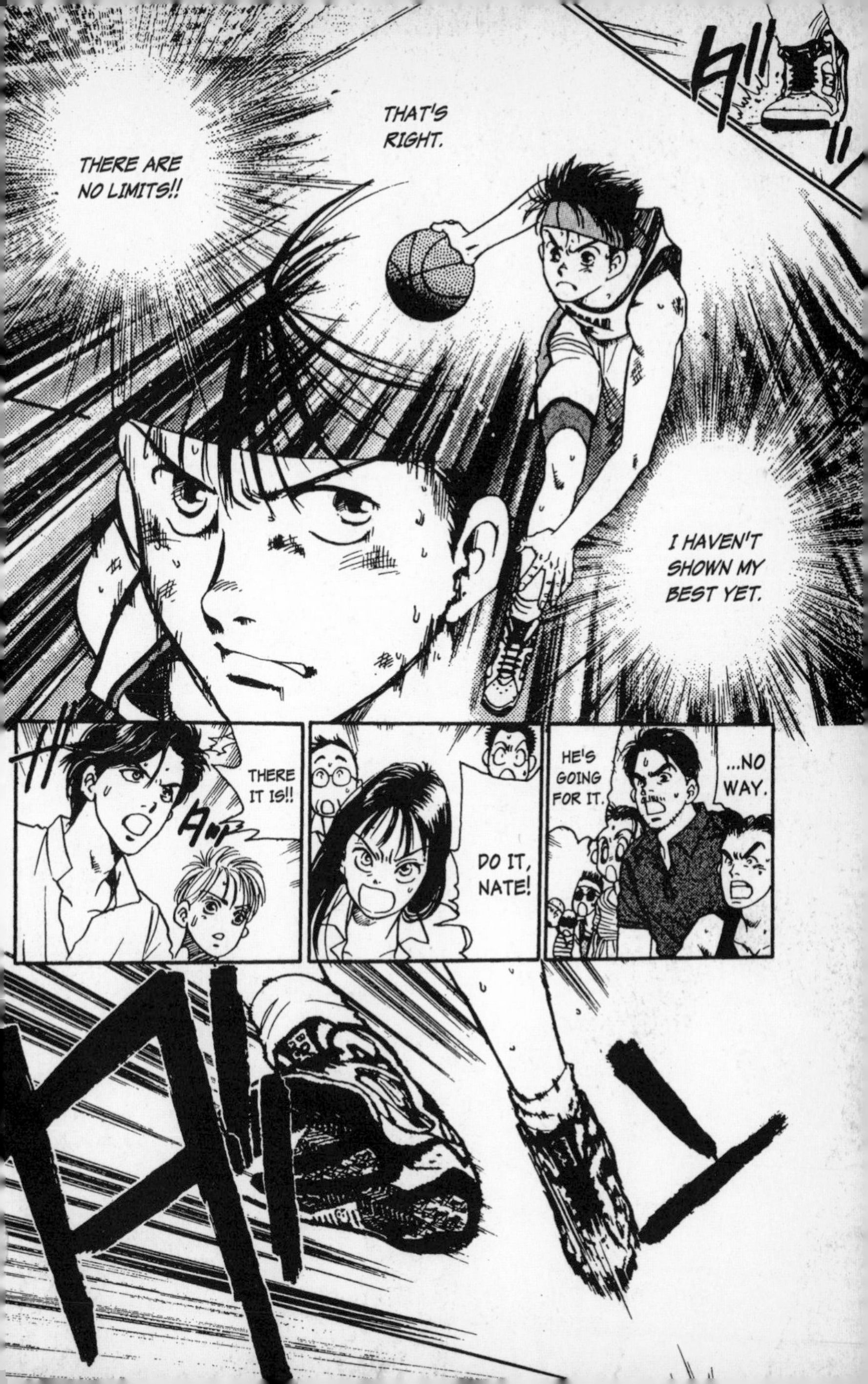
THAT'S RIGHT.
THERE ARE NO LIMITS!!
I HAVEN'T SHOWN MY BEST YET.
...NO WAY.
HE'S GOING FOR IT.
DO IT, NATE!
THERE IT IS!!

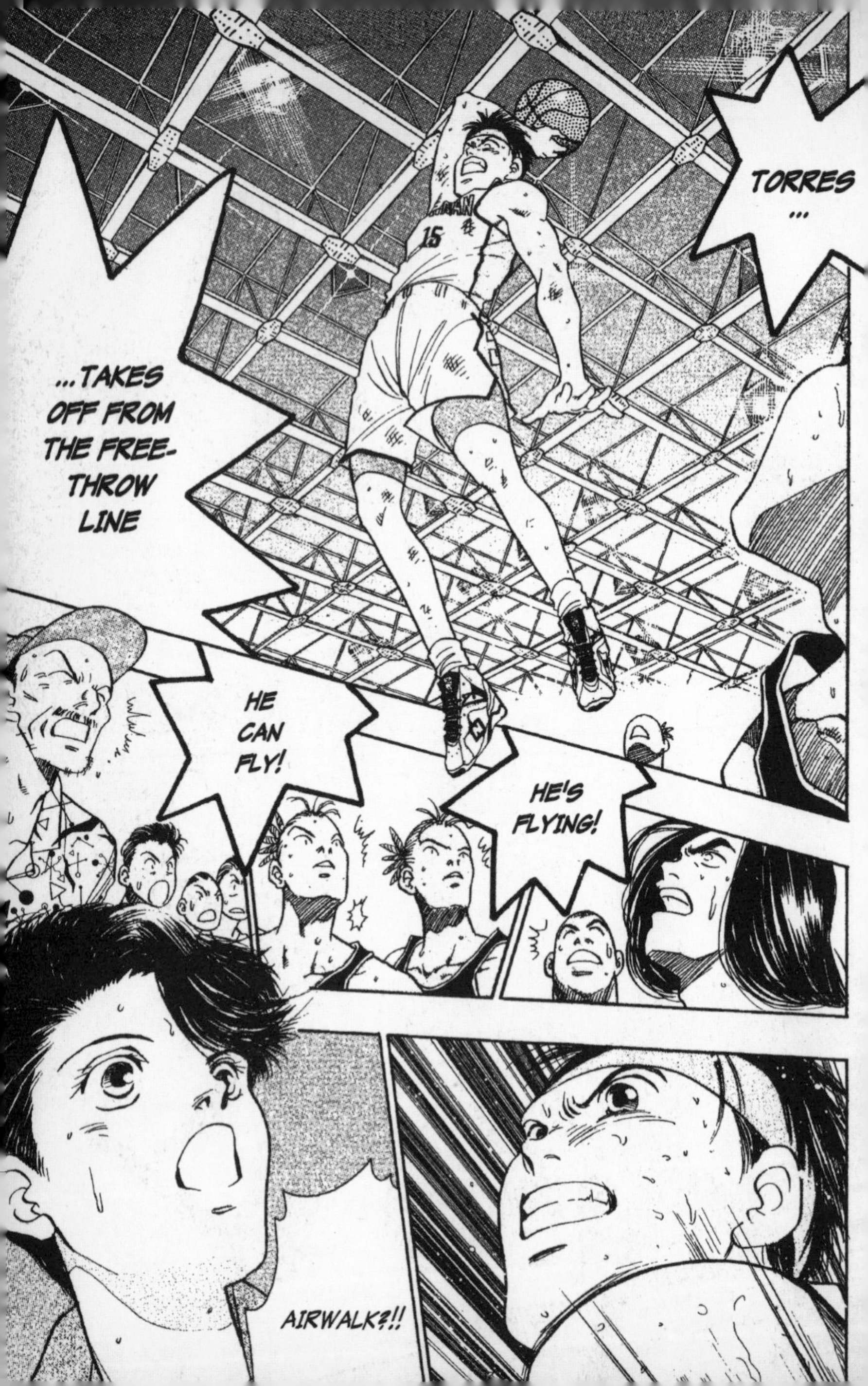
TORRES ...
...TAKES OFF FROM THE FREE-THROW LINE
HE'S FLYING!
HE CAN FLY!
AIRWALK?!!

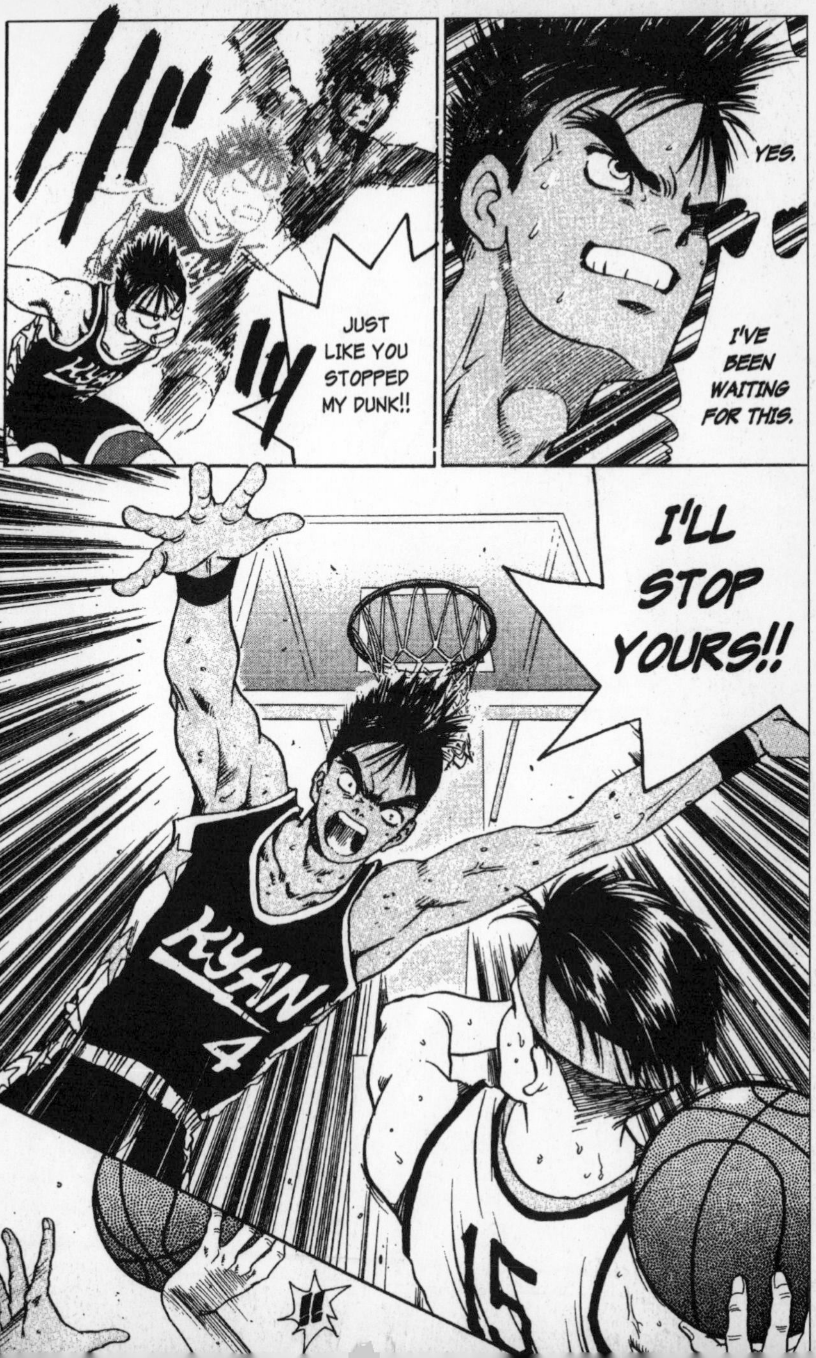
YES.
I'VE BEEN WAITING FOR THIS.
JUST LIKE YOU STOPPED MY DUNK!!
I'LL STOP YOURS!!
!!

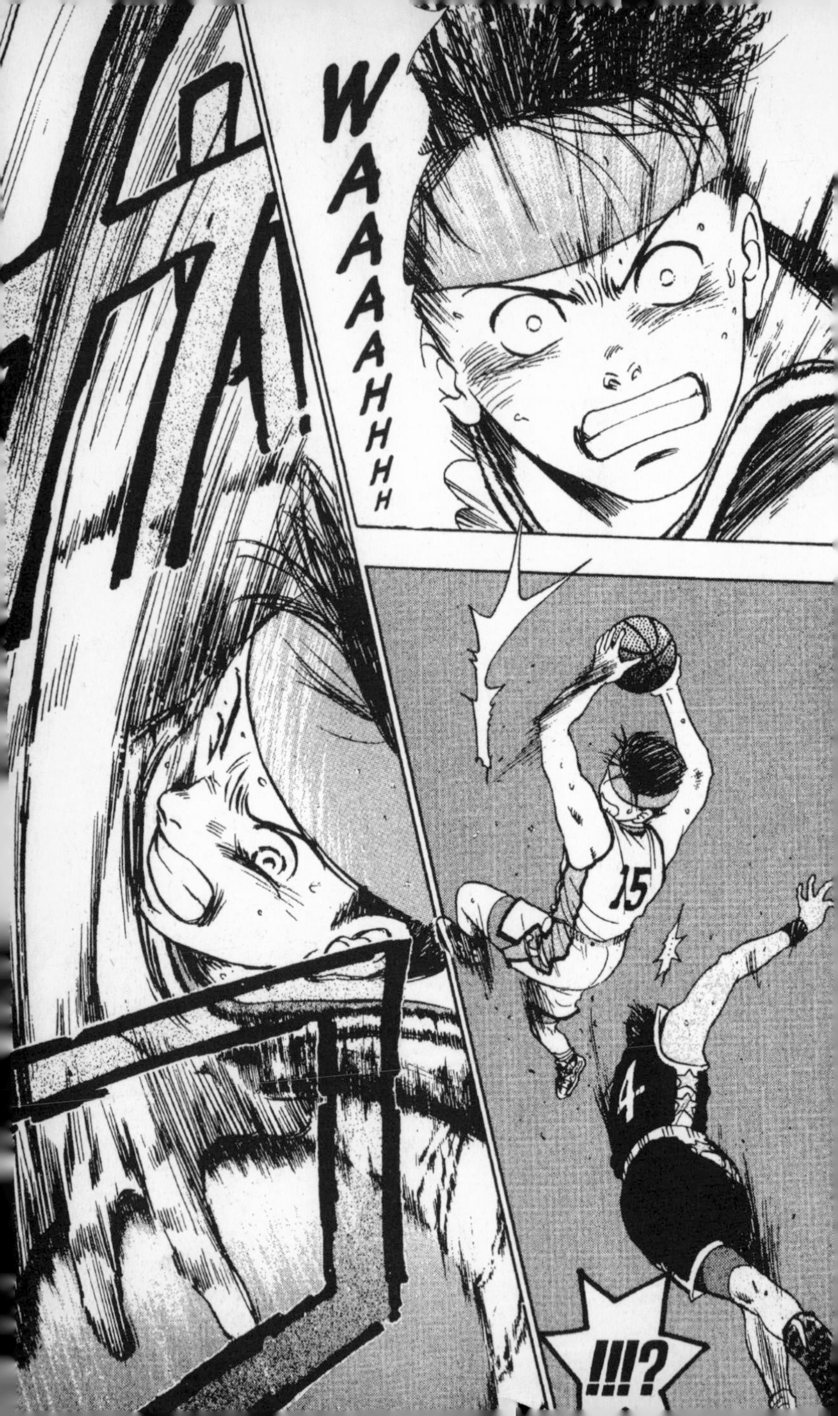
WAAAAHHHH
!!!?

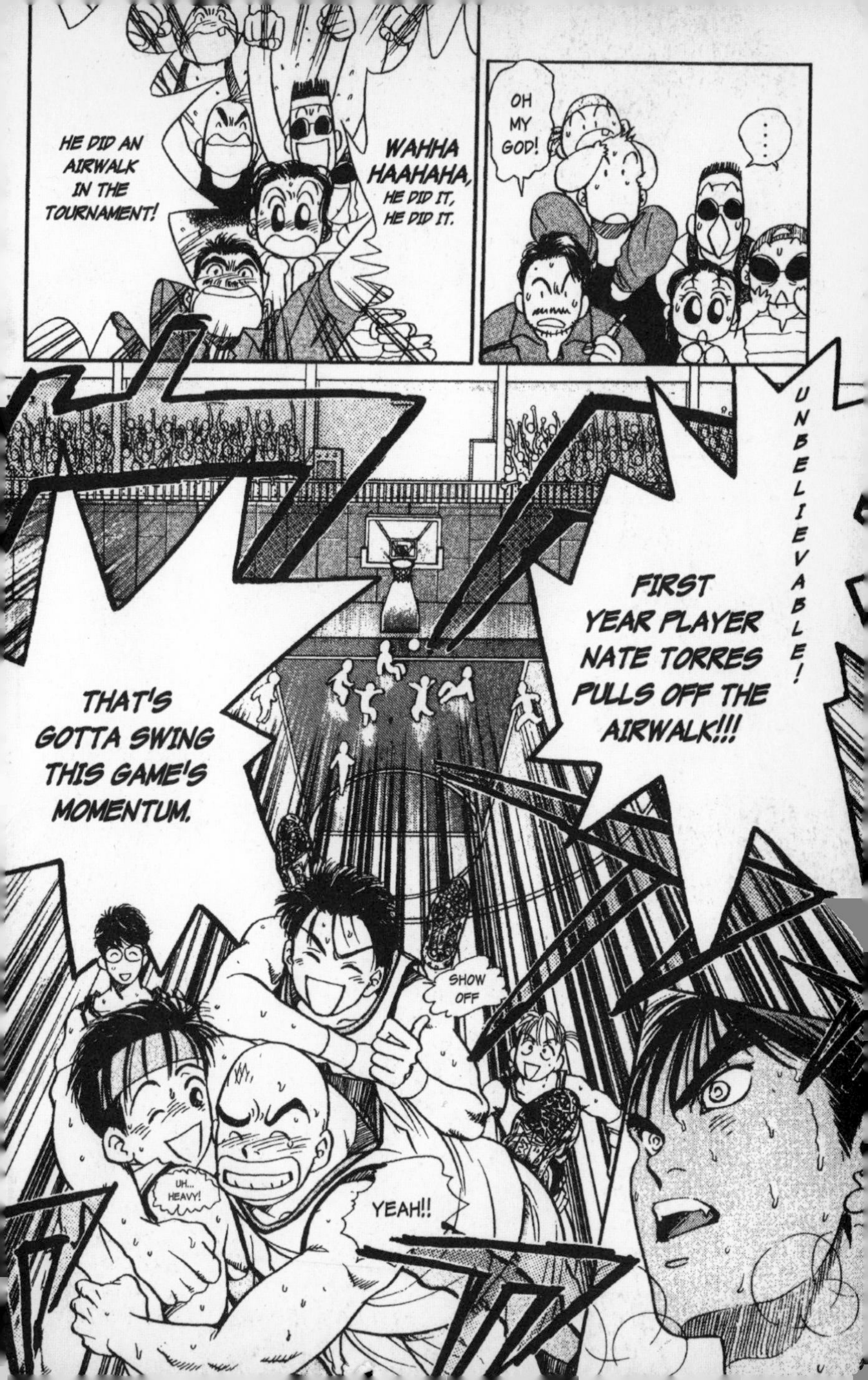

. . . .
OH MY GOD!
WAHHA HAAHAHA,
HE DID IT, HE DID IT.
HE DID AN AIRWALK IN THE TOURNAMENT!
UNBELIEVABLE!
FIRST YEAR PLAYER NATE TORRES PULLS OFF THE AIRWALK!!!
THAT'S GOTTA SWING THIS GAME'S MOMENTUM.
SHOW OFF
YEAH!!
UH... HEAVY!

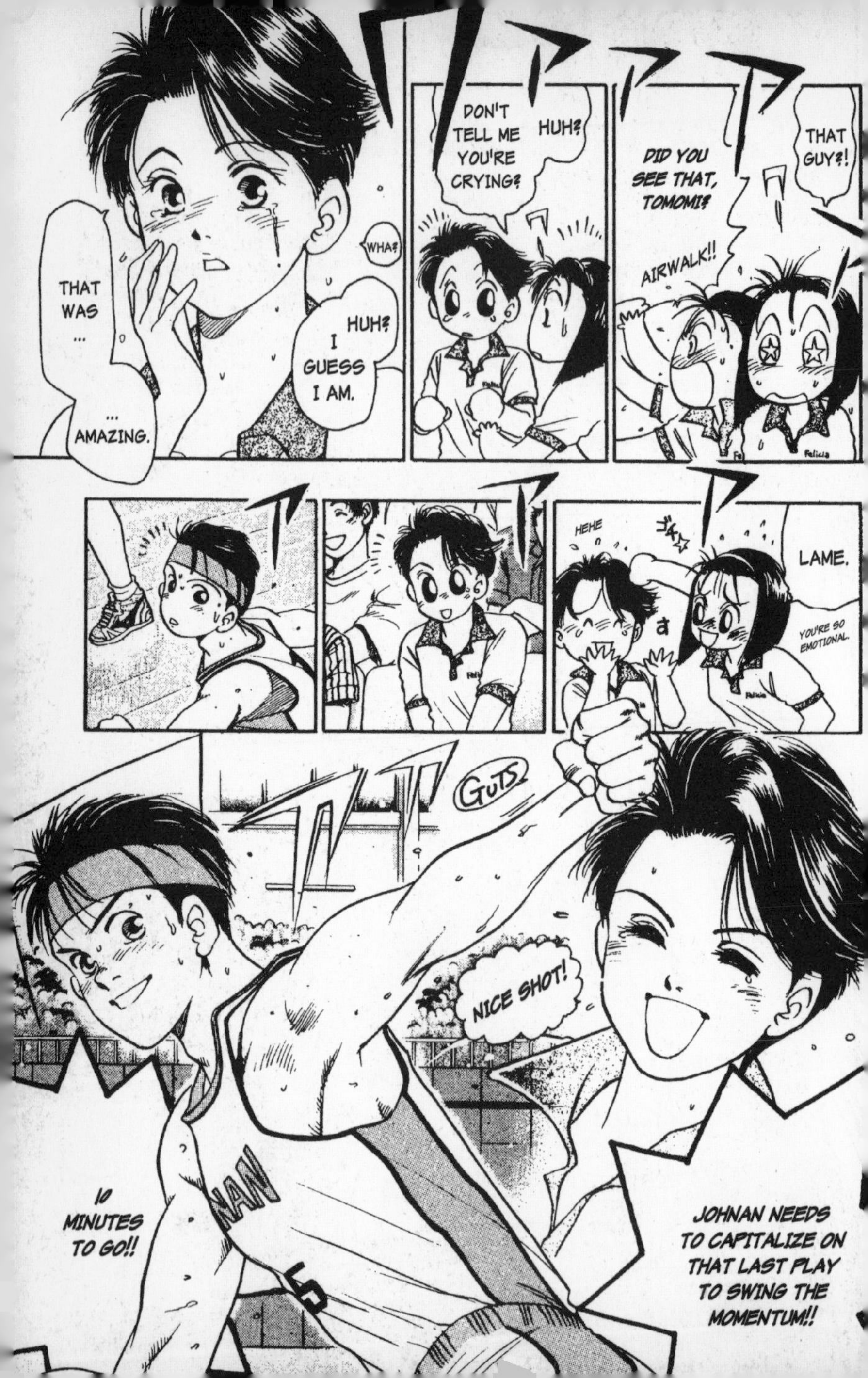
THAT GUY?!
DID YOU SEE THAT, TOMOMI?
AIRWALK!!
HUH?
DON'T TELL ME YOU'RE CRYING?
WHA?
HUH? I GUESS I AM.
THAT WAS ...
... AMAZING.
LAME.
YOU'RE SO EMOTIONAL.
HEHE
GUTS
NICE SHOT!
JOHNAN NEEDS TO CAPITALIZE ON THAT LAST PLAY TO SWING THE MOMENTUM!!
10 MINUTES TO GO!!

Ballad of Coach

There once was a boozer,
who liked to coach losers,
like Hoosiers without the old
coot.

And like many
a teacher,
he stole under
the bleachers,
to sneak a quick
sip of the juice.

But he loved his bad boys,
and gave them the joy
of charging the court
to cut loose.

Now to get them to win
he says, with a grin,
"If you don't shut your big
mouth you'll lose."

You're reading...
REBOUND

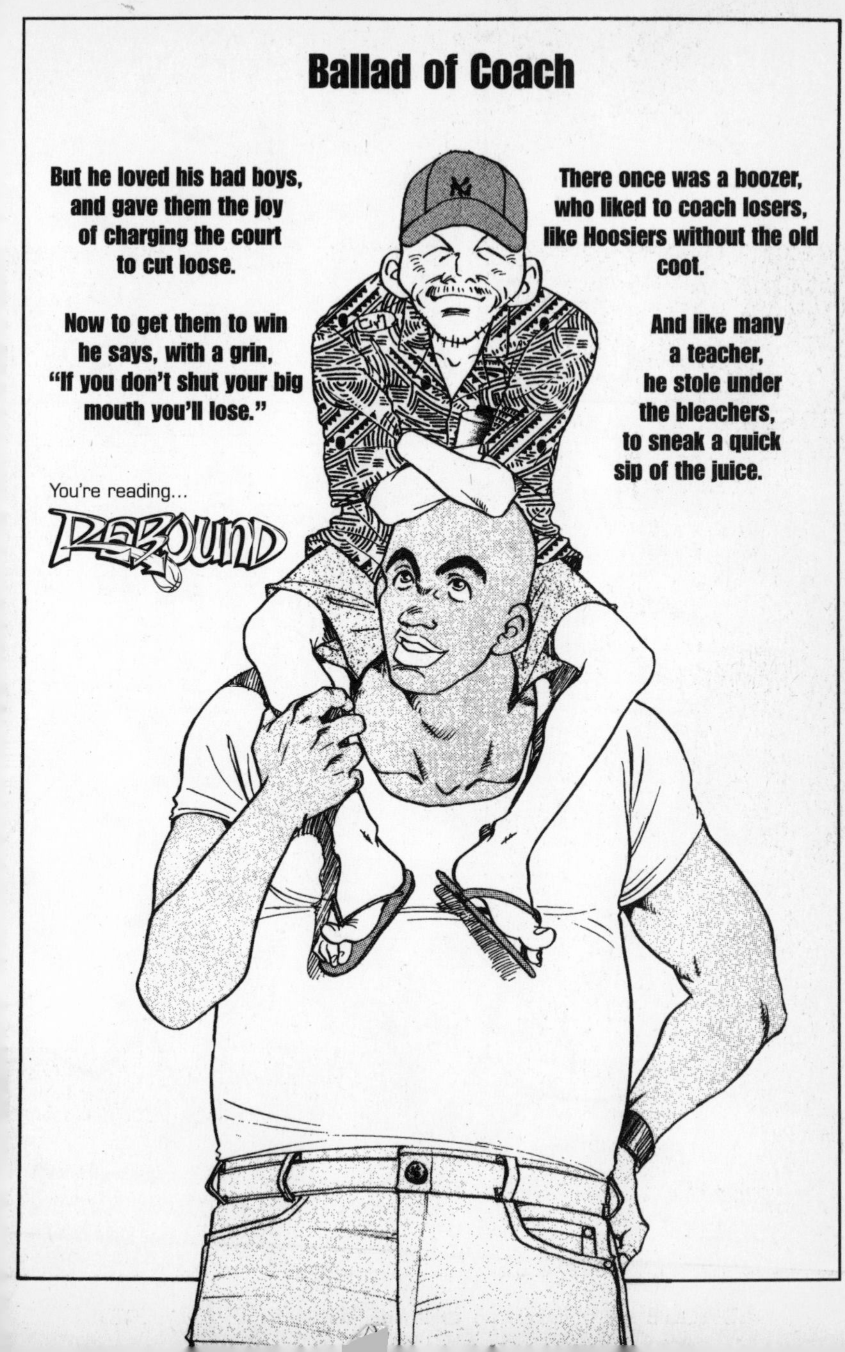

REBOUND

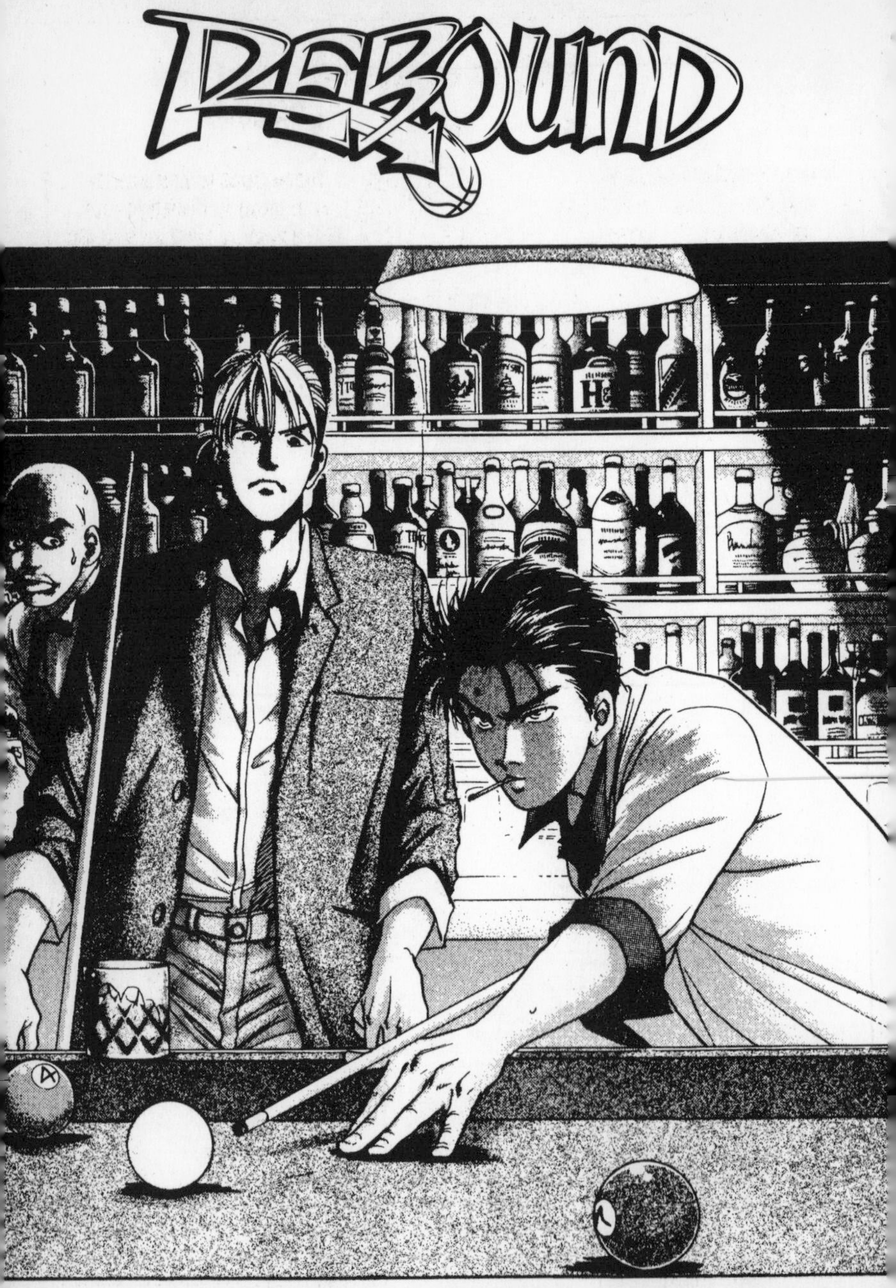

Episode 16: Let Us Spend the Time Together

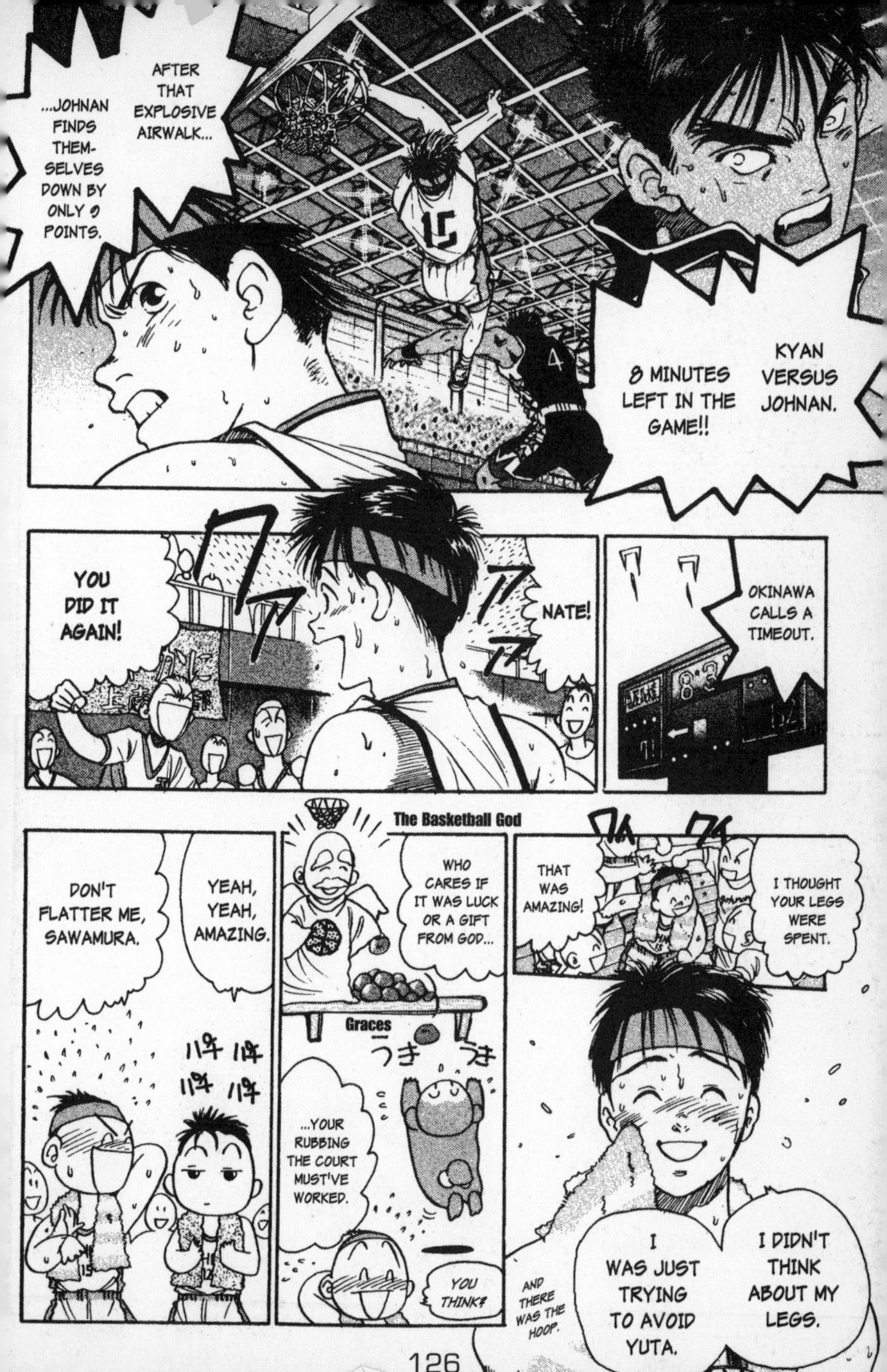
KYAN VERSUS JOHNAN.
8 MINUTES LEFT IN THE GAME!!
AFTER THAT EXPLOSIVE AIRWALK...
...JOHNAN FINDS THEM-SELVES DOWN BY ONLY 9 POINTS.
OKINAWA CALLS A TIMEOUT.
NATE!
YOU DID IT AGAIN!
I THOUGHT YOUR LEGS WERE SPENT.
THAT WAS AMAZING!
I DIDN'T THINK ABOUT MY LEGS.
I WAS JUST TRYING TO AVOID YUTA.
AND THERE WAS THE HOOP.
The Basketball God
WHO CARES IF IT WAS LUCK OR A GIFT FROM GOD...
Graces
うき うき
...YOUR RUBBING THE COURT MUST'VE WORKED.
YOU THINK?
YEAH, YEAH, AMAZING.
DON'T FLATTER ME, SAWAMURA.

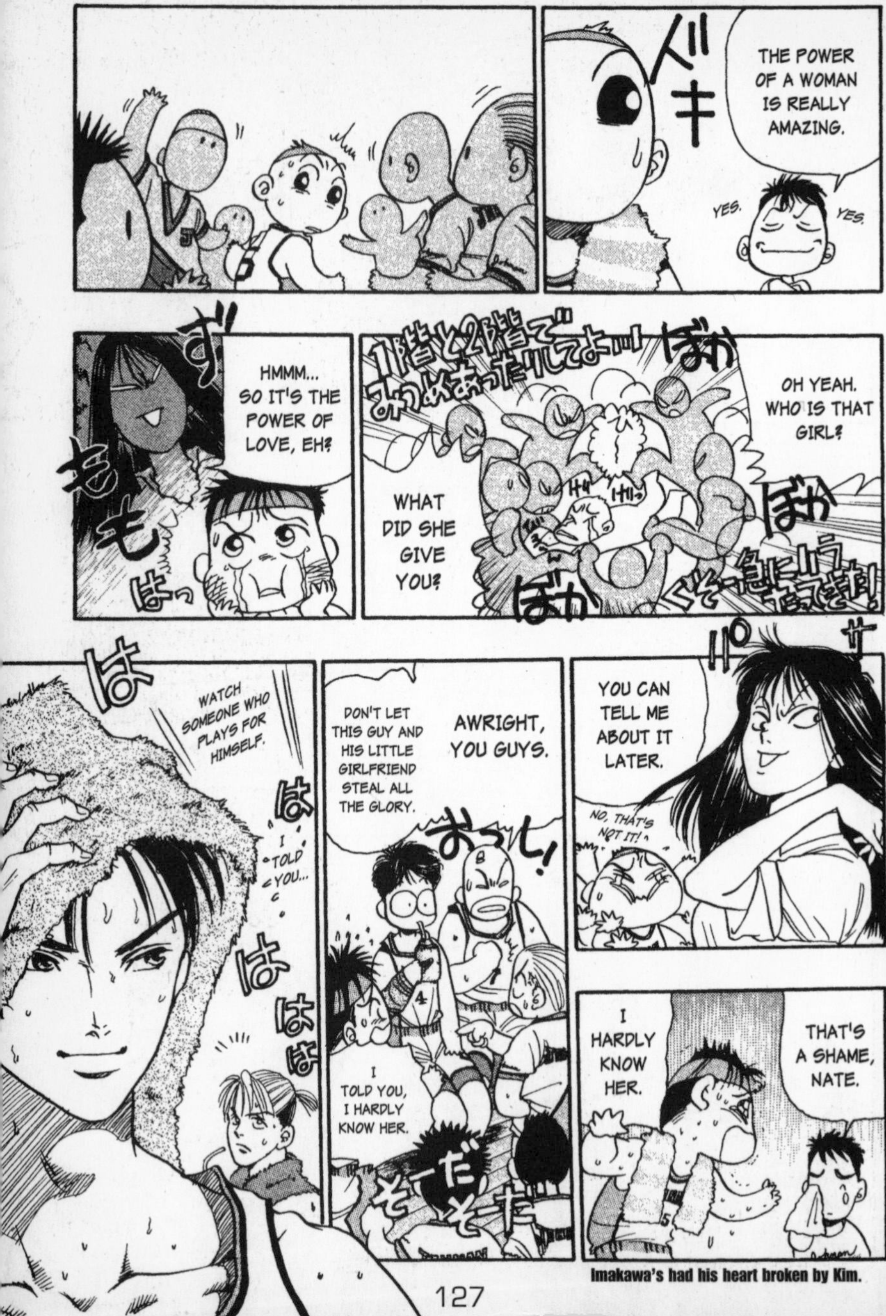
THE POWER OF A WOMAN IS REALLY AMAZING.
YES.
YES.
OH YEAH. WHO IS THAT GIRL?
WHAT DID SHE GIVE YOU?
HMMM... SO IT'S THE POWER OF LOVE, EH?
YOU CAN TELL ME ABOUT IT LATER.
NO, THAT'S NOT IT!
THAT'S A SHAME, NATE.
I HARDLY KNOW HER.
AWRIGHT, YOU GUYS.
DON'T LET THIS GUY AND HIS LITTLE GIRLFRIEND STEAL ALL THE GLORY.
I TOLD YOU, I HARDLY KNOW HER.
I TOLD YOU...
WATCH SOMEONE WHO PLAYS FOR HIMSELF.

Imakawa's had his heart broken by Kim.

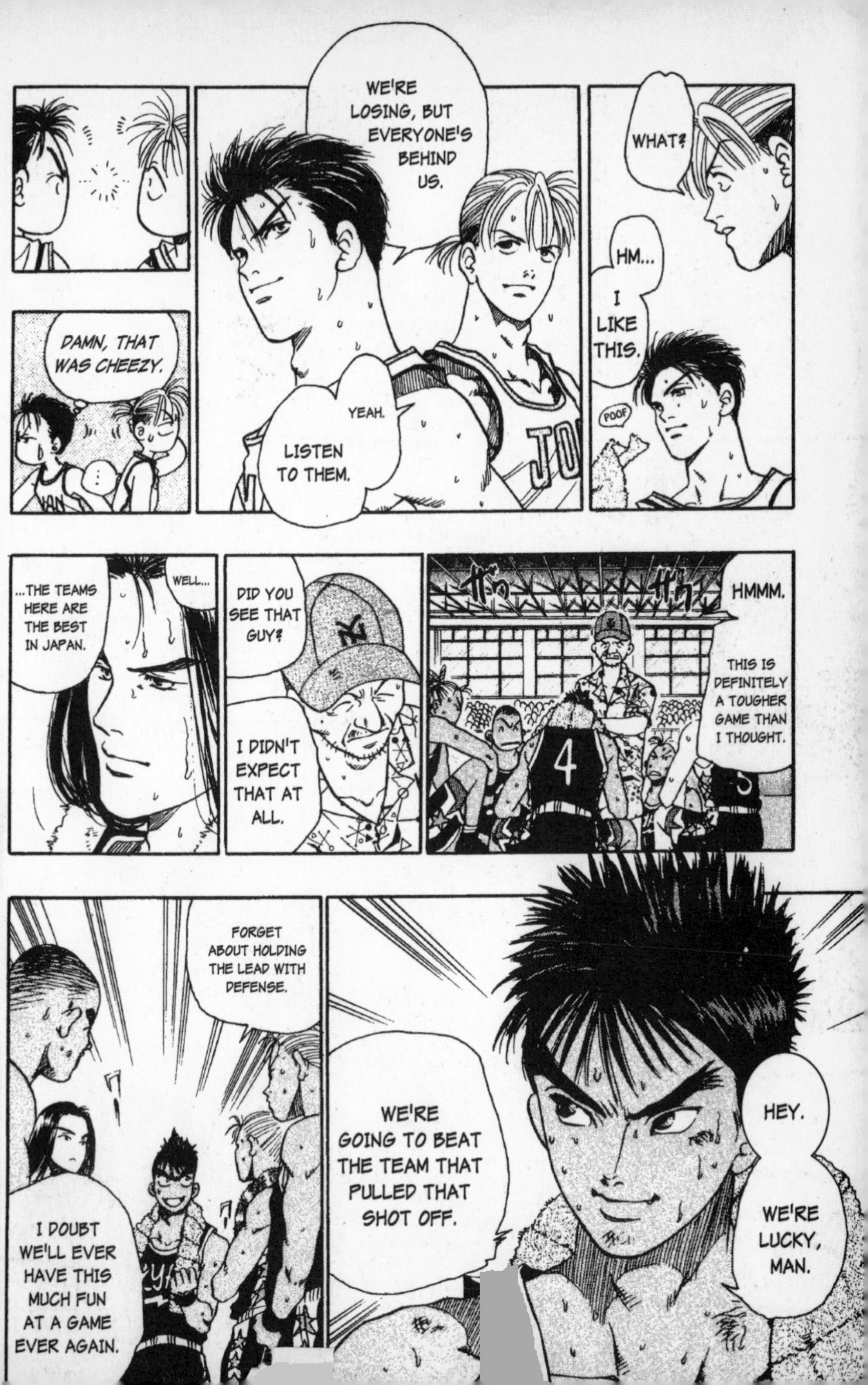
WHAT?
HM...
I LIKE THIS.
POOF
WE'RE LOSING, BUT EVERYONE'S BEHIND US.
YEAH.
LISTEN TO THEM.
DAMN, THAT WAS CHEEZY.
...
HMMM.
THIS IS DEFINITELY A TOUGHER GAME THAN I THOUGHT.
DID YOU SEE THAT GUY?
I DIDN'T EXPECT THAT AT ALL.
WELL...
...THE TEAMS HERE ARE THE BEST IN JAPAN.
HEY.
WE'RE LUCKY, MAN.
WE'RE GOING TO BEAT THE TEAM THAT PULLED THAT SHOT OFF.
FORGET ABOUT HOLDING THE LEAD WITH DEFENSE.
I DOUBT WE'LL EVER HAVE THIS MUCH FUN AT A GAME EVER AGAIN.

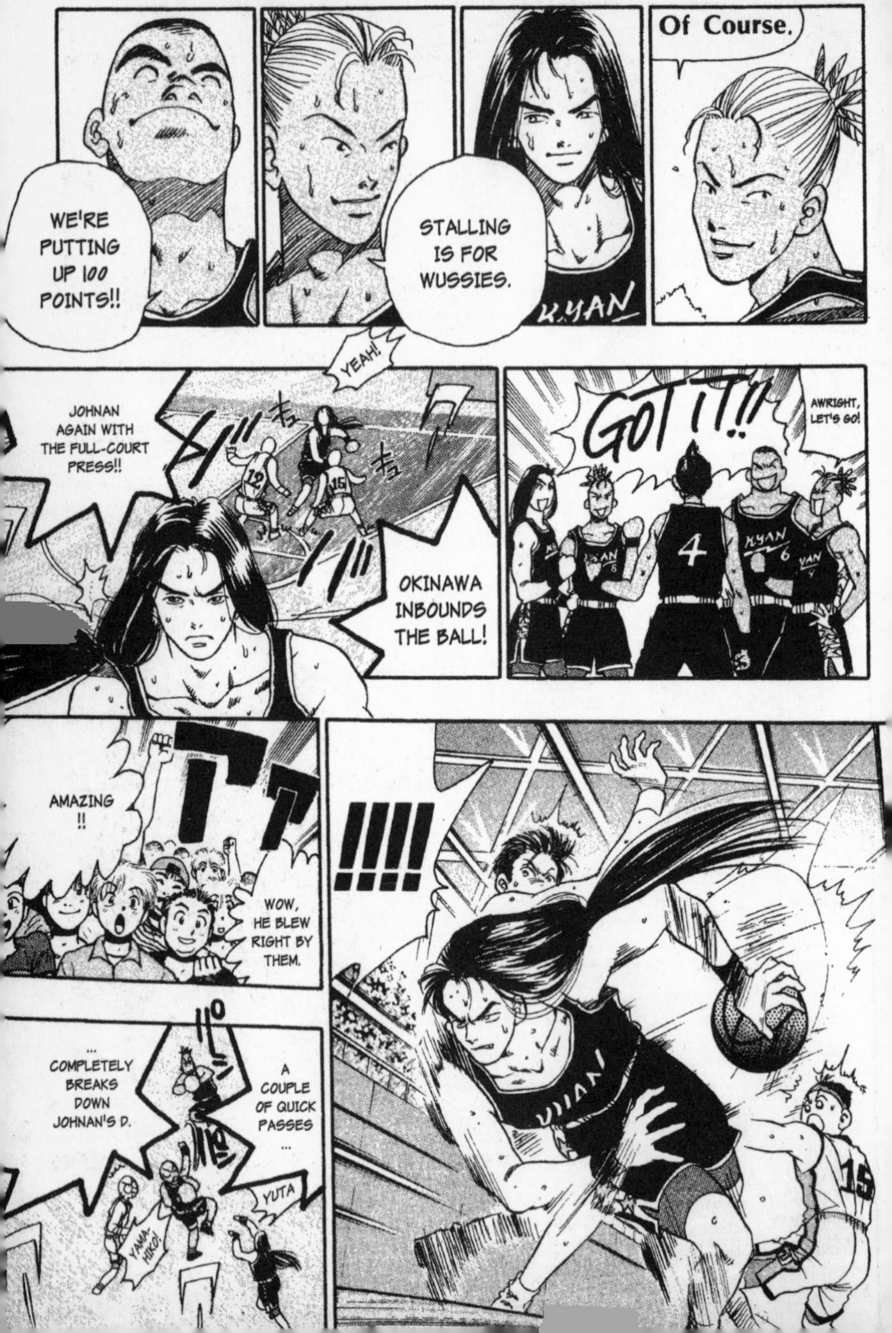
Of Course.
STALLING IS FOR WUSSIES.
WE'RE PUTTING UP 100 POINTS!!
AWRIGHT, LET'S GO!
GOT IT!!
YEAH!
JOHNAN AGAIN WITH THE FULL-COURT PRESS!!
OKINAWA INBOUNDS THE BALL!
!!!!
AMAZING !!
WOW, HE BLEW RIGHT BY THEM.
A COUPLE OF QUICK PASSES ...
... COMPLETELY BREAKS DOWN JOHNAN'S D.
YUTA
YAMA-HIKO!

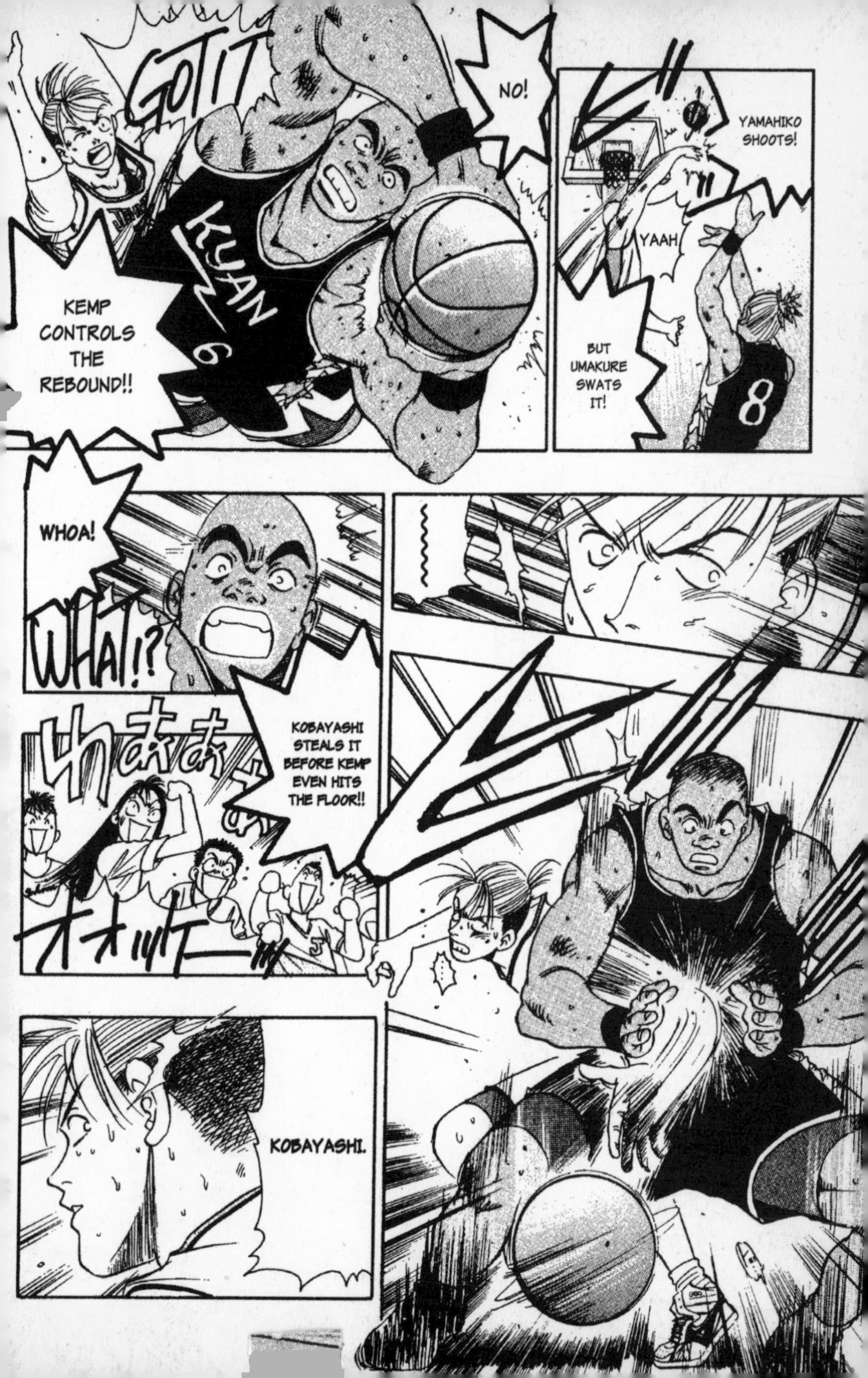
YAMAHIKO SHOOTS!
YAAH
BUT UMAKURE SWATS IT!
NO!
GOT IT
KEMP CONTROLS THE REBOUND!!
WHOA!
WHAT!?
KOBAYASHI STEALS IT BEFORE KEMP EVEN HITS THE FLOOR!!
KOBAYASHI.

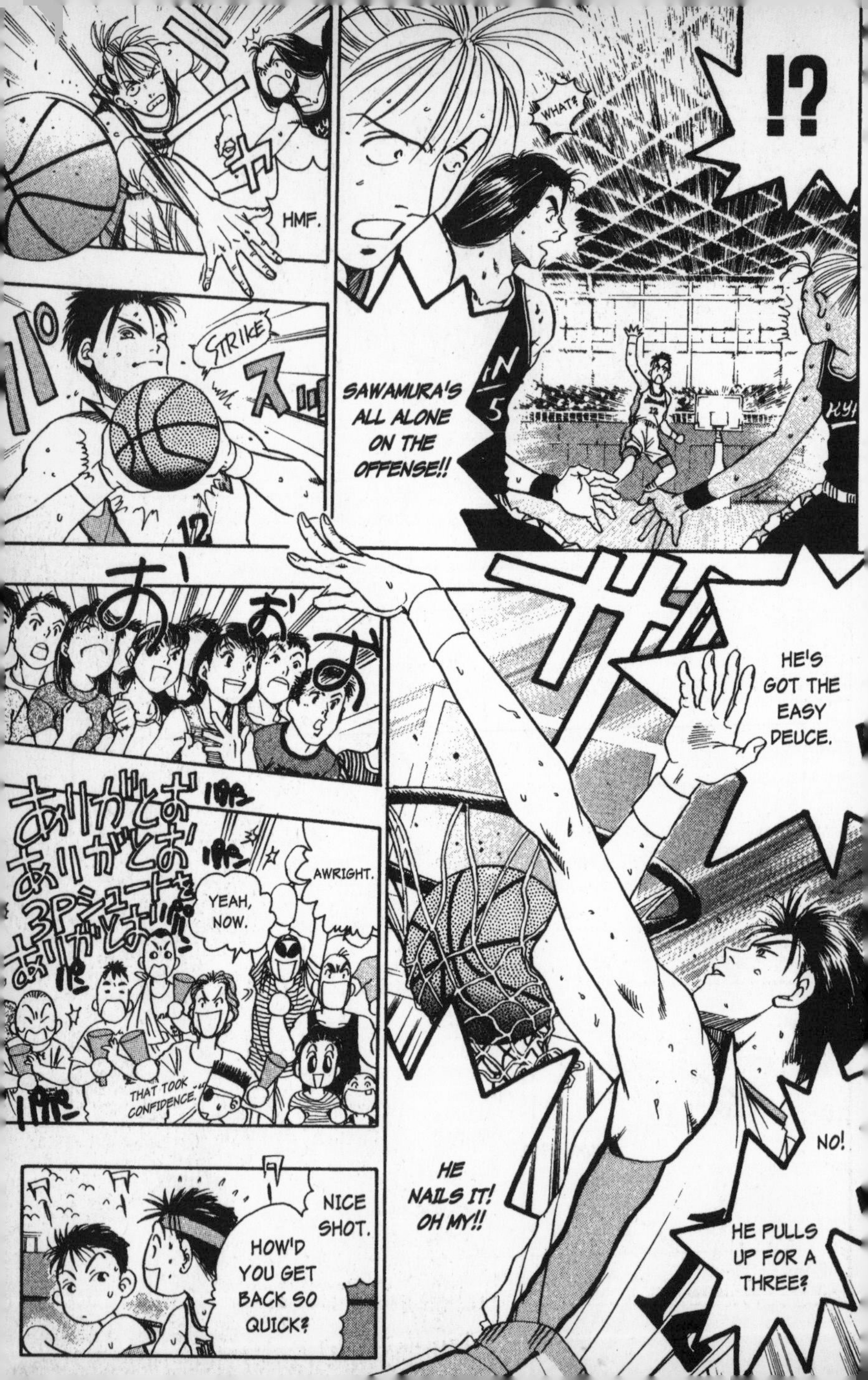
!?
WHAT?
SAWAMURA'S ALL ALONE ON THE OFFENSE!!
HMF.
STRIKE
HE'S GOT THE EASY DEUCE.
NO!
HE PULLS UP FOR A THREE?
HE NAILS IT! OH MY!!
ありがとお ありがとお 3Pシュートを ありがとお
AWRIGHT.
YEAH, NOW.
THAT TOOK CONFIDENCE.
NICE SHOT.
HOW'D YOU GET BACK SO QUICK?

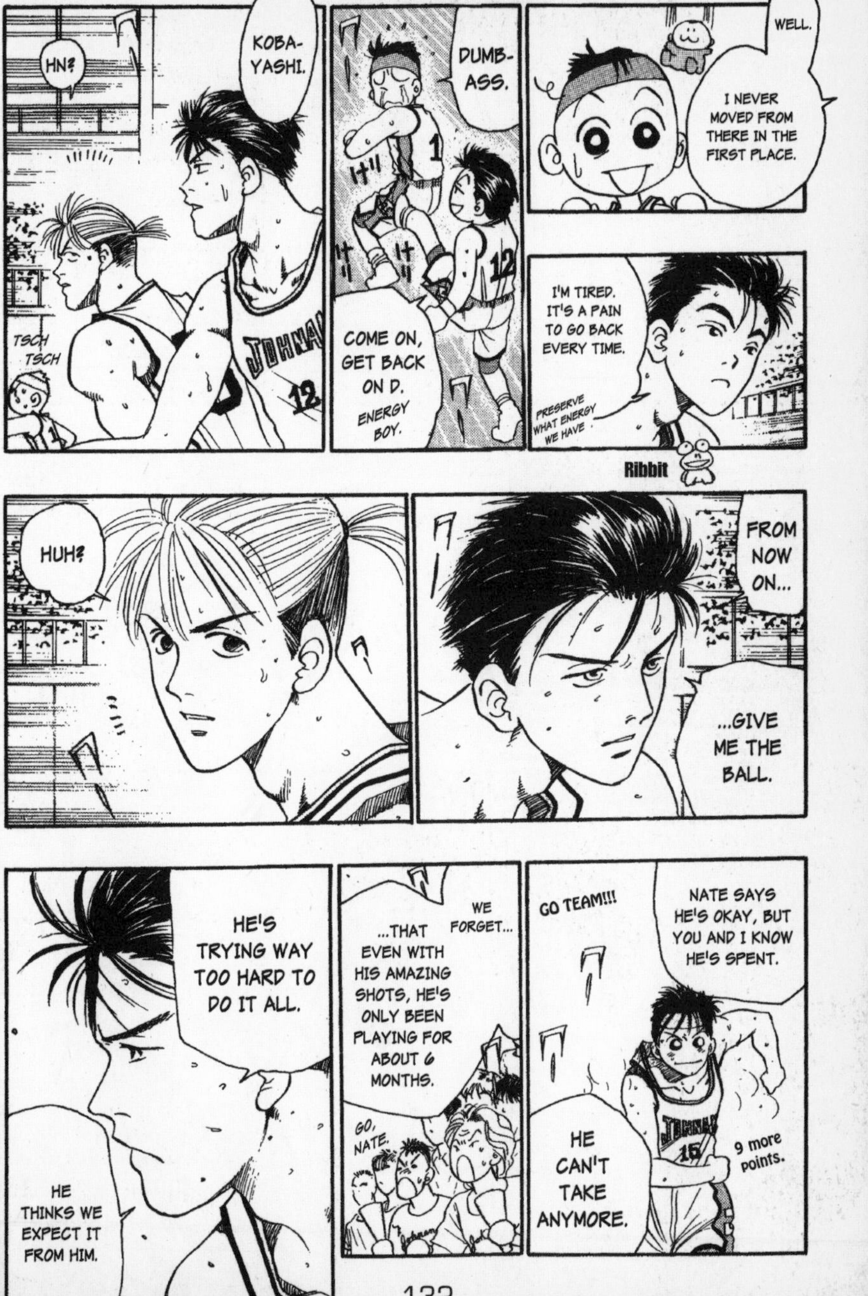
WELL.
I NEVER MOVED FROM THERE IN THE FIRST PLACE.
I'M TIRED. IT'S A PAIN TO GO BACK EVERY TIME.
PRESERVE WHAT ENERGY WE HAVE
Ribbit
DUMB-ASS.
COME ON, GET BACK ON D.
ENERGY BOY.
KOBA-YASHI.
HN?
TSCH TSCH
FROM NOW ON...
...GIVE ME THE BALL.
HUH?
NATE SAYS HE'S OKAY, BUT YOU AND I KNOW HE'S SPENT.
GO TEAM!!!
HE CAN'T TAKE ANYMORE.
9 more points.
WE FORGET...
...THAT EVEN WITH HIS AMAZING SHOTS, HE'S ONLY BEEN PLAYING FOR ABOUT 6 MONTHS.
GO, NATE.
HE'S TRYING WAY TOO HARD TO DO IT ALL.
HE THINKS WE EXPECT IT FROM HIM.

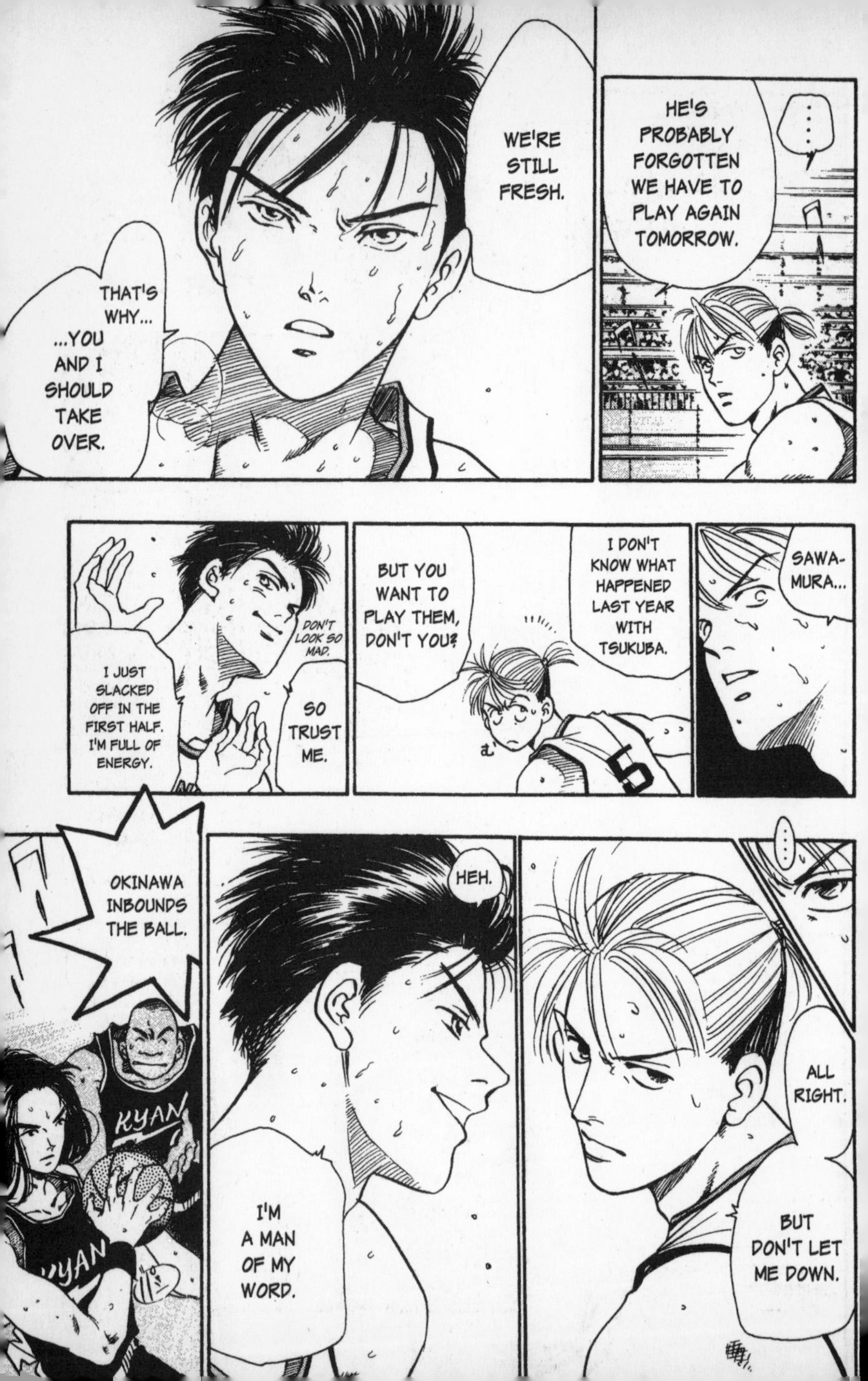
. . . .
HE'S PROBABLY FORGOTTEN WE HAVE TO PLAY AGAIN TOMORROW.
WE'RE STILL FRESH.
THAT'S WHY...
...YOU AND I SHOULD TAKE OVER.
SAWA-MURA...
I DON'T KNOW WHAT HAPPENED LAST YEAR WITH TSUKUBA.
BUT YOU WANT TO PLAY THEM, DON'T YOU?
DON'T LOOK SO MAD.
I JUST SLACKED OFF IN THE FIRST HALF. I'M FULL OF ENERGY.
SO TRUST ME.
. . .
ALL RIGHT.
BUT DON'T LET ME DOWN.
HEH.
I'M A MAN OF MY WORD.
OKINAWA INBOUNDS THE BALL.
KYAN
KYAN

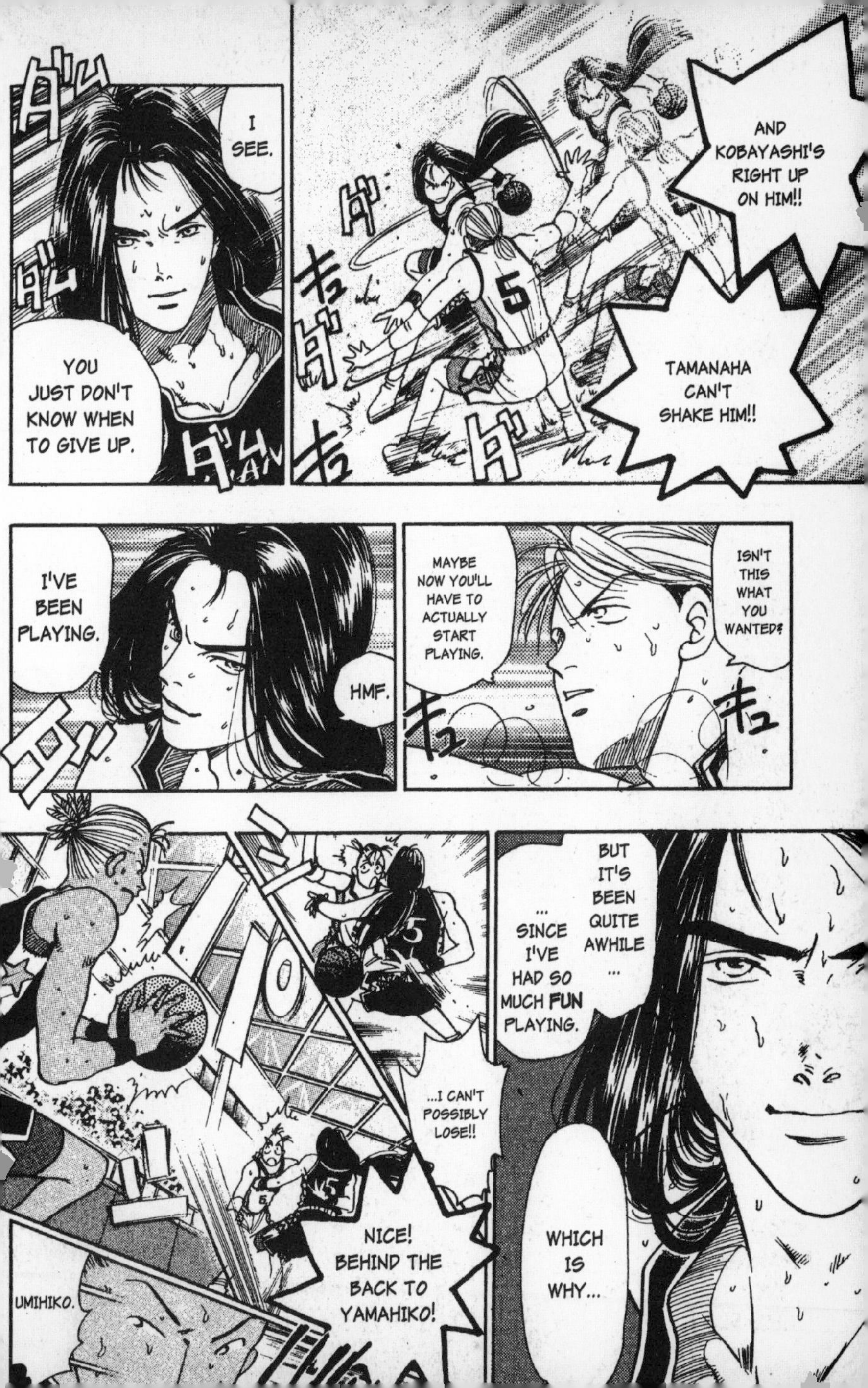
AND KOBAYASHI'S RIGHT UP ON HIM!!
TAMANAHA CAN'T SHAKE HIM!!
I SEE.
YOU JUST DON'T KNOW WHEN TO GIVE UP.
ISN'T THIS WHAT YOU WANTED?
MAYBE NOW YOU'LL HAVE TO ACTUALLY START PLAYING.
HMF.
I'VE BEEN PLAYING.
BUT IT'S BEEN QUITE AWHILE ...
... SINCE I'VE HAD SO MUCH FUN PLAYING.
WHICH IS WHY...
...I CAN'T POSSIBLY LOSE!!
NICE! BEHIND THE BACK TO YAMAHIKO!
UMIHIKO.

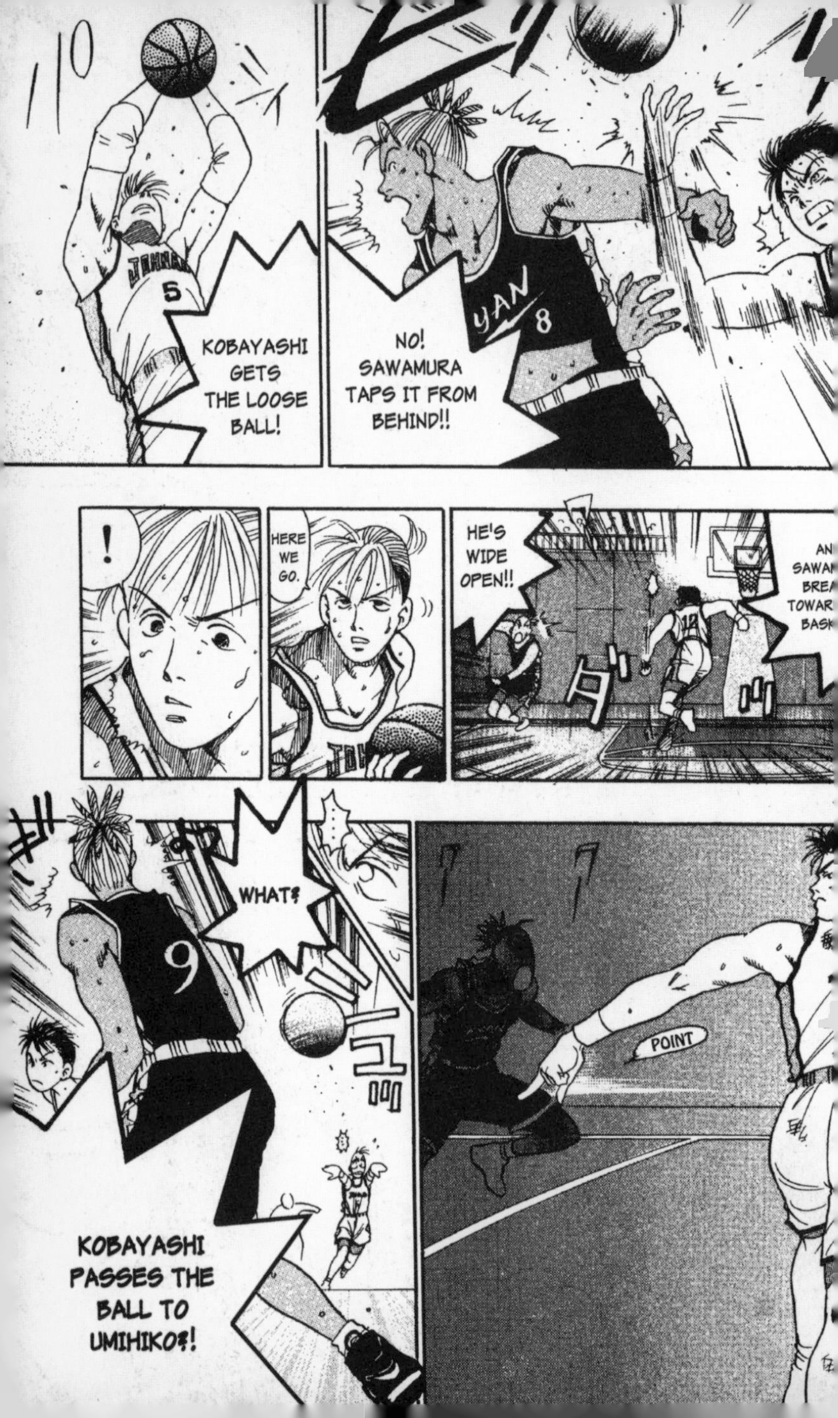
NO! SAWAMURA TAPS IT FROM BEHIND!!
KOBAYASHI GETS THE LOOSE BALL!
HE'S WIDE OPEN!!
HERE WE GO.
!
POINT
WHAT?
KOBAYASHI PASSES THE BALL TO UMIHIKO?!

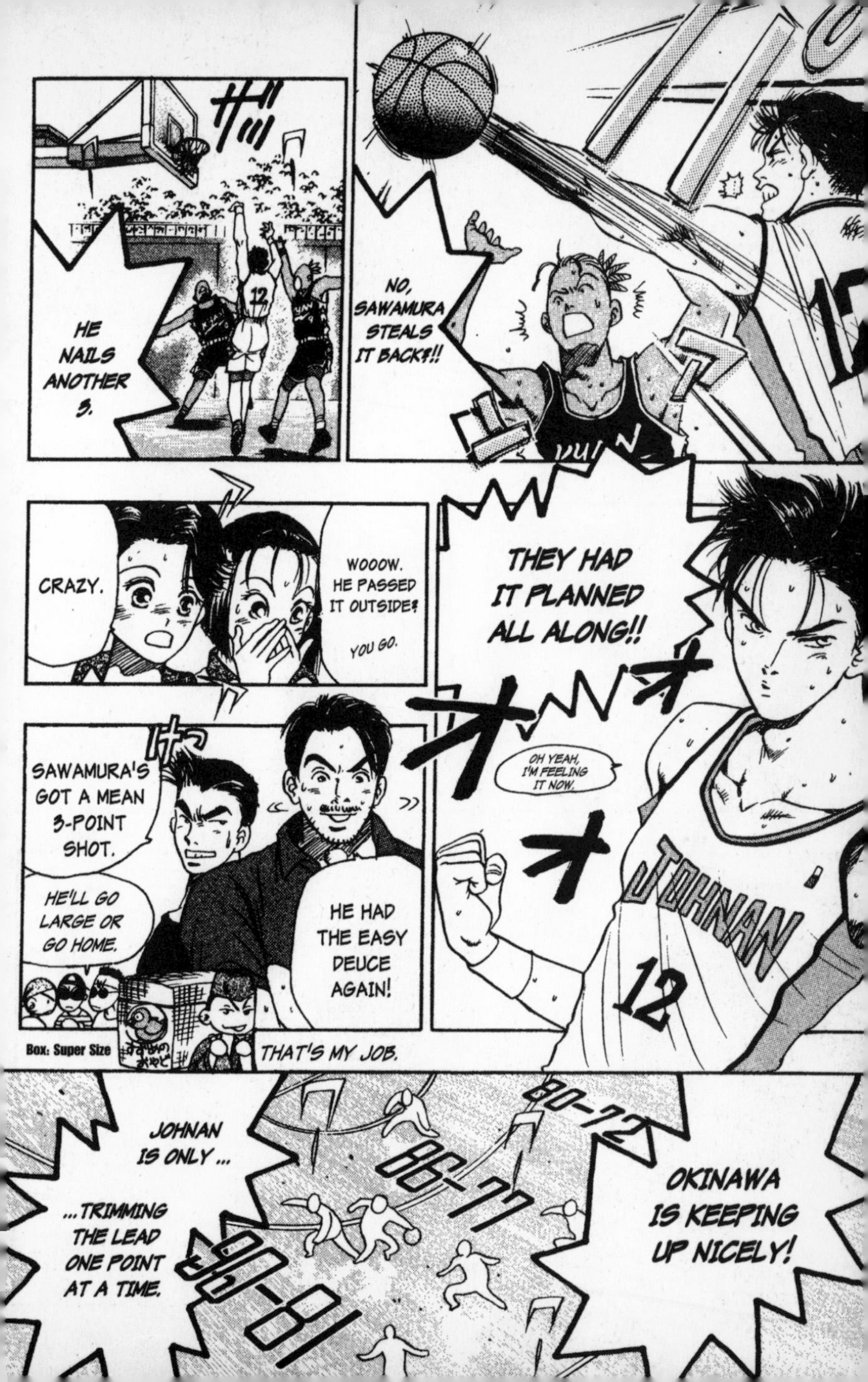
NO, SAWAMURA STEALS IT BACK?!!
HE NAILS ANOTHER 3.
THEY HAD IT PLANNED ALL ALONG!!
OH YEAH, I'M FEELING IT NOW.
WOOOW. HE PASSED IT OUTSIDE?
YOU GO.
CRAZY.
HE HAD THE EASY DEUCE AGAIN!
SAWAMURA'S GOT A MEAN 3-POINT SHOT.
HE'LL GO LARGE OR GO HOME.
Box: Super Size
THAT'S MY JOB.
OKINAWA IS KEEPING UP NICELY!
80-72
86-77
96-81
JOHNAN IS ONLY ...
...TRIMMING THE LEAD ONE POINT AT A TIME.

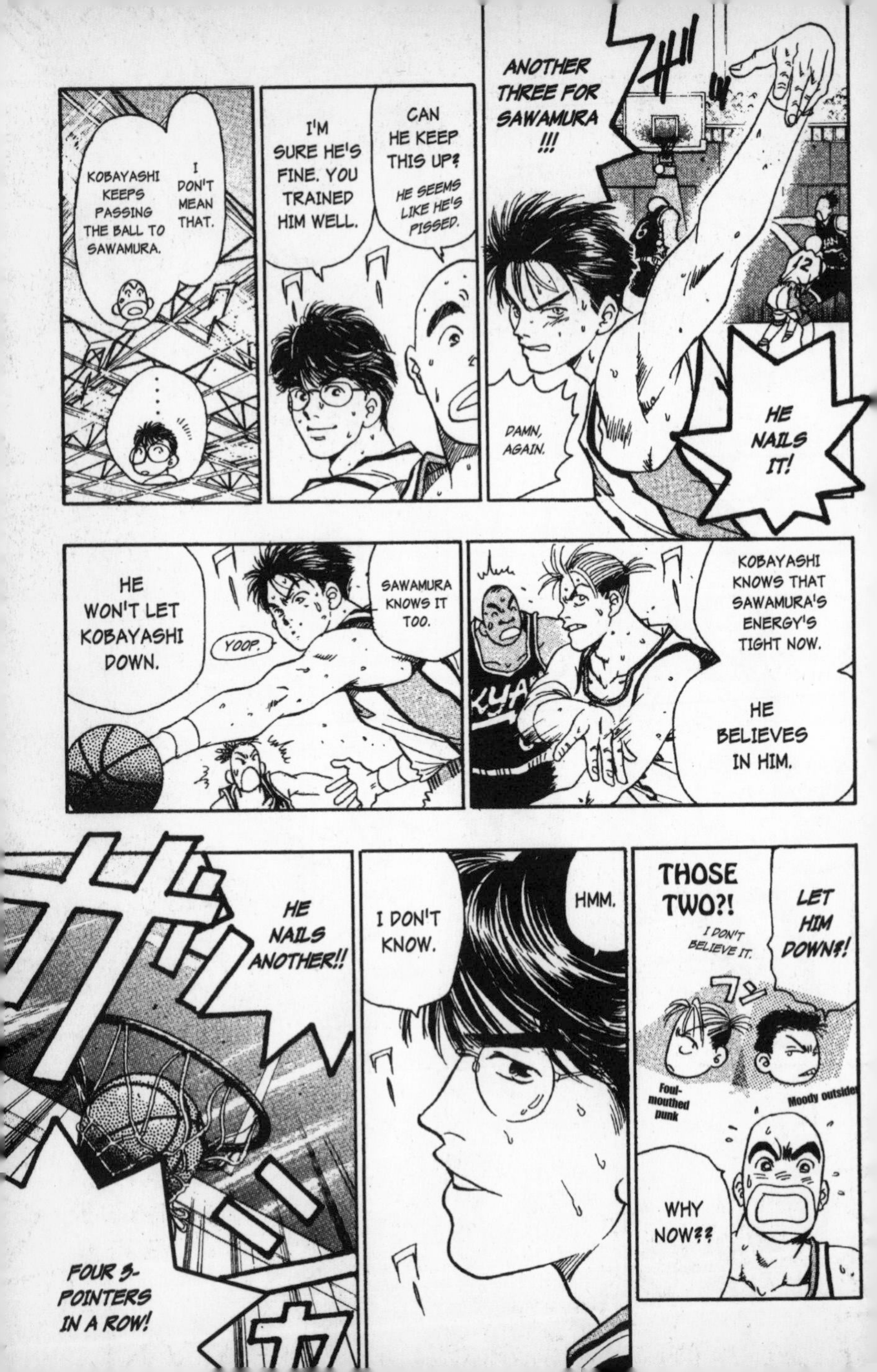
ANOTHER THREE FOR SAWAMURA !!!
HE NAILS IT!
DAMN, AGAIN.
CAN HE KEEP THIS UP?
HE SEEMS LIKE HE'S PISSED.
I'M SURE HE'S FINE. YOU TRAINED HIM WELL.
I DON'T MEAN THAT.
KOBAYASHI KEEPS PASSING THE BALL TO SAWAMURA.
...
KOBAYASHI KNOWS THAT SAWAMURA'S ENERGY'S TIGHT NOW.
HE BELIEVES IN HIM.
SAWAMURA KNOWS IT TOO.
HE WON'T LET KOBAYASHI DOWN.
YOOP.
LET HIM DOWN?!
THOSE TWO?!
I DON'T BELIEVE IT.
Foul-mouthed punk
Moody outside
WHY NOW??
HMM.
I DON'T KNOW.
HE NAILS ANOTHER!!
FOUR 3-POINTERS IN A ROW!

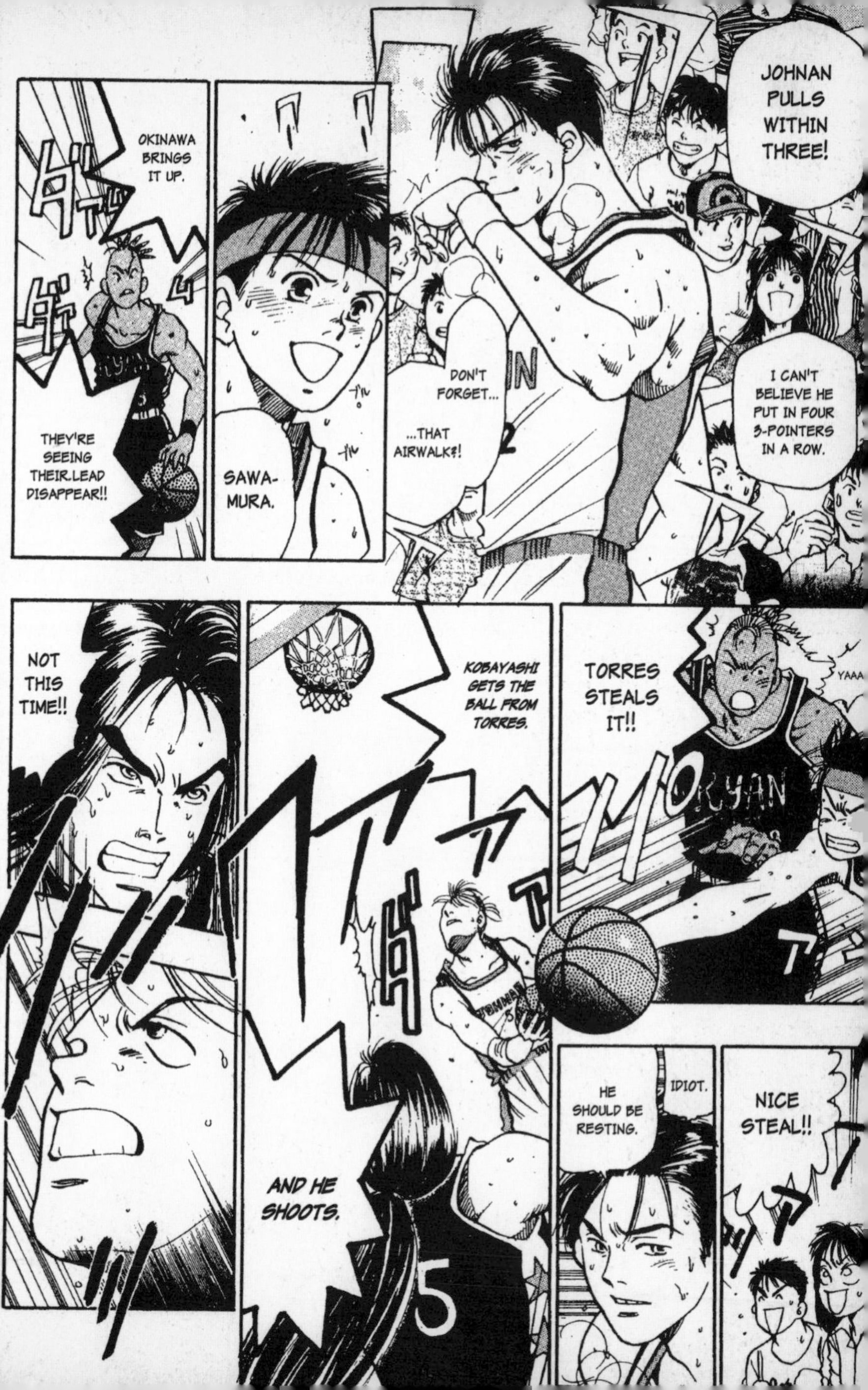
JOHNAN PULLS WITHIN THREE!
I CAN'T BELIEVE HE PUT IN FOUR 3-POINTERS IN A ROW.
DON'T FORGET...
...THAT AIRWALK?!
SAWA-MURA.
OKINAWA BRINGS IT UP.
THEY'RE SEEING THEIR LEAD DISAPPEAR!!
TORRES STEALS IT!!
NICE STEAL!!
IDIOT.
HE SHOULD BE RESTING.
KOBAYASHI GETS THE BALL FROM TORRES.
AND HE SHOOTS.
NOT THIS TIME!!

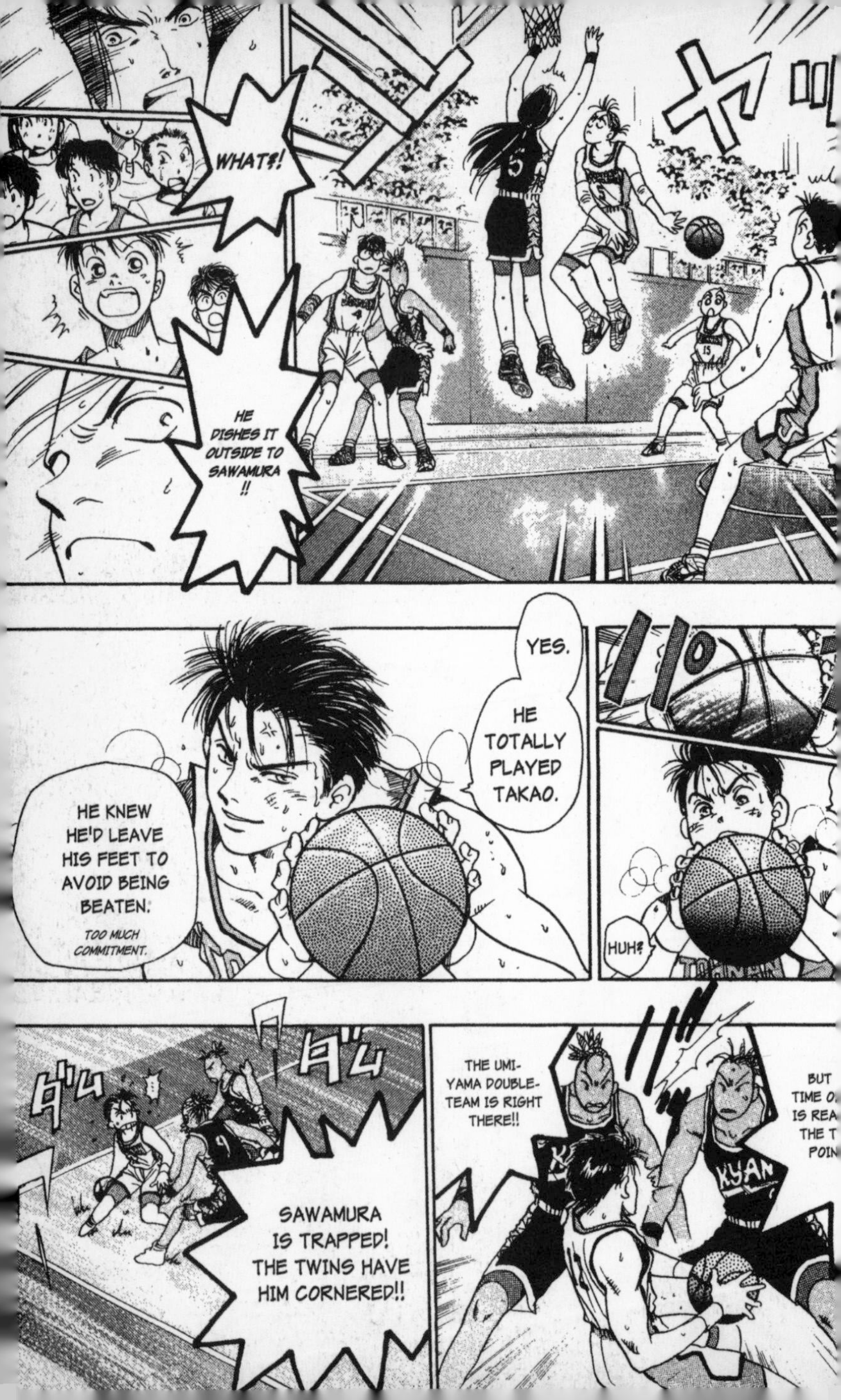
WHAT?!
HE DISHES IT OUTSIDE TO SAWAMURA !!
HUH?
YES.
HE TOTALLY PLAYED TAKAO.
HE KNEW HE'D LEAVE HIS FEET TO AVOID BEING BEATEN.
TOO MUCH COMMITMENT.
BUT TIME O IS REA THE T POIN
THE UMI-YAMA DOUBLE-TEAM IS RIGHT THERE!!
SAWAMURA IS TRAPPED! THE TWINS HAVE HIM CORNERED!!

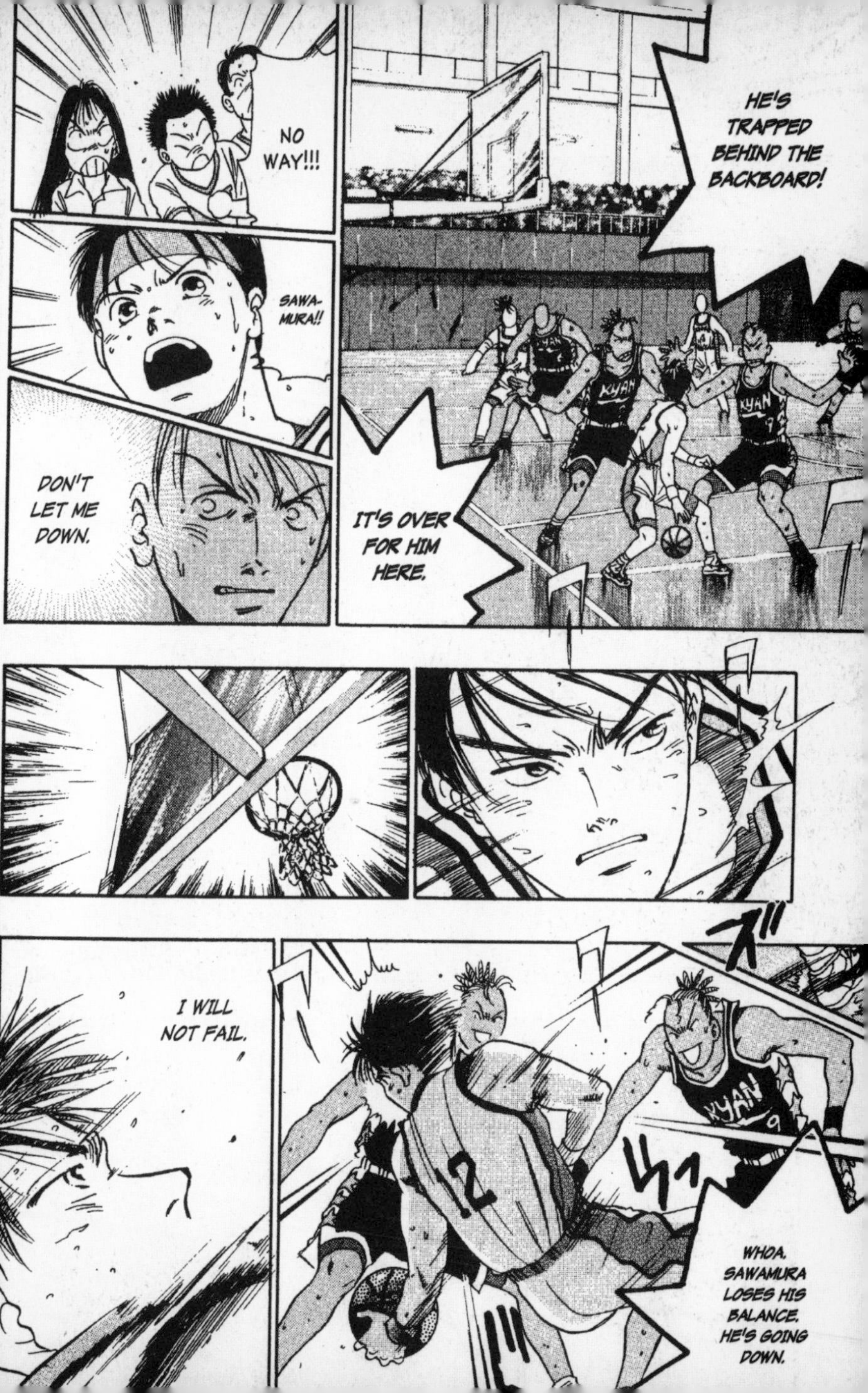
HE'S TRAPPED BEHIND THE BACKBOARD!
IT'S OVER FOR HIM HERE.
NO WAY!!!
SAWAMURA!!
DON'T LET ME DOWN.
WHOA. SAWAMURA LOSES HIS BALANCE. HE'S GOING DOWN.
I WILL NOT FAIL.

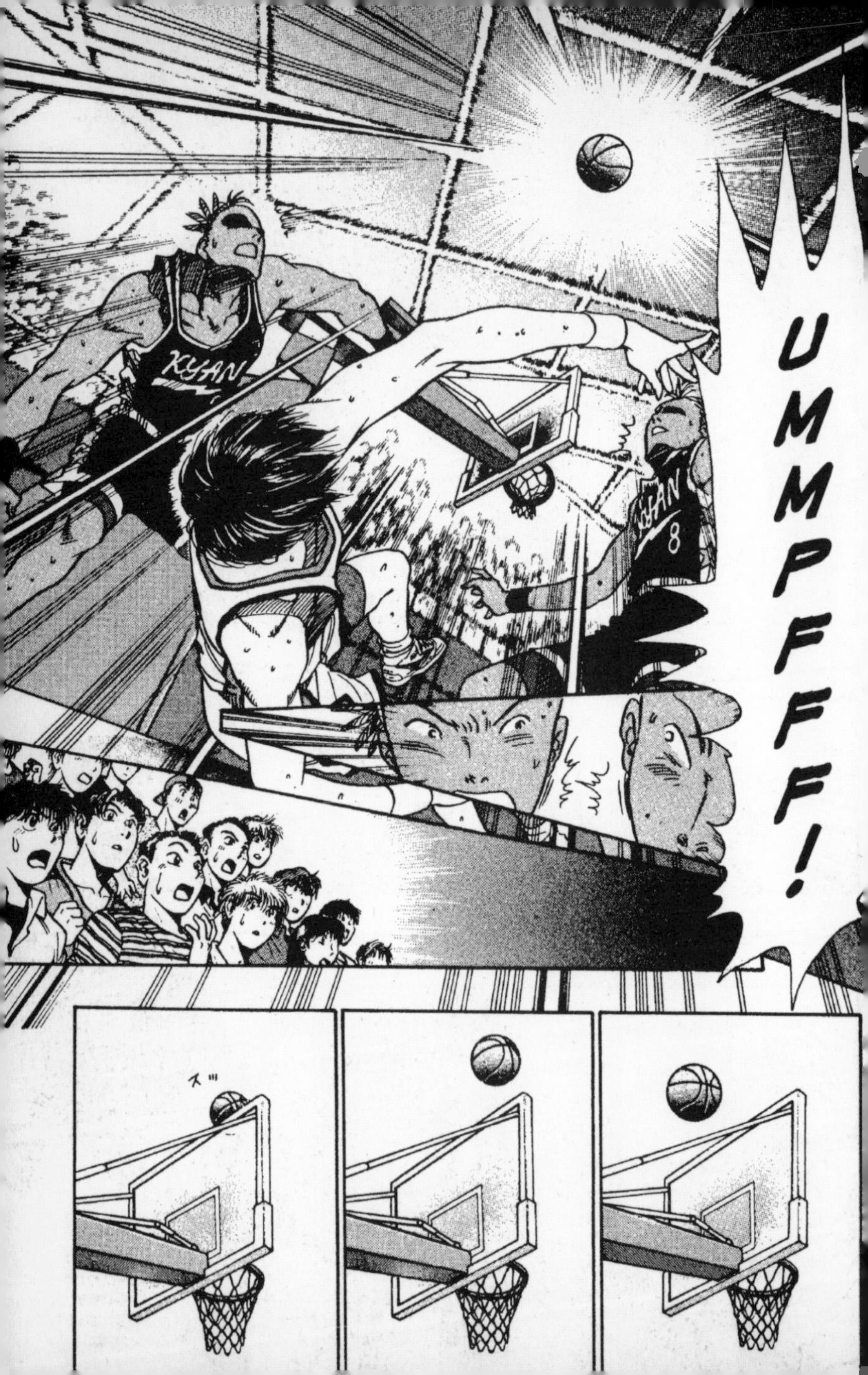
UMMPFFF!
ズッ

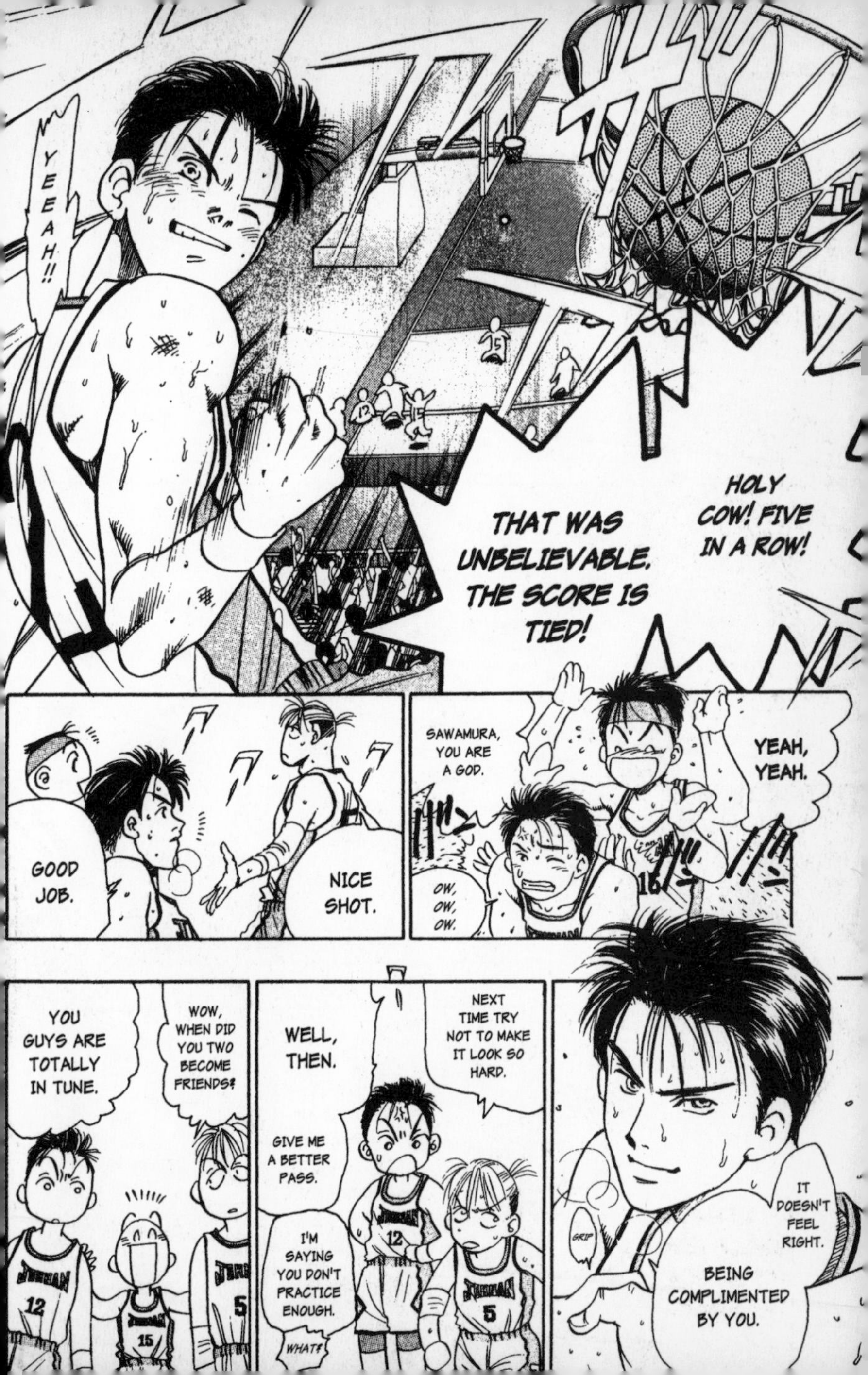
HOLY COW! FIVE IN A ROW!
THAT WAS UNBELIEVABLE. THE SCORE IS TIED!
YEEEAH!!
YEAH, YEAH.
SAWAMURA, YOU ARE A GOD.
OW, OW, OW.
NICE SHOT.
GOOD JOB.
IT DOESN'T FEEL RIGHT.
GRIP
BEING COMPLIMENTED BY YOU.
NEXT TIME TRY NOT TO MAKE IT LOOK SO HARD.
WELL, THEN.
GIVE ME A BETTER PASS.
I'M SAYING YOU DON'T PRACTICE ENOUGH.
WHAT?
WOW, WHEN DID YOU TWO BECOME FRIENDS?
YOU GUYS ARE TOTALLY IN TUNE.

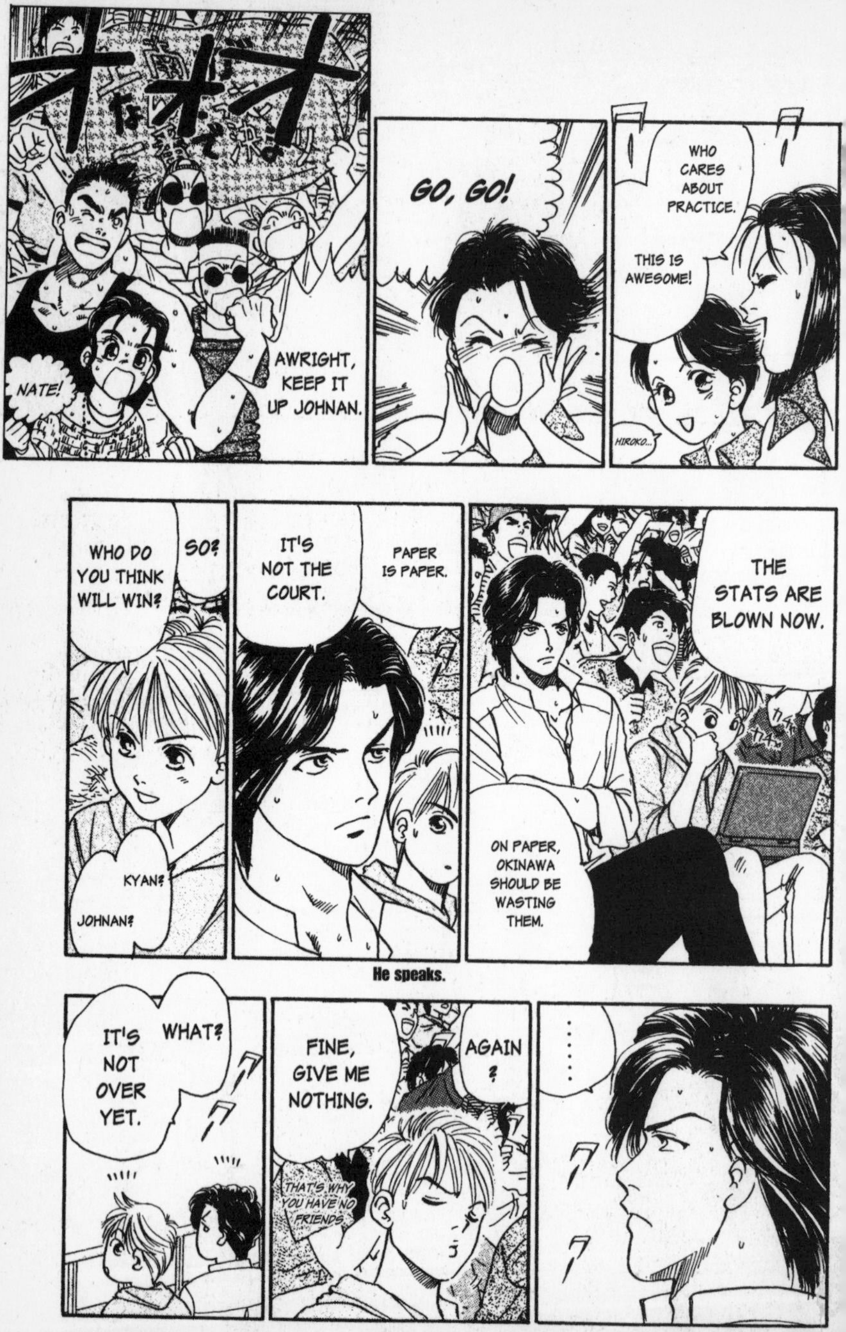
WHO CARES ABOUT PRACTICE.
THIS IS AWESOME!
HIROKO...
GO, GO!
AWRIGHT, KEEP IT UP JOHNAN.
NATE!
THE STATS ARE BLOWN NOW.
ON PAPER, OKINAWA SHOULD BE WASTING THEM.
PAPER IS PAPER.
IT'S NOT THE COURT.
SO?
WHO DO YOU THINK WILL WIN?
KYAN?
JOHNAN?
He speaks.
......
AGAIN?
FINE, GIVE ME NOTHING.
THAT'S WHY YOU HAVE NO FRIENDS.
WHAT?
IT'S NOT OVER YET.

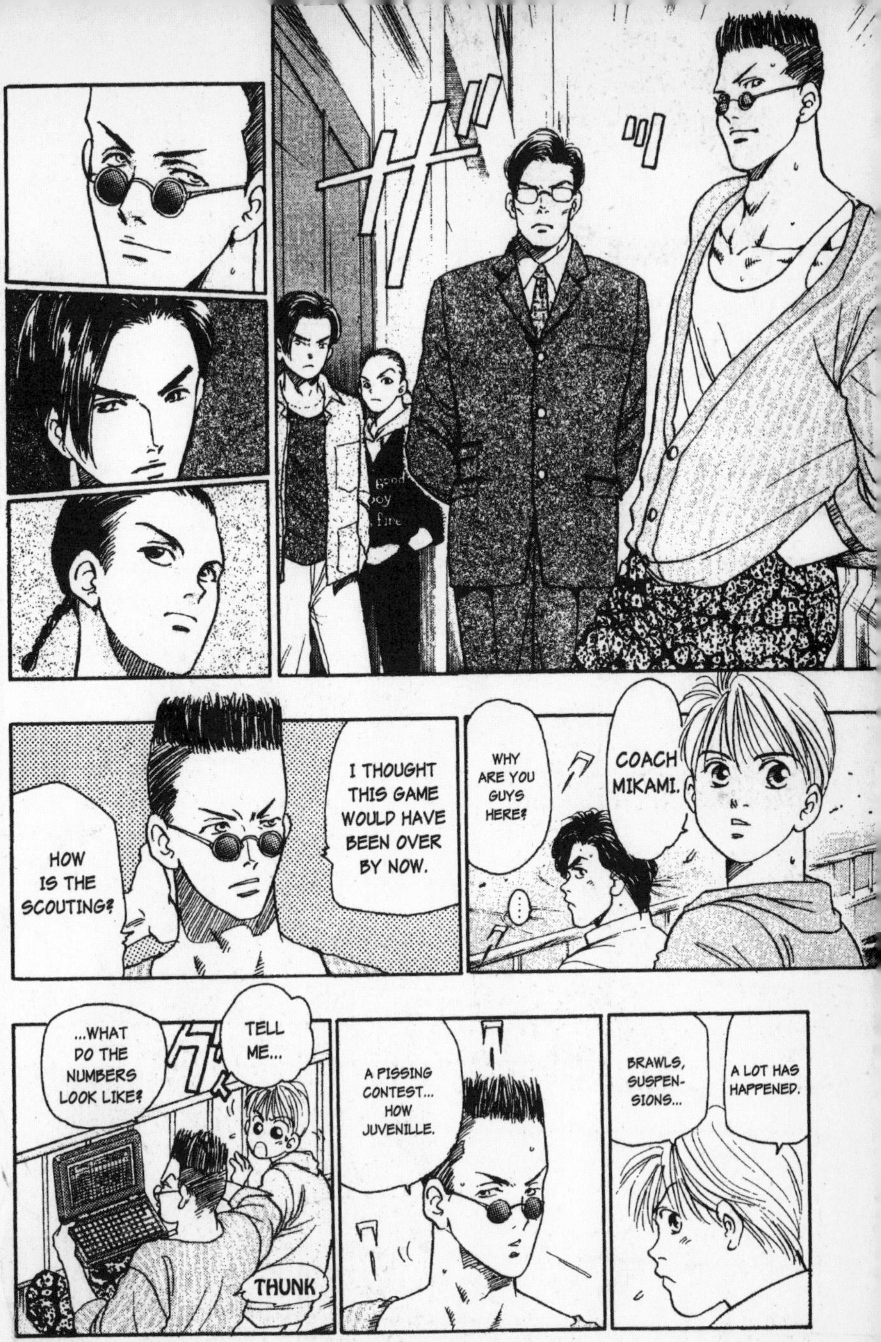
COACH MIKAMI.
WHY ARE YOU GUYS HERE?
...
I THOUGHT THIS GAME WOULD HAVE BEEN OVER BY NOW.
HOW IS THE SCOUTING?
A LOT HAS HAPPENED.
BRAWLS, SUSPEN-SIONS...
A PISSING CONTEST... HOW JUVENILLE.
TELL ME...
...WHAT DO THE NUMBERS LOOK LIKE?
THUNK

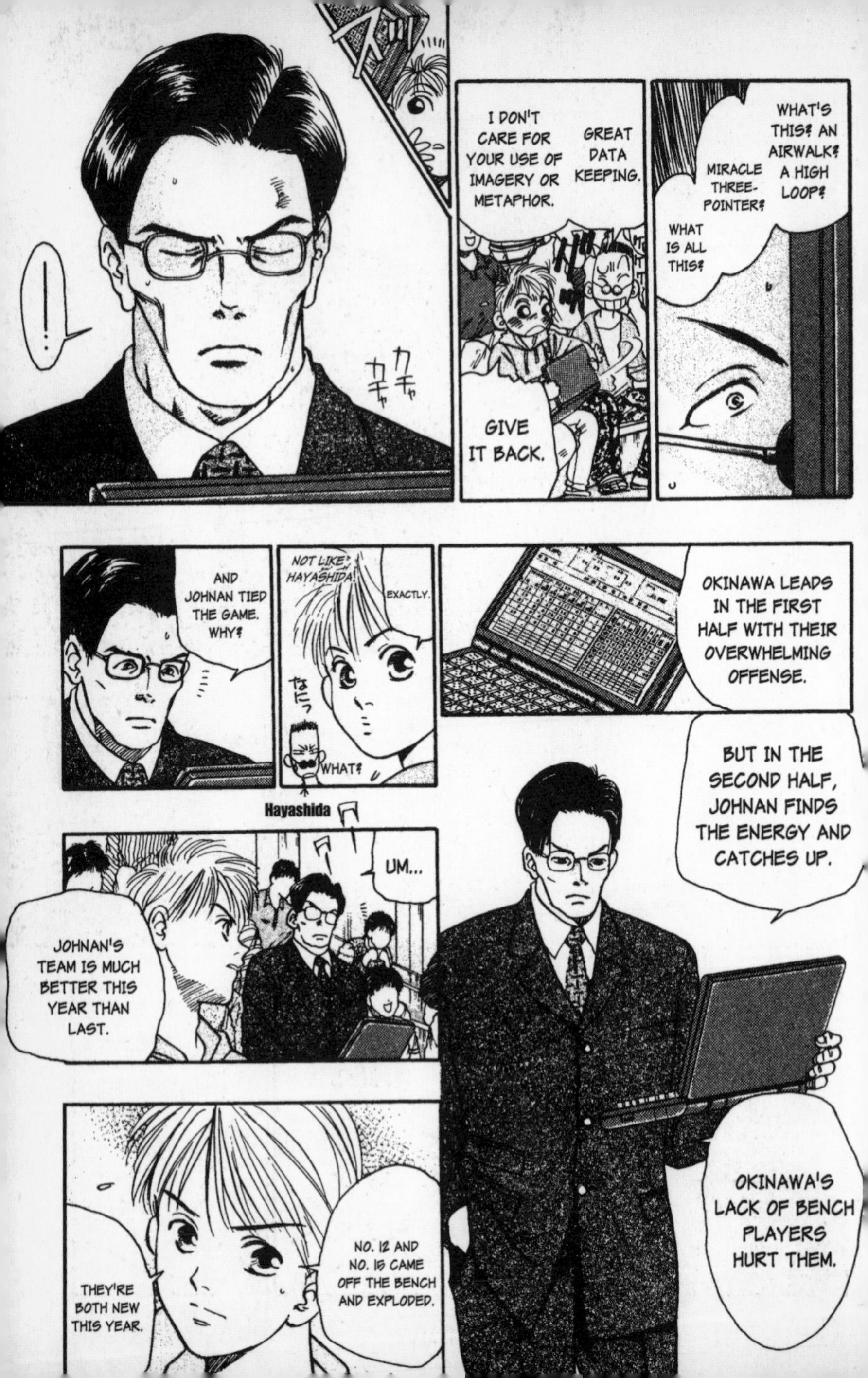
WHAT'S THIS? AN AIRWALK? A HIGH LOOP?
MIRACLE THREE-POINTER?
WHAT IS ALL THIS?
GREAT DATA KEEPING.
I DON'T CARE FOR YOUR USE OF IMAGERY OR METAPHOR.
GIVE IT BACK.
カチャカチャ
!
OKINAWA LEADS IN THE FIRST HALF WITH THEIR OVERWHELMING OFFENSE.
EXACTLY.
NOT LIKE HAYASHIDA!
なにっ
WHAT?
Hayashida
AND JOHNAN TIED THE GAME. WHY?
BUT IN THE SECOND HALF, JOHNAN FINDS THE ENERGY AND CATCHES UP.
UM...
JOHNAN'S TEAM IS MUCH BETTER THIS YEAR THAN LAST.
NO. 12 AND NO. 15 CAME OFF THE BENCH AND EXPLODED.
THEY'RE BOTH NEW THIS YEAR.
OKINAWA'S LACK OF BENCH PLAYERS HURT THEM.

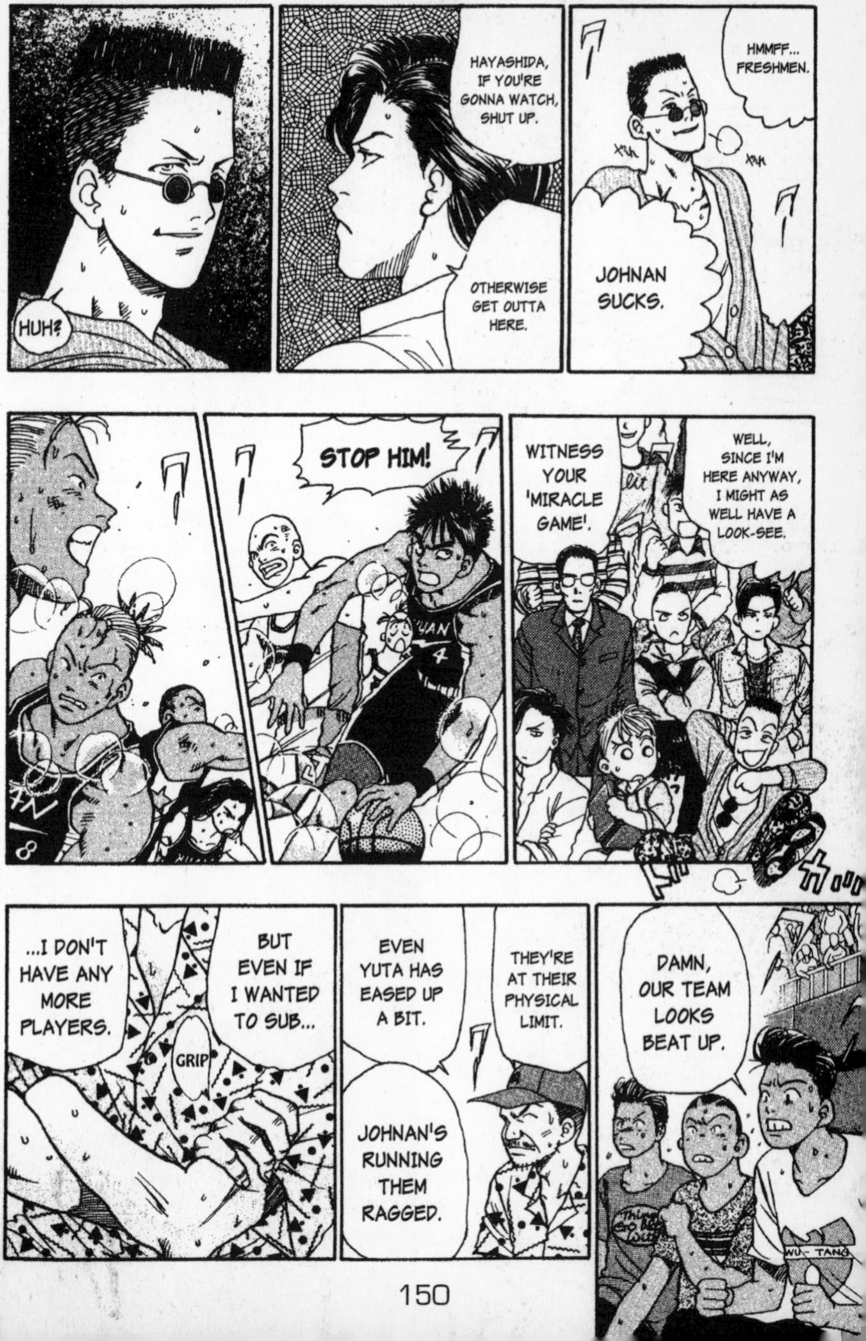
HMMFF... FRESHMEN.
JOHNAN SUCKS.
HAYASHIDA, IF YOU'RE GONNA WATCH, SHUT UP.
OTHERWISE GET OUTTA HERE.
HUH?
WELL, SINCE I'M HERE ANYWAY, I MIGHT AS WELL HAVE A LOOK-SEE.
WITNESS YOUR 'MIRACLE GAME'.
STOP HIM!
DAMN, OUR TEAM LOOKS BEAT UP.
WU-TANG
THEY'RE AT THEIR PHYSICAL LIMIT.
EVEN YUTA HAS EASED UP A BIT.
JOHNAN'S RUNNING THEM RAGGED.
BUT EVEN IF I WANTED TO SUB...
GRIP
...I DON'T HAVE ANY MORE PLAYERS.

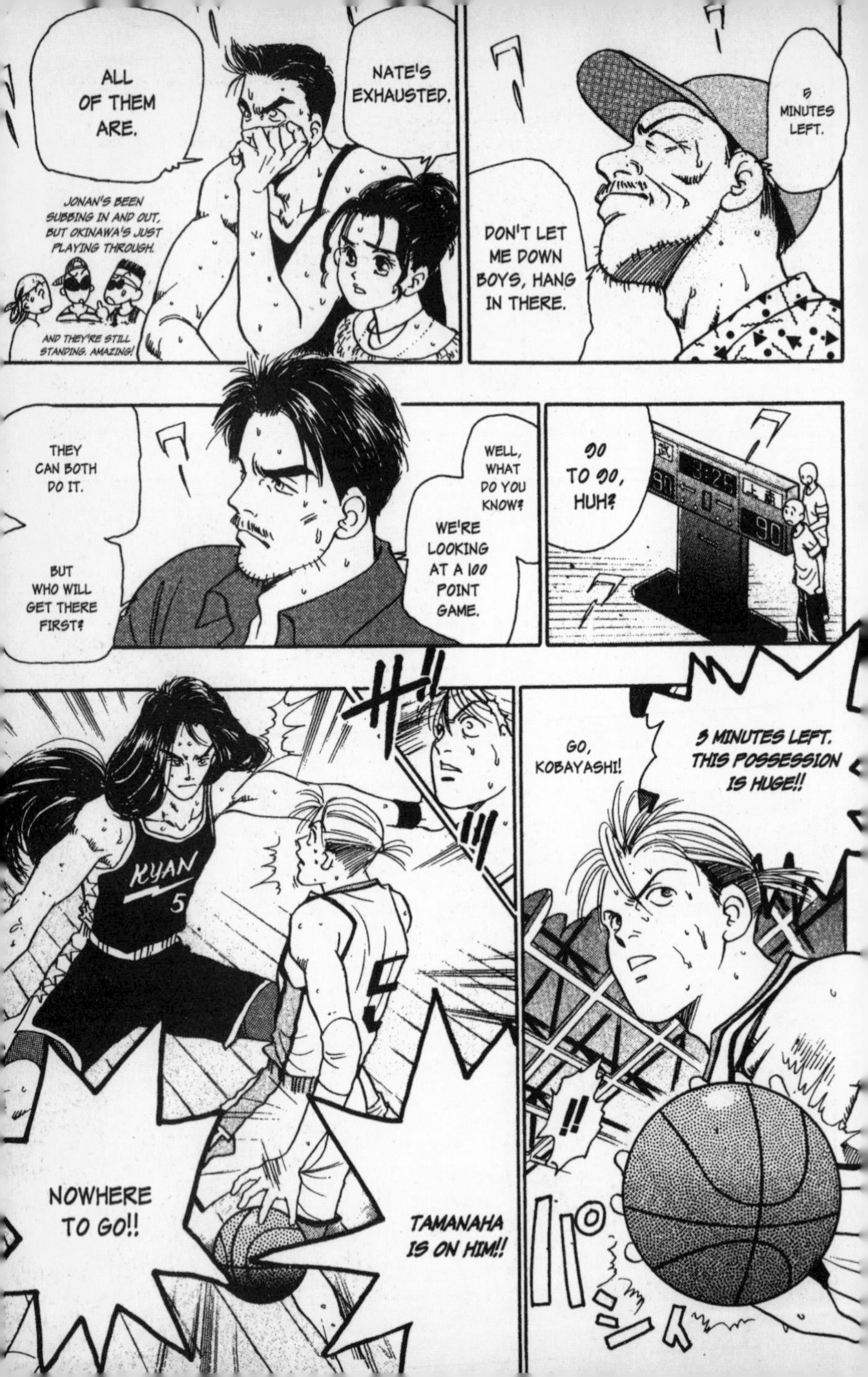
5 MINUTES LEFT.
DON'T LET ME DOWN BOYS, HANG IN THERE.
NATE'S EXHAUSTED.
ALL OF THEM ARE.
JONAN'S BEEN SUBBING IN AND OUT, BUT OKINAWA'S JUST PLAYING THROUGH.
AND THEY'RE STILL STANDING. AMAZING!
90 TO 90, HUH?
WELL, WHAT DO YOU KNOW?
WE'RE LOOKING AT A 100 POINT GAME.
THEY CAN BOTH DO IT.
BUT WHO WILL GET THERE FIRST?
3 MINUTES LEFT. THIS POSSESSION IS HUGE!!
GO, KOBAYASHI!
TAMANAHA IS ON HIM!!
NOWHERE TO GO!!

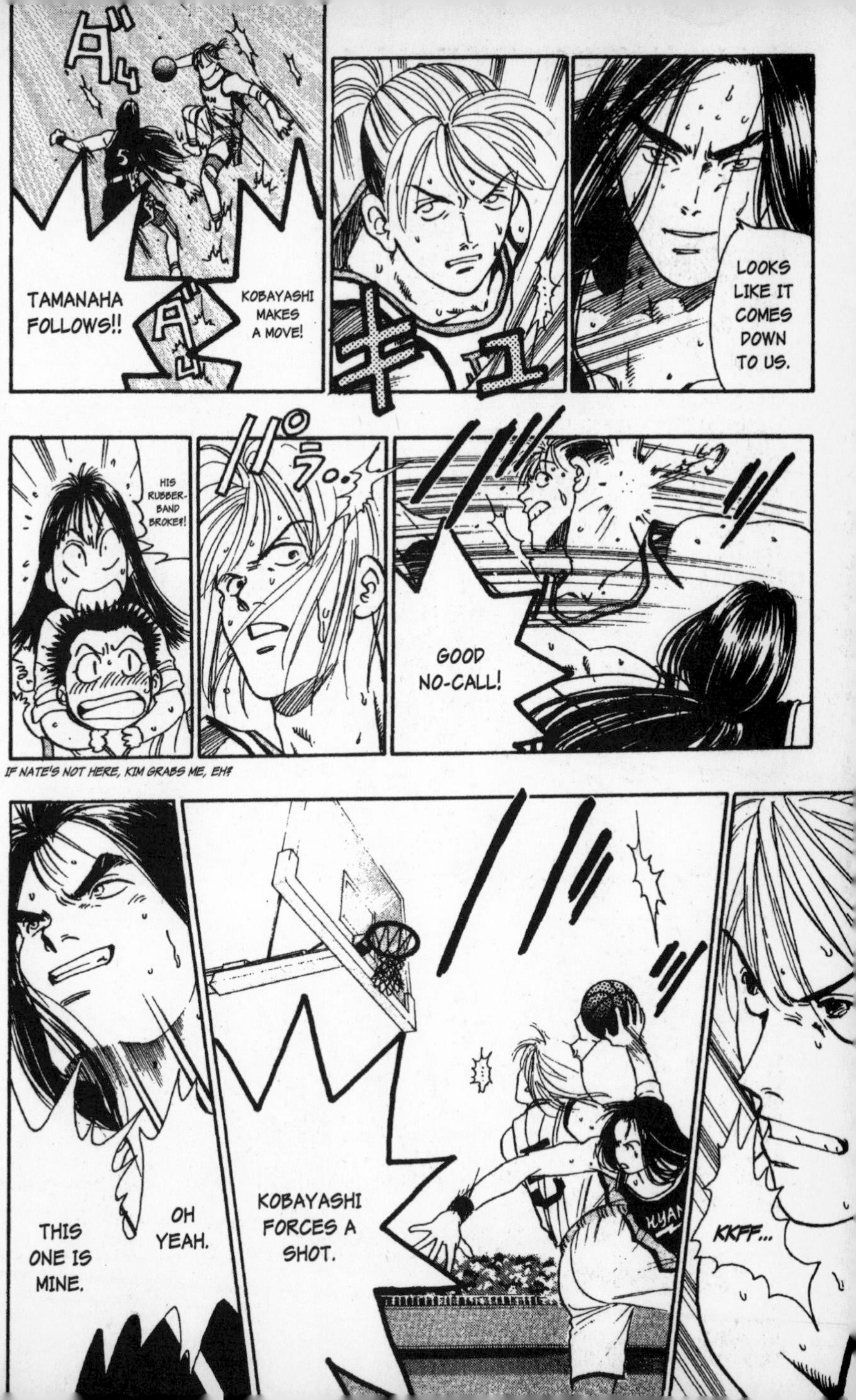
LOOKS LIKE IT COMES DOWN TO US.
KOBAYASHI MAKES A MOVE!
TAMANAHA FOLLOWS!!
GOOD NO-CALL!
HIS RUBBER-BAND BROKE?!
IF NATE'S NOT HERE, KIM GRABS ME, EH?
KKFF...
KOBAYASHI FORCES A SHOT.
OH YEAH.
THIS ONE IS MINE.

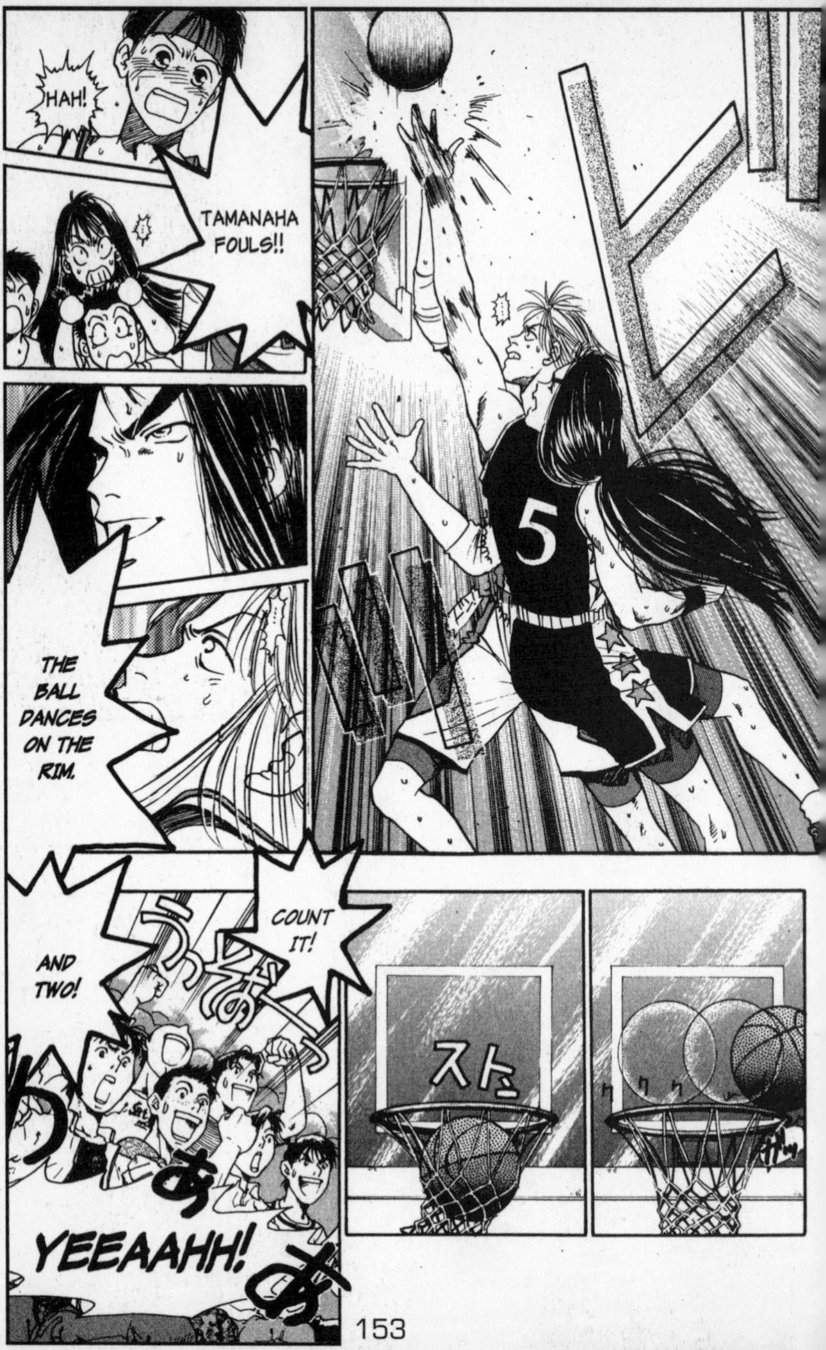

HAH!
TAMANAHA FOULS!!
THE BALL DANCES ON THE RIM.
スト
COUNT IT!
AND TWO!
YEEAAHH!

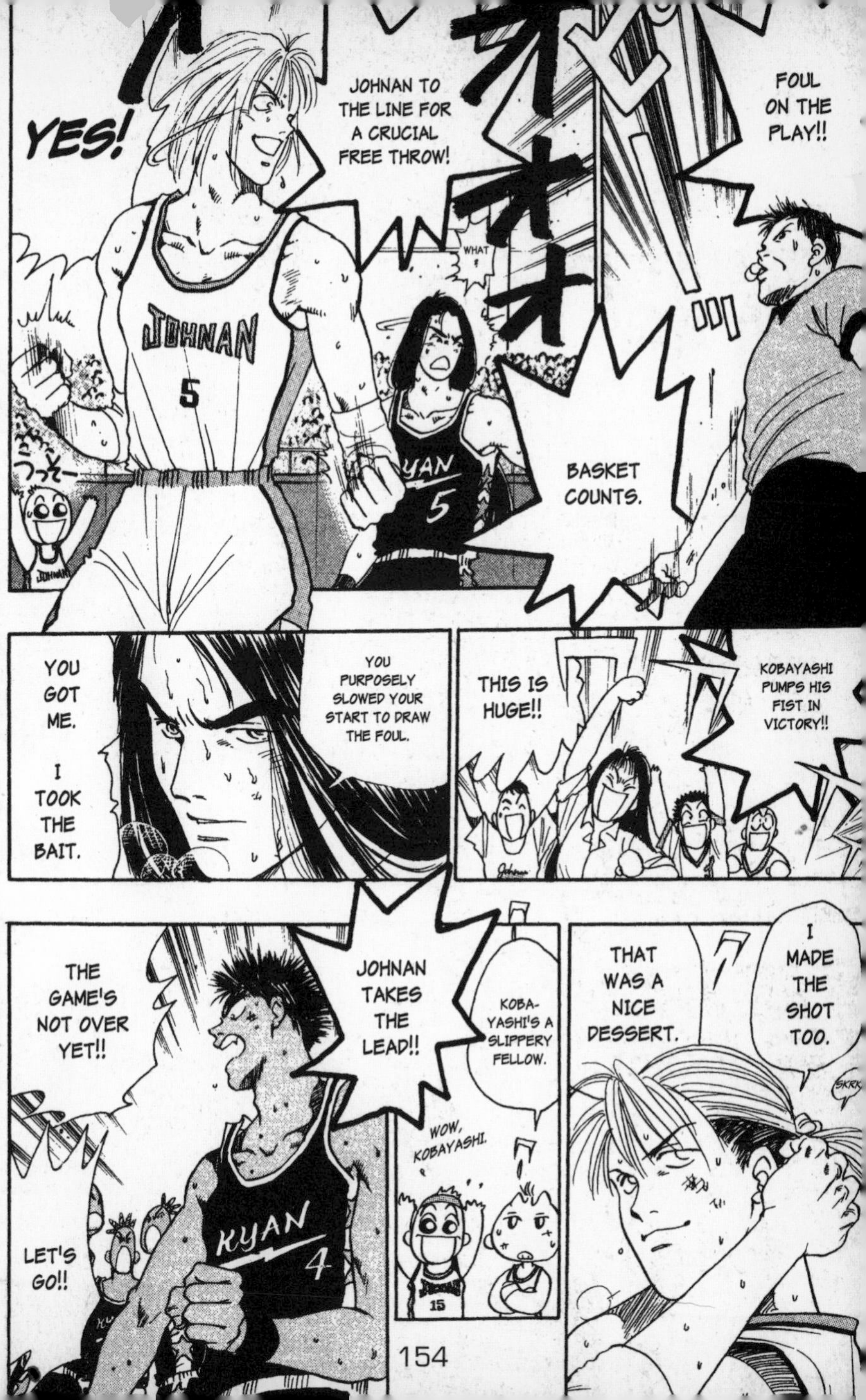
FOUL ON THE PLAY!!
オオオ
JOHNAN TO THE LINE FOR A CRUCIAL FREE THROW!
YES!
WHAT!
BASKET COUNTS.
KOBAYASHI PUMPS HIS FIST IN VICTORY!!
THIS IS HUGE!!
YOU PURPOSELY SLOWED YOUR START TO DRAW THE FOUL.
YOU GOT ME.
I TOOK THE BAIT.
I MADE THE SHOT TOO.
SKRK
THAT WAS A NICE DESSERT.
KOBA-YASHI'S A SLIPPERY FELLOW.
WOW, KOBAYASHI.
JOHNAN TAKES THE LEAD!!
THE GAME'S NOT OVER YET!!
LET'S GO!!

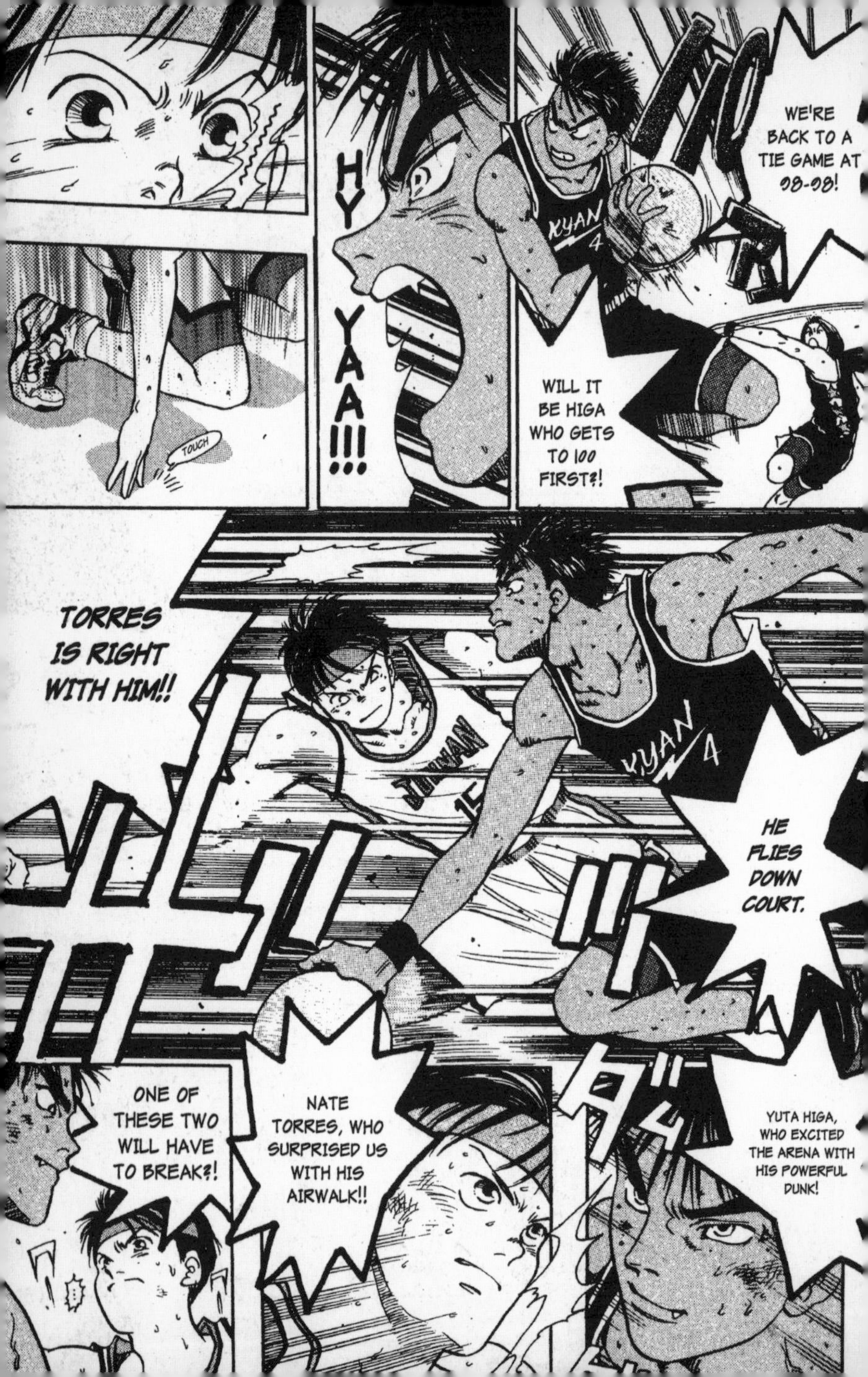
WE'RE BACK TO A TIE GAME AT 98-98!
WILL IT BE HIGA WHO GETS TO 100 FIRST?!
HYYAA!!!
TOUCH
HE FLIES DOWN COURT.
TORRES IS RIGHT WITH HIM!!
YUTA HIGA, WHO EXCITED THE ARENA WITH HIS POWERFUL DUNK!
NATE TORRES, WHO SURPRISED US WITH HIS AIRWALK!!
ONE OF THESE TWO WILL HAVE TO BREAK?!

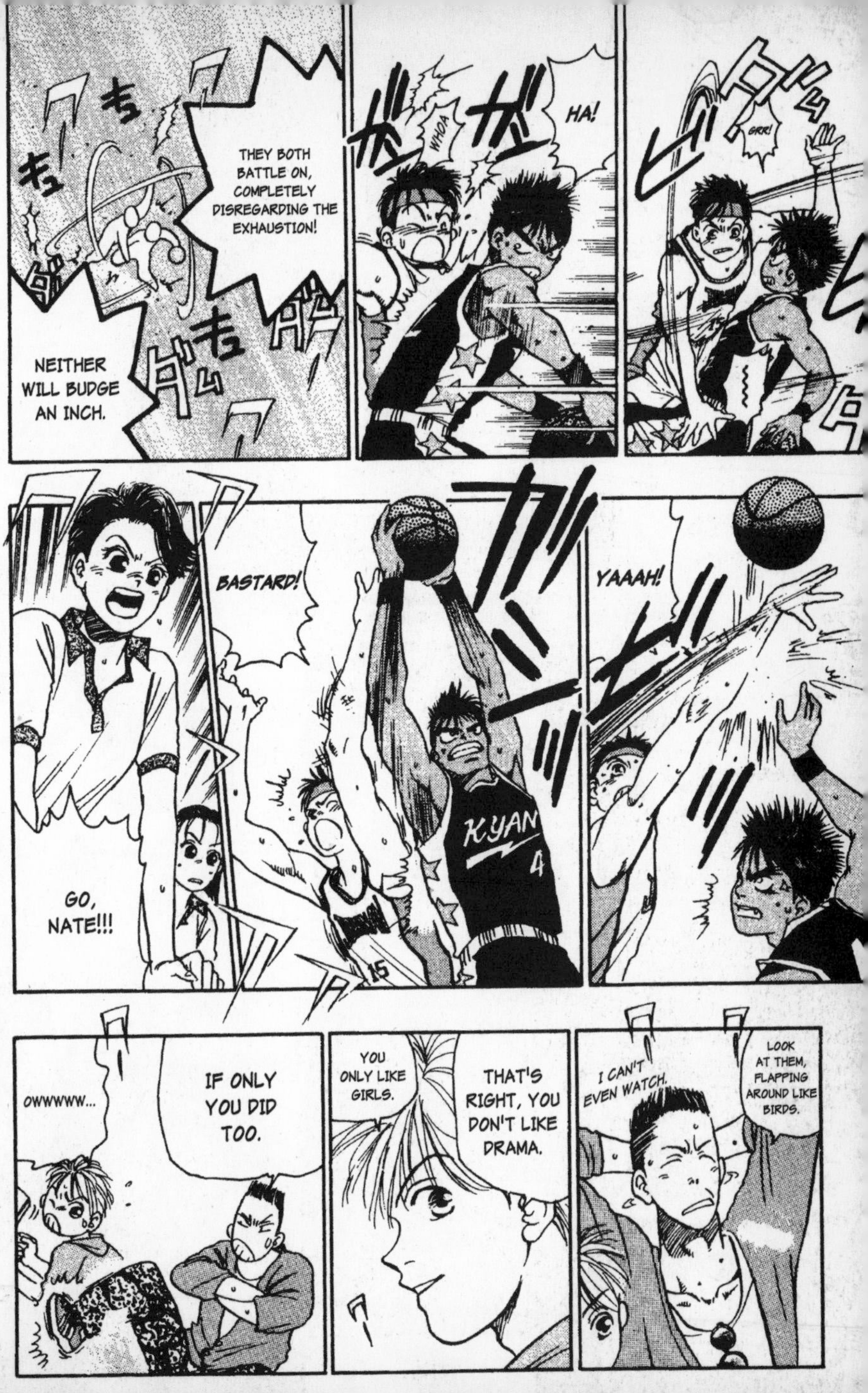
GRR!
HA!
WHOA
THEY BOTH BATTLE ON, COMPLETELY DISREGARDING THE EXHAUSTION!
NEITHER WILL BUDGE AN INCH.
YAAAH!
BASTARD!
GO, NATE!!!
LOOK AT THEM, FLAPPING AROUND LIKE BIRDS.
I CAN'T EVEN WATCH.
THAT'S RIGHT, YOU DON'T LIKE DRAMA.
YOU ONLY LIKE GIRLS.
IF ONLY YOU DID TOO.
OWWWWW...

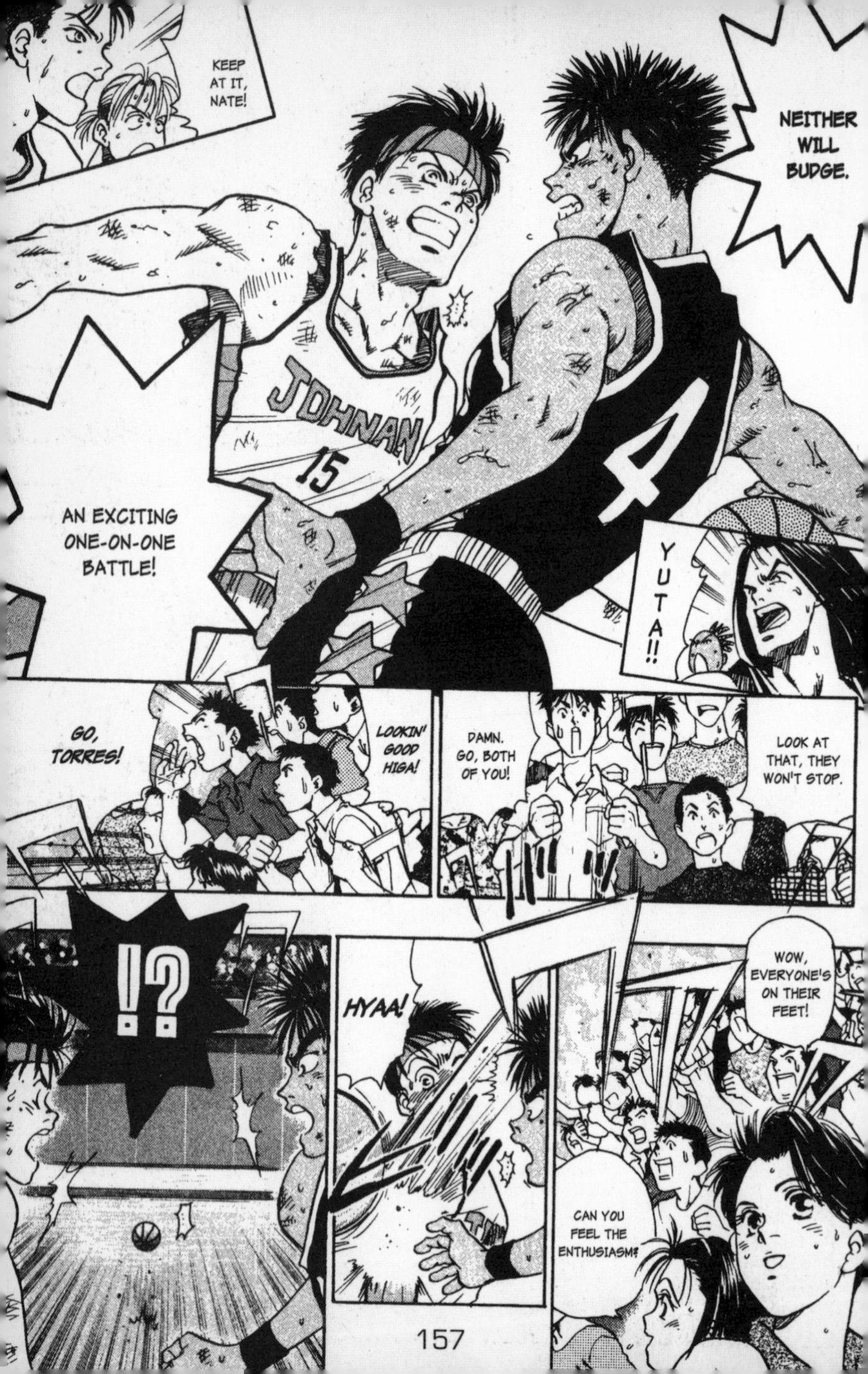
NEITHER WILL BUDGE.
KEEP AT IT, NATE!
YUTA!!
AN EXCITING ONE-ON-ONE BATTLE!
LOOK AT THAT, THEY WON'T STOP.
DAMN. GO, BOTH OF YOU!
LOOKIN' GOOD HIGA!
GO, TORRES!
WOW, EVERYONE'S ON THEIR FEET!
CAN YOU FEEL THE ENTHUSIASM?
HYAA!
!?

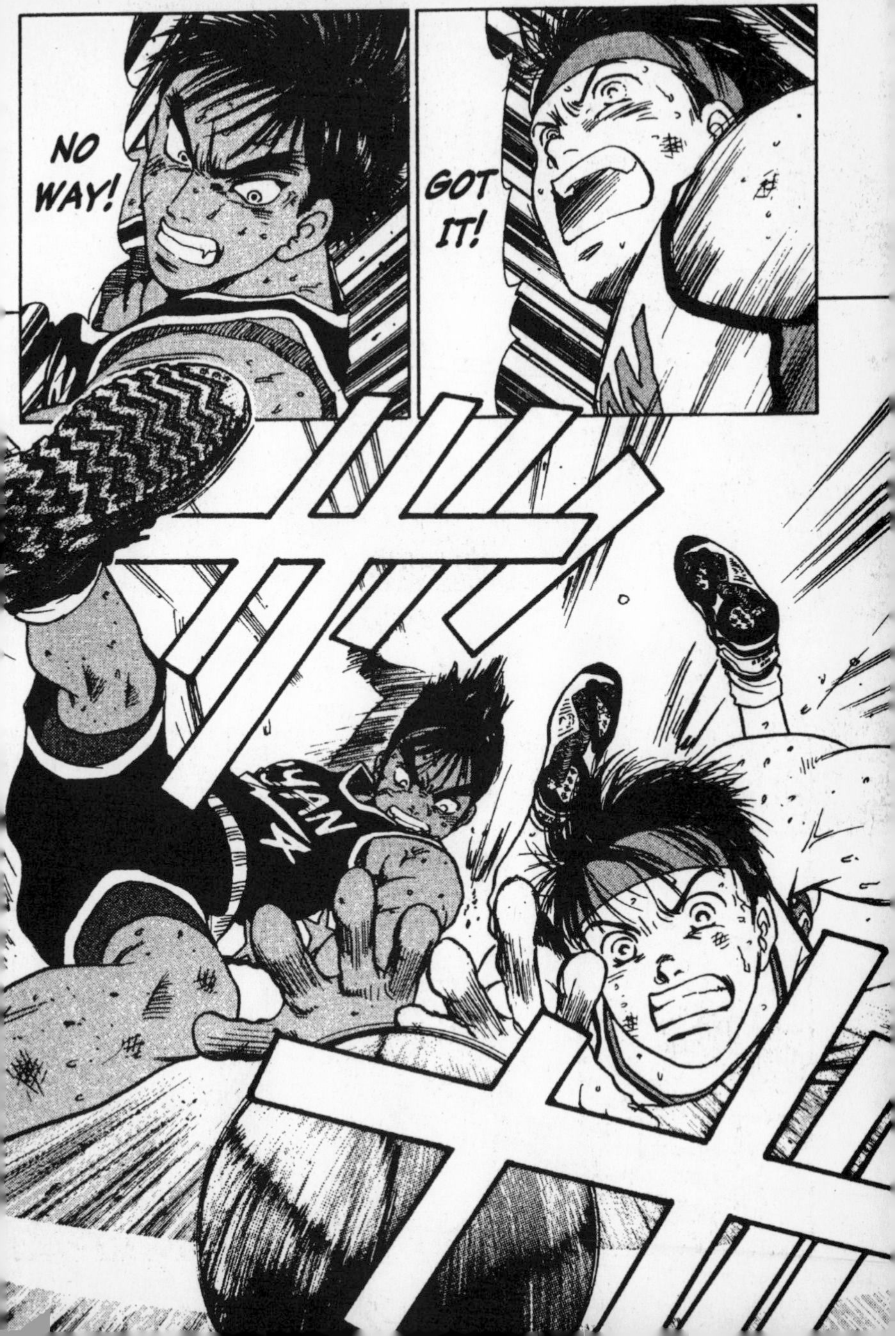
GOT IT!
NO WAY!

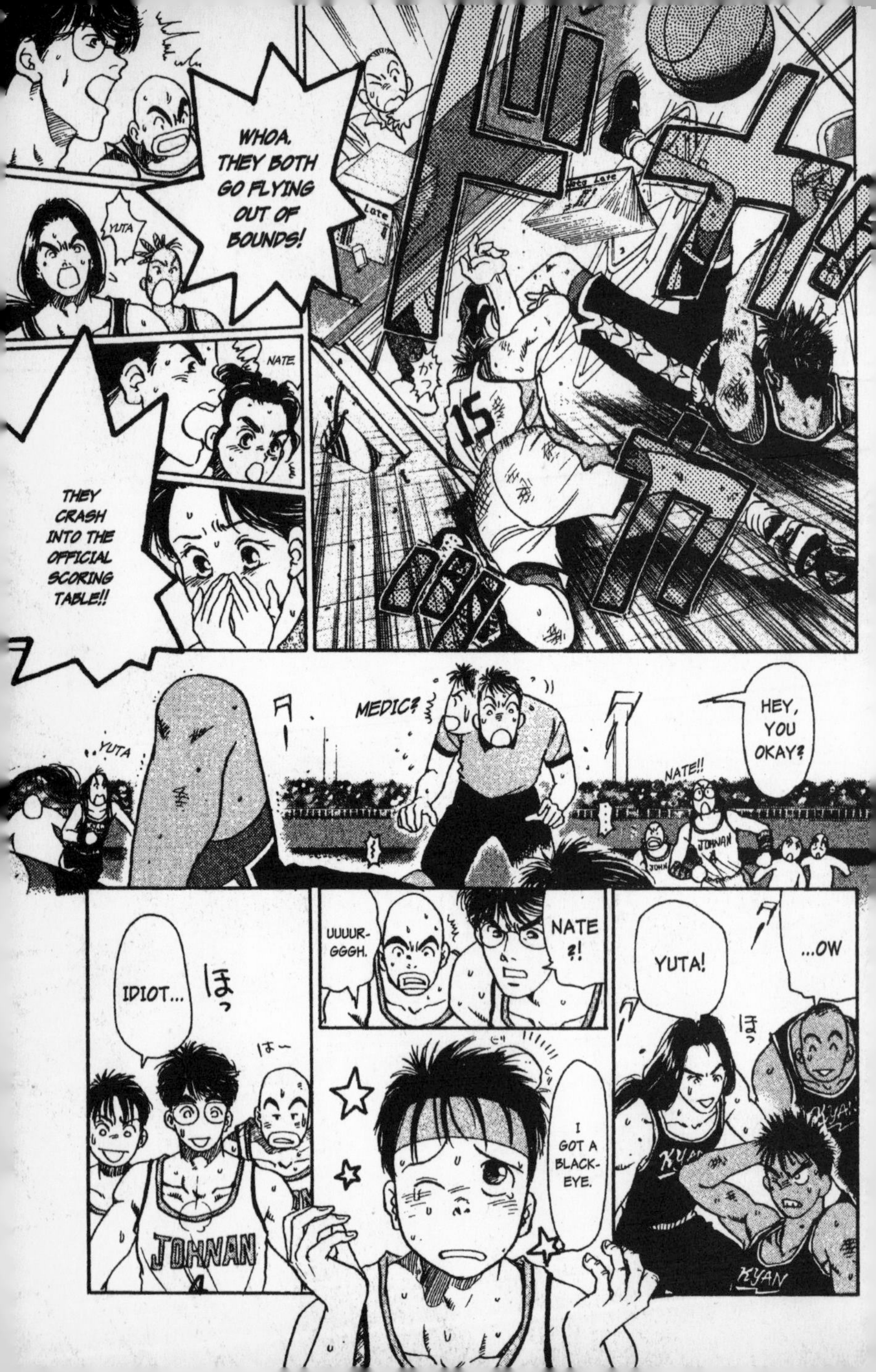
がっ
WHOA. THEY BOTH GO FLYING OUT OF BOUNDS!
YUTA
NATE.
THEY CRASH INTO THE OFFICIAL SCORING TABLE!!
HEY, YOU OKAY?
NATE!!
MEDIC?
...YUTA
...OW
YUTA!
ほっ
NATE?!
UUUUR-GGGH.
I GOT A BLACK-EYE.
IDIOT...
ほっ
はー

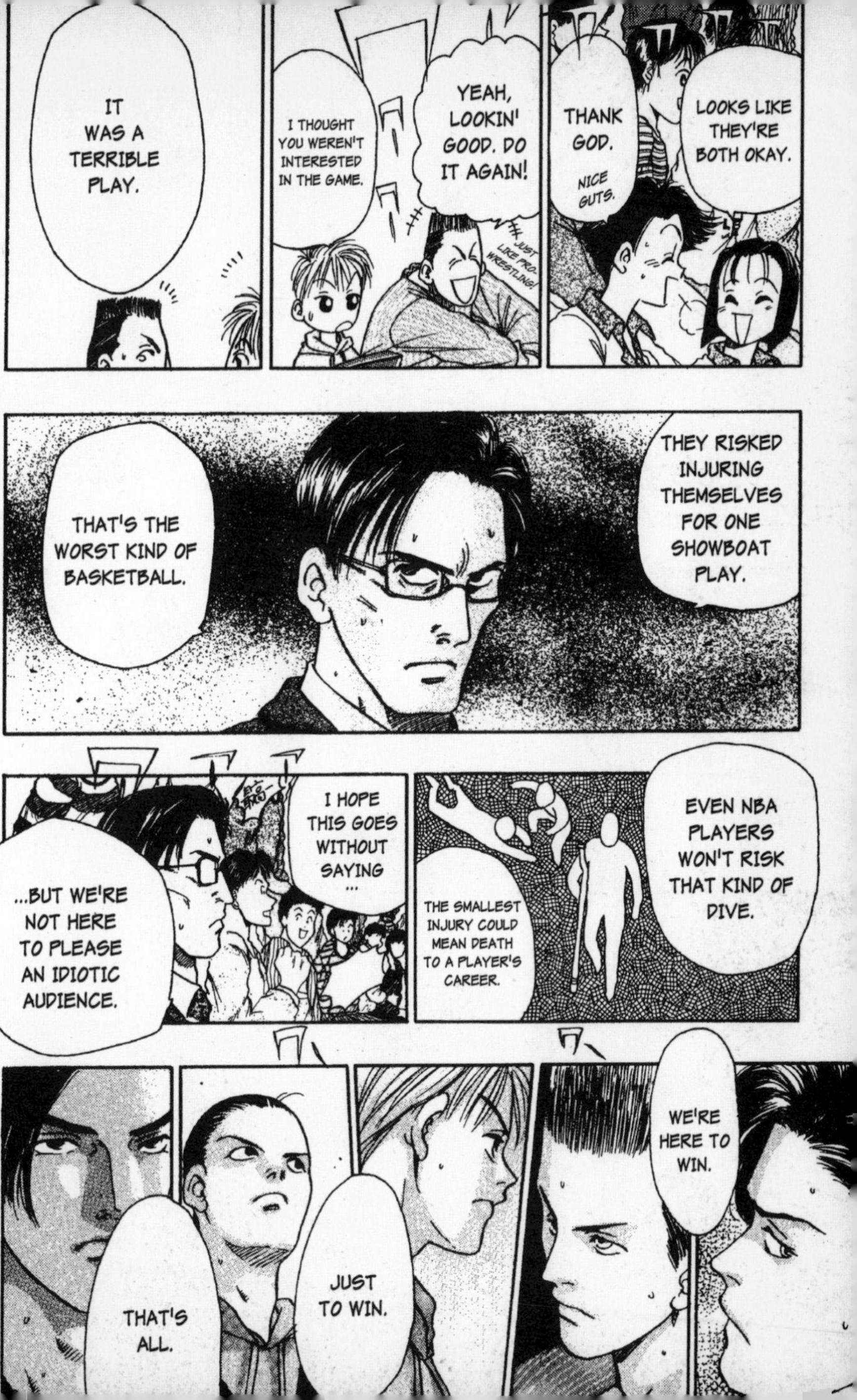
LOOKS LIKE THEY'RE BOTH OKAY.
THANK GOD.
NICE GUTS.
YEAH, LOOKIN' GOOD. DO IT AGAIN!
JUST LIKE PRO-WRESTLING!
I THOUGHT YOU WEREN'T INTERESTED IN THE GAME.
IT WAS A TERRIBLE PLAY.
THEY RISKED INJURING THEMSELVES FOR ONE SHOWBOAT PLAY.
THAT'S THE WORST KIND OF BASKETBALL.
EVEN NBA PLAYERS WON'T RISK THAT KIND OF DIVE.
THE SMALLEST INJURY COULD MEAN DEATH TO A PLAYER'S CAREER.
I HOPE THIS GOES WITHOUT SAYING ...
...BUT WE'RE NOT HERE TO PLEASE AN IDIOTIC AUDIENCE.
WE'RE HERE TO WIN.
JUST TO WIN.
THAT'S ALL.

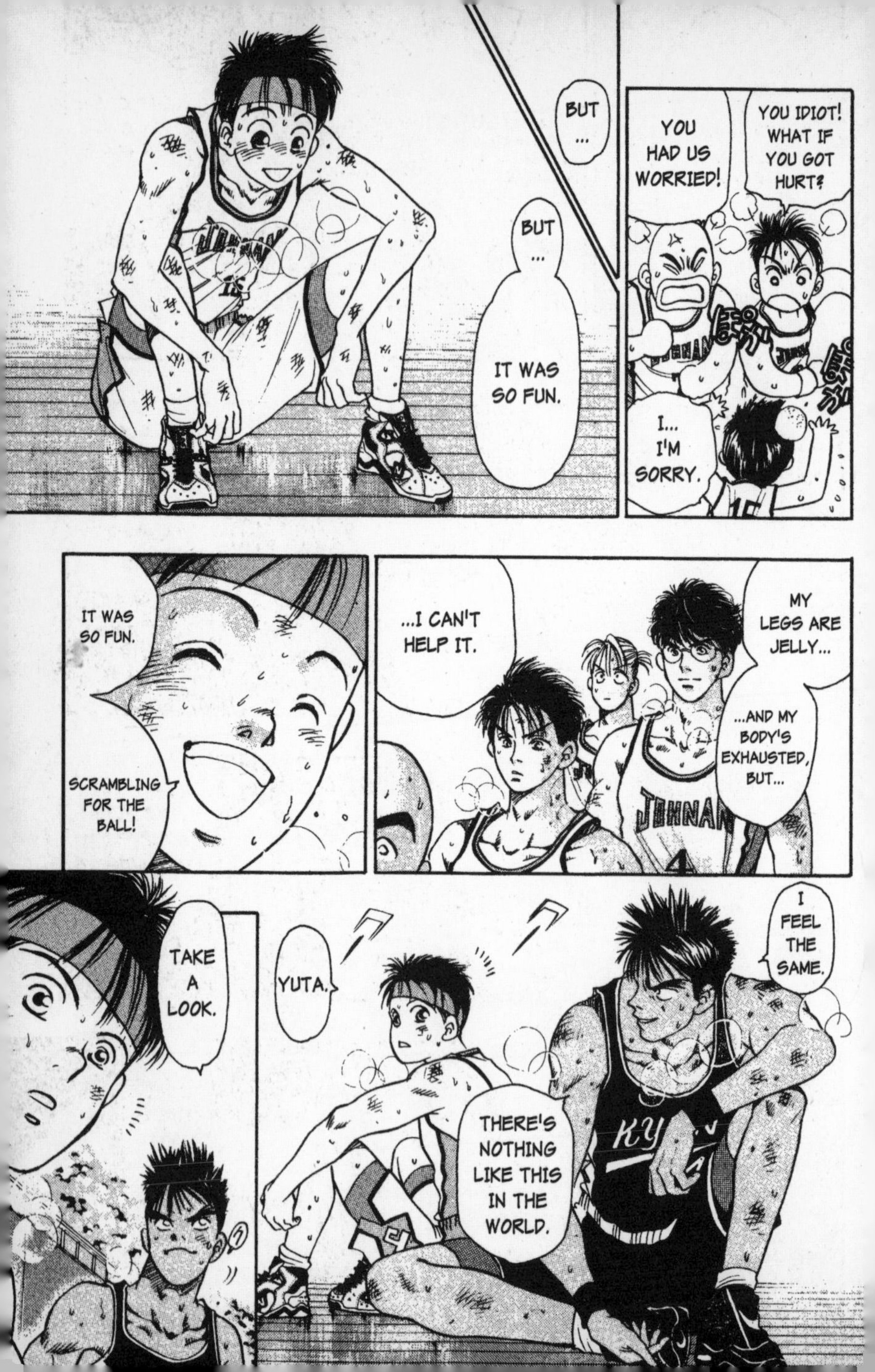
YOU IDIOT! WHAT IF YOU GOT HURT?
YOU HAD US WORRIED!
I... I'M SORRY.
BUT ...
BUT ...
IT WAS SO FUN.
MY LEGS ARE JELLY...
...AND MY BODY'S EXHAUSTED, BUT...
...I CAN'T HELP IT.
IT WAS SO FUN.
SCRAMBLING FOR THE BALL!
I FEEL THE SAME.
THERE'S NOTHING LIKE THIS IN THE WORLD.
YUTA.
TAKE A LOOK.

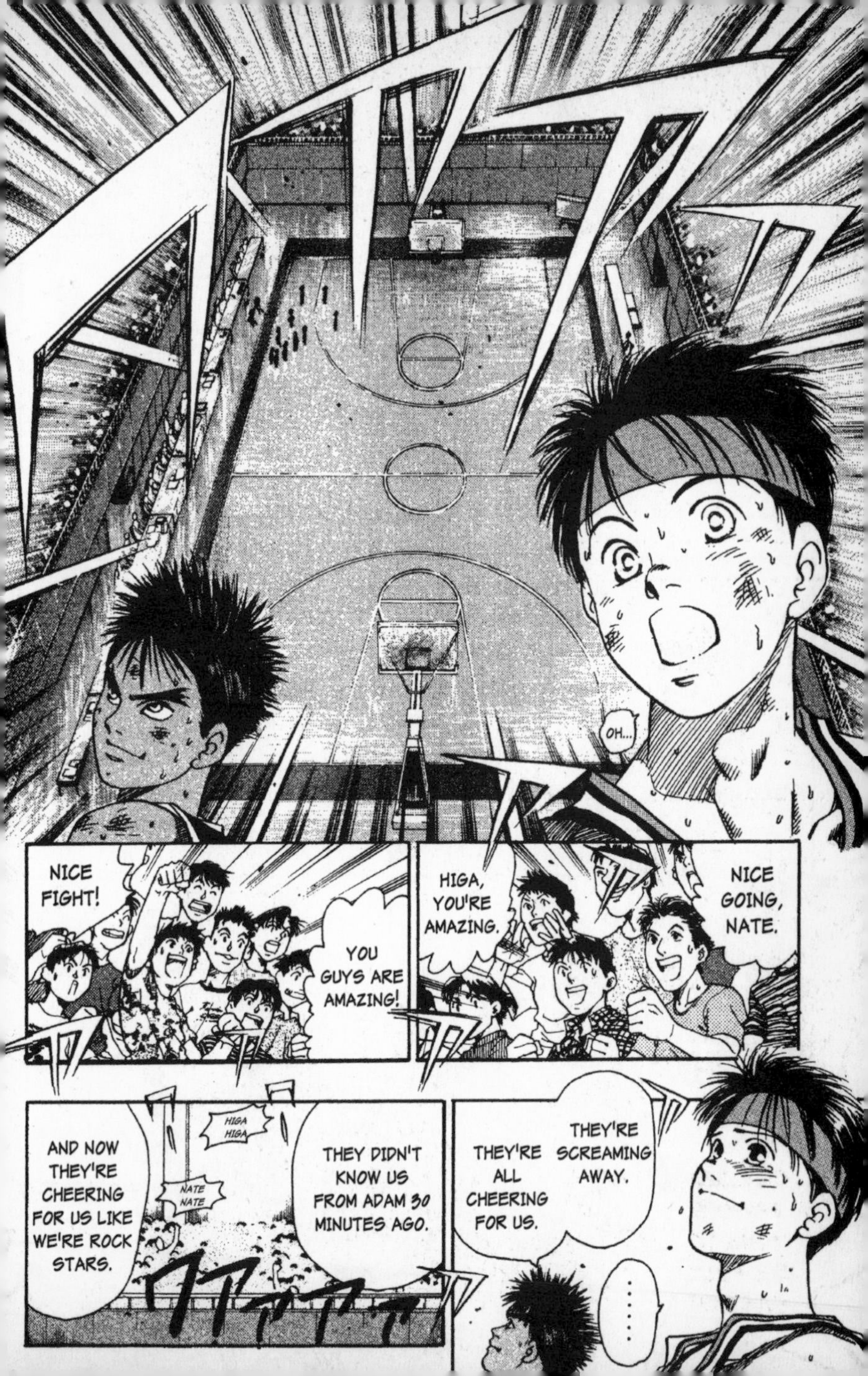
OH...
NICE GOING, NATE.
HIGA, YOU'RE AMAZING.
NICE FIGHT!
YOU GUYS ARE AMAZING!
THEY'RE SCREAMING AWAY.
THEY'RE ALL CHEERING FOR US.
......
HIGA HIGA
THEY DIDN'T KNOW US FROM ADAM 30 MINUTES AGO.
NATE NATE
AND NOW THEY'RE CHEERING FOR US LIKE WE'RE ROCK STARS.

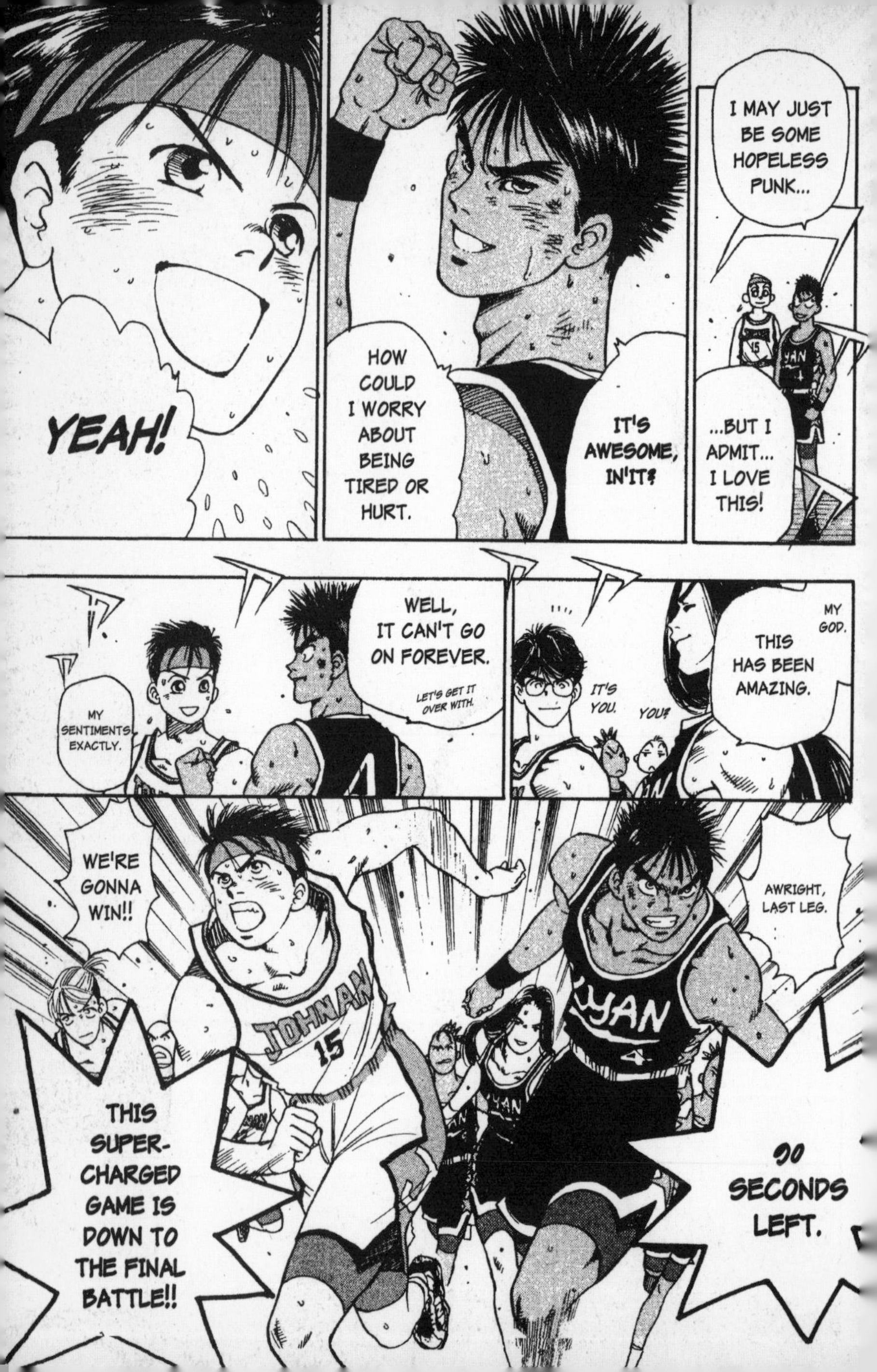
I MAY JUST BE SOME HOPELESS PUNK...
...BUT I ADMIT... I LOVE THIS!
IT'S AWESOME, IN'IT?
HOW COULD I WORRY ABOUT BEING TIRED OR HURT.
YEAH!
MY GOD.
THIS HAS BEEN AMAZING.
IT'S YOU.
YOU?
WELL, IT CAN'T GO ON FOREVER.
LET'S GET IT OVER WITH.
MY SENTIMENTS EXACTLY.
AWRIGHT, LAST LEG.
WE'RE GONNA WIN!!
90 SECONDS LEFT.
THIS SUPER-CHARGED GAME IS DOWN TO THE FINAL BATTLE!!

You're reading...

See the adventures of Kim the Witch serialized in her own monthly manga: Itchy, Twitchy, Witch.

I AM KIM, THE WITCH.

I CAPTURE AND CRUSH THE HEARTS OF MEN.

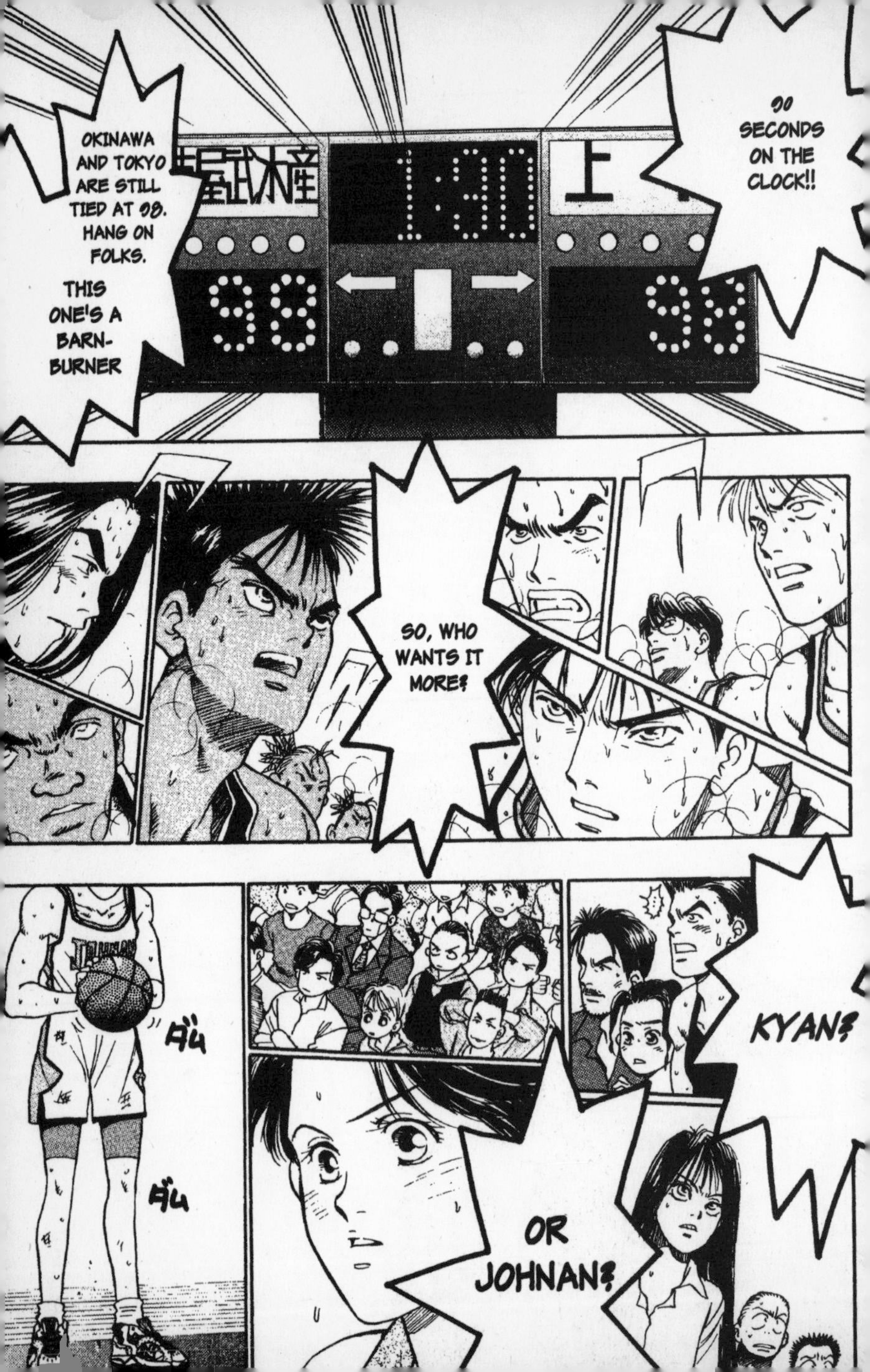
90 SECONDS ON THE CLOCK!!
OKINAWA AND TOKYO ARE STILL TIED AT 98. HANG ON FOLKS.
THIS ONE'S A BARN-BURNER
SO, WHO WANTS IT MORE?
KYAN?
OR JOHNAN?

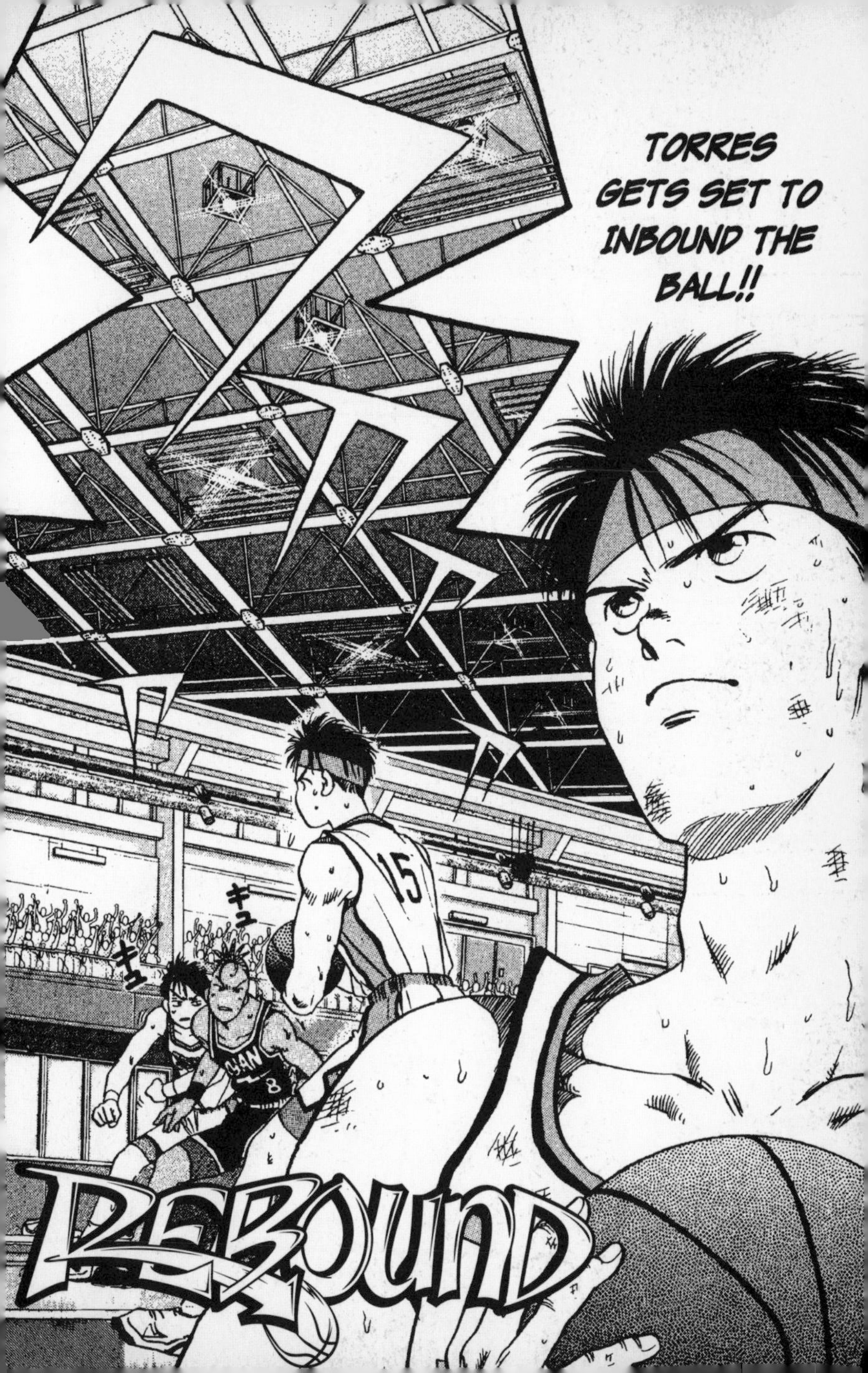
TORRES GETS SET TO INBOUND THE BALL!!
キュ
キュ
REBOUND

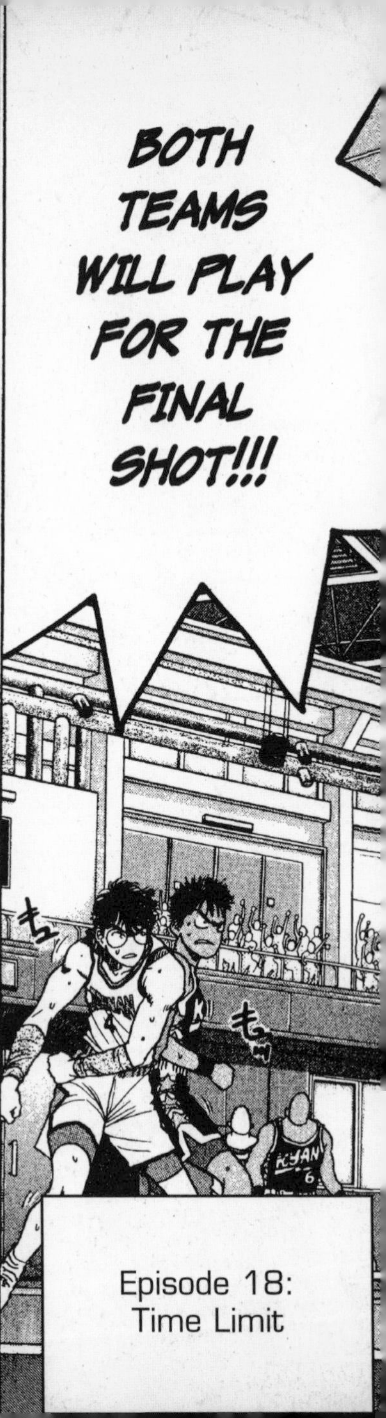
BOTH TEAMS WILL PLAY FOR THE FINAL SHOT!!!
Episode 18: Time Limit

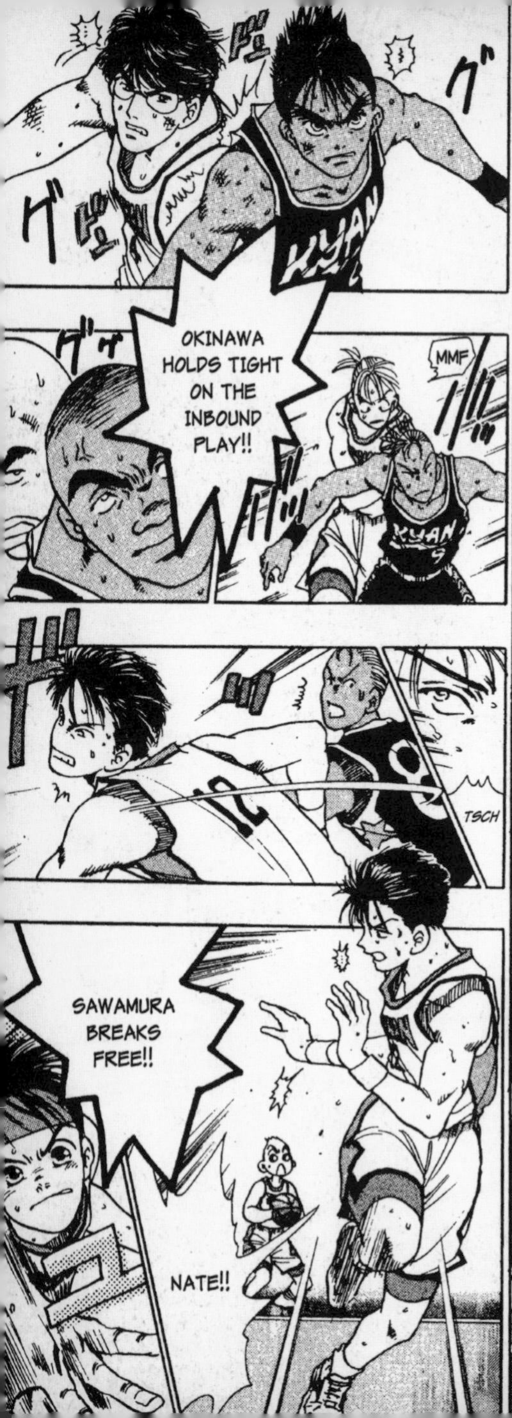
MMF
OKINAWA HOLDS TIGHT ON THE INBOUND PLAY!!
TSCH
SAWAMURA BREAKS FREE!!
NATE!!

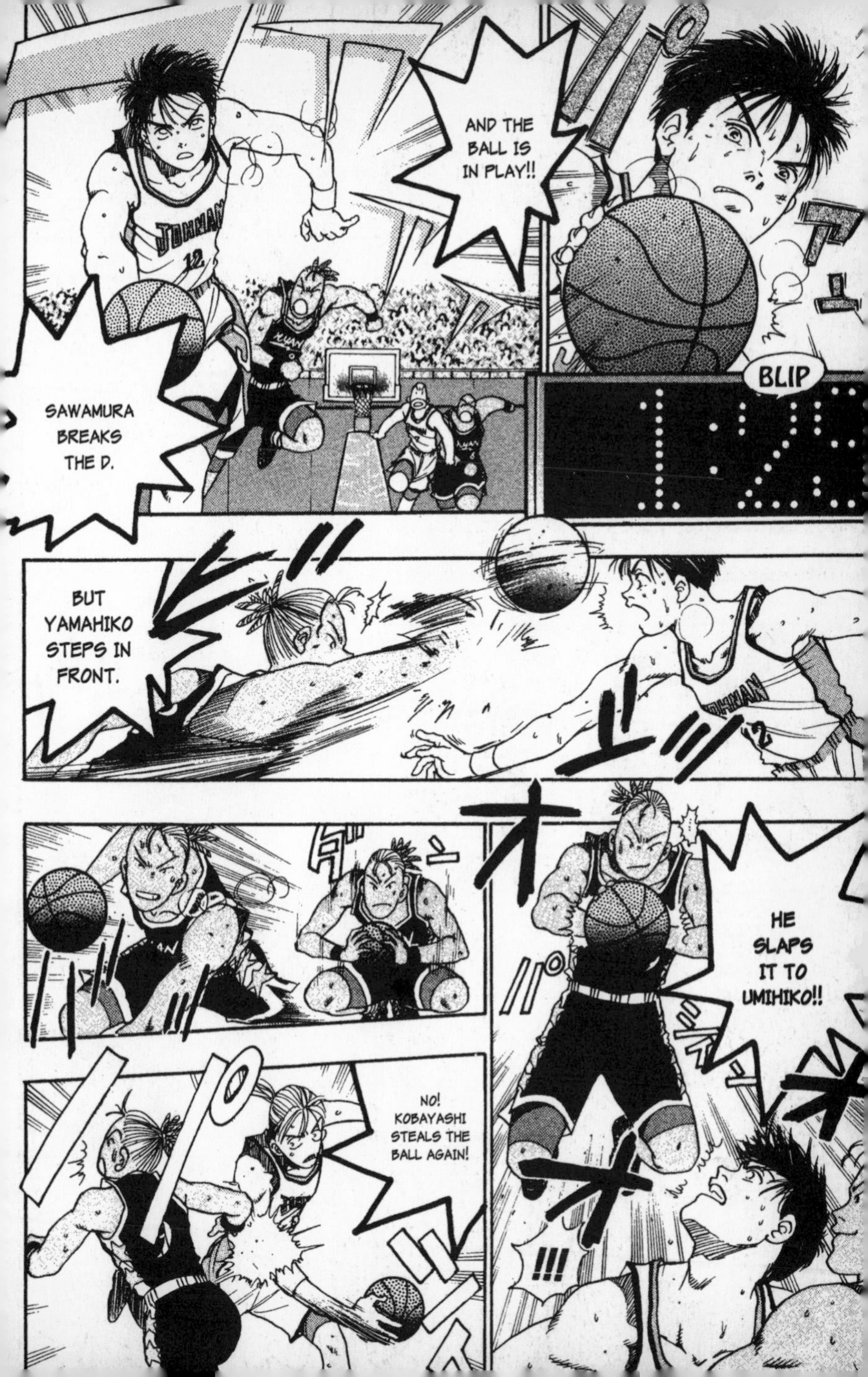
AND THE BALL IS IN PLAY!!
BLIP
SAWAMURA BREAKS THE D.
BUT YAMAHIKO STEPS IN FRONT.
HE SLAPS IT TO UMIHIKO!!
!!!
NO! KOBAYASHI STEALS THE BALL AGAIN!

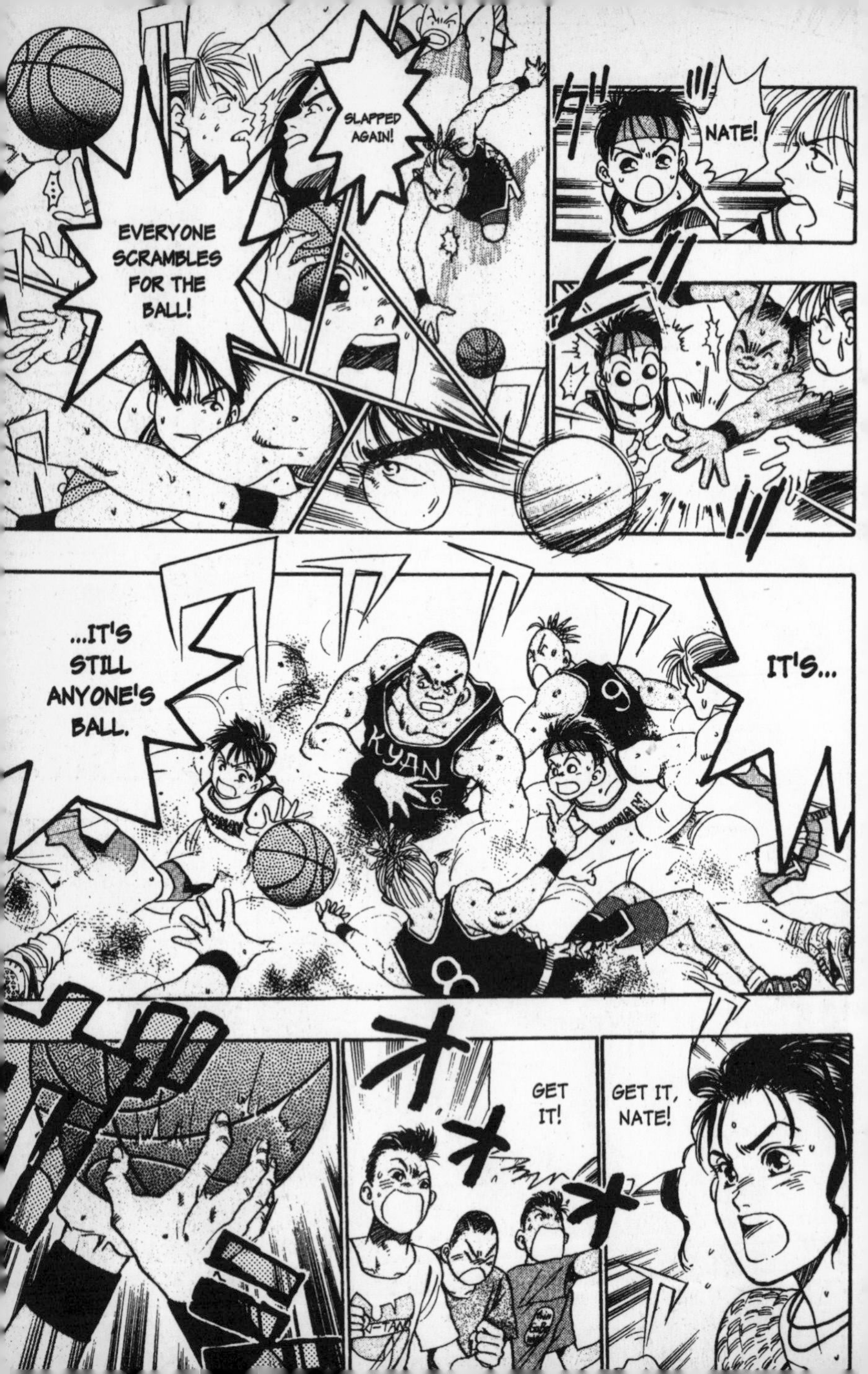
NATE!
SLAPPED AGAIN!
EVERYONE SCRAMBLES FOR THE BALL!
IT'S...
...IT'S STILL ANYONE'S BALL.
GET IT, NATE!
GET IT!

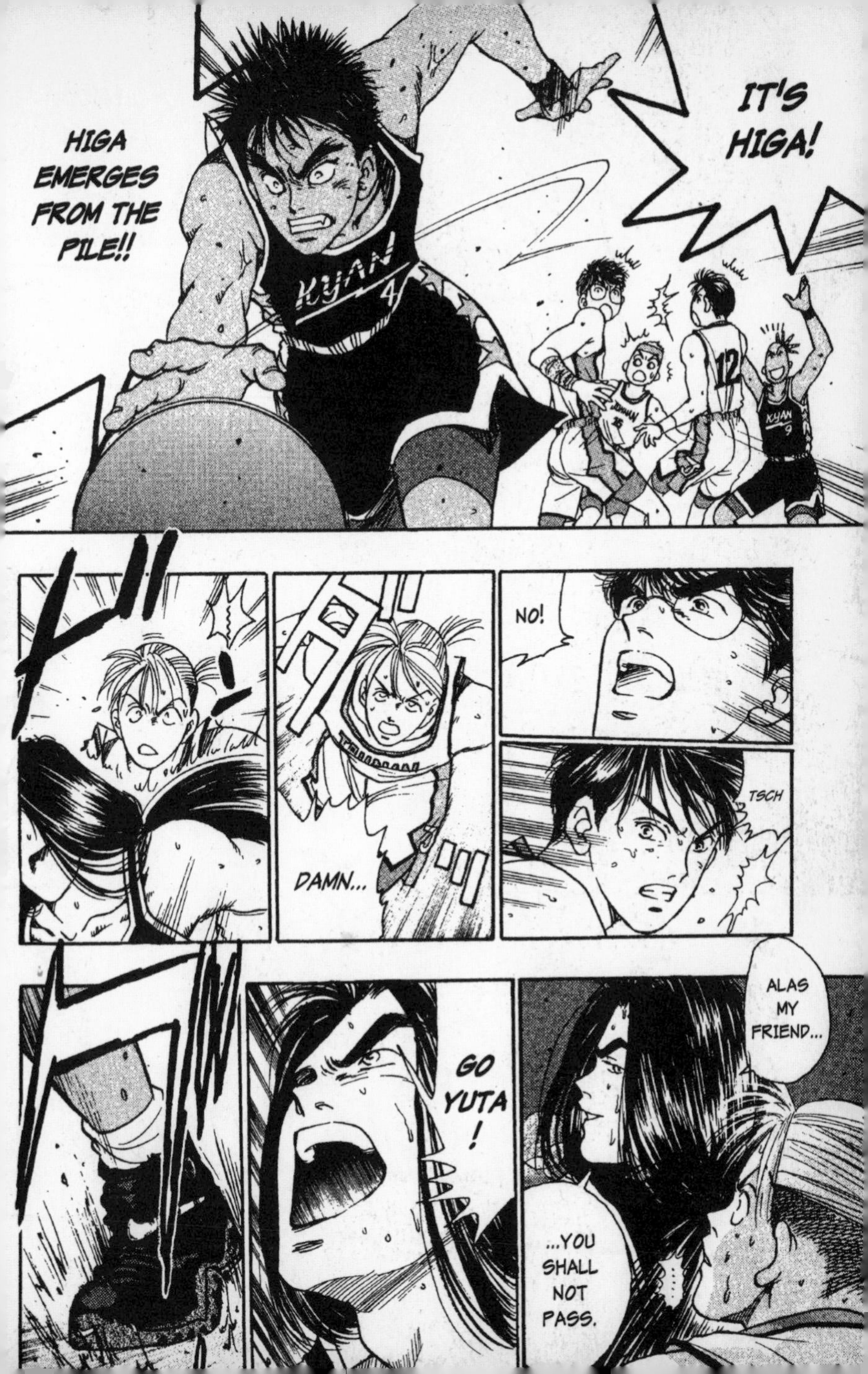
IT'S HIGA!
HIGA EMERGES FROM THE PILE!!
NO!
TSCH
DAMN...
ALAS MY FRIEND...
...YOU SHALL NOT PASS.
GO YUTA!

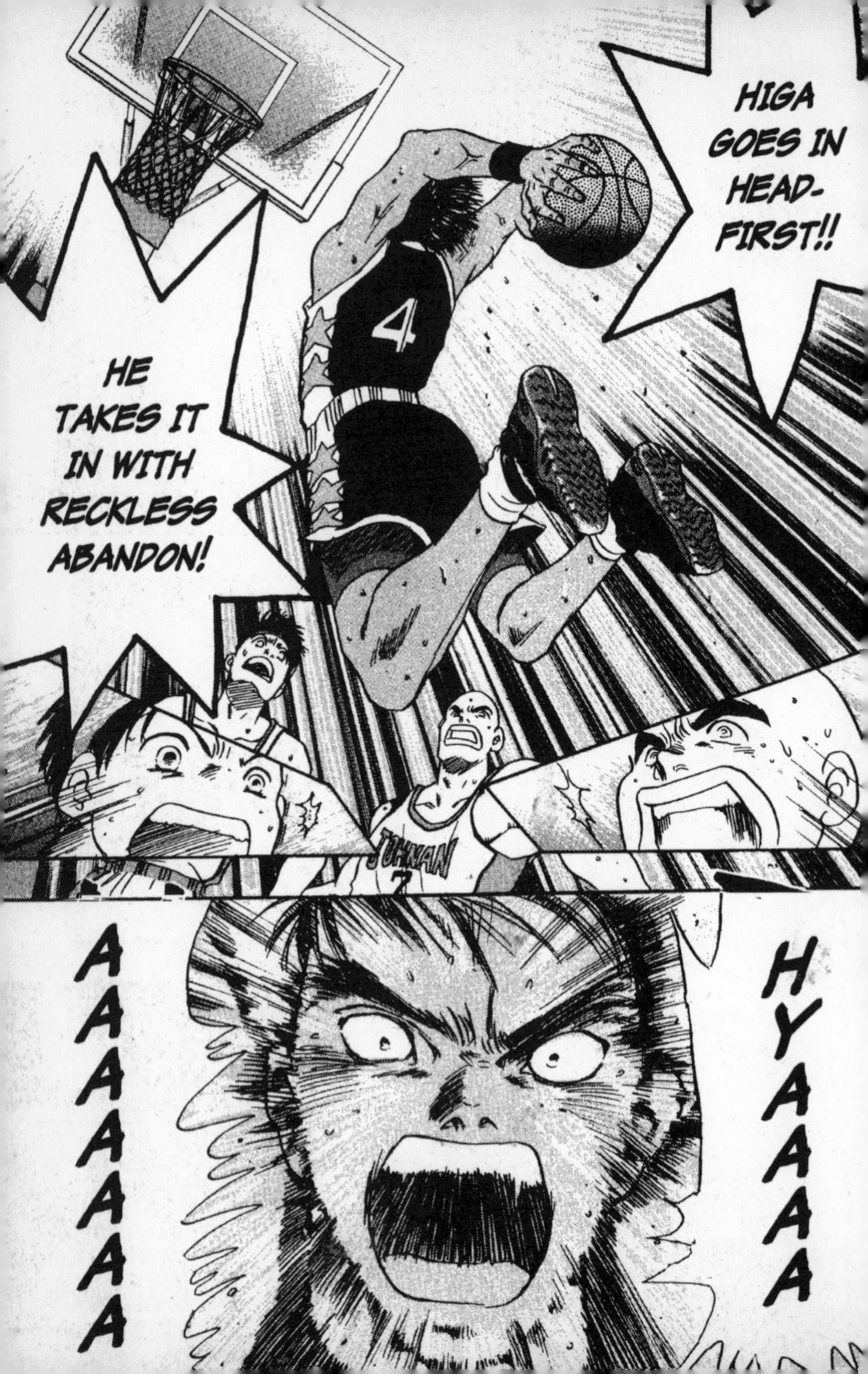
HIGA GOES IN HEAD-FIRST!!
HE TAKES IT IN WITH RECKLESS ABANDON!
HYAAAAAA
AAAAAAAA

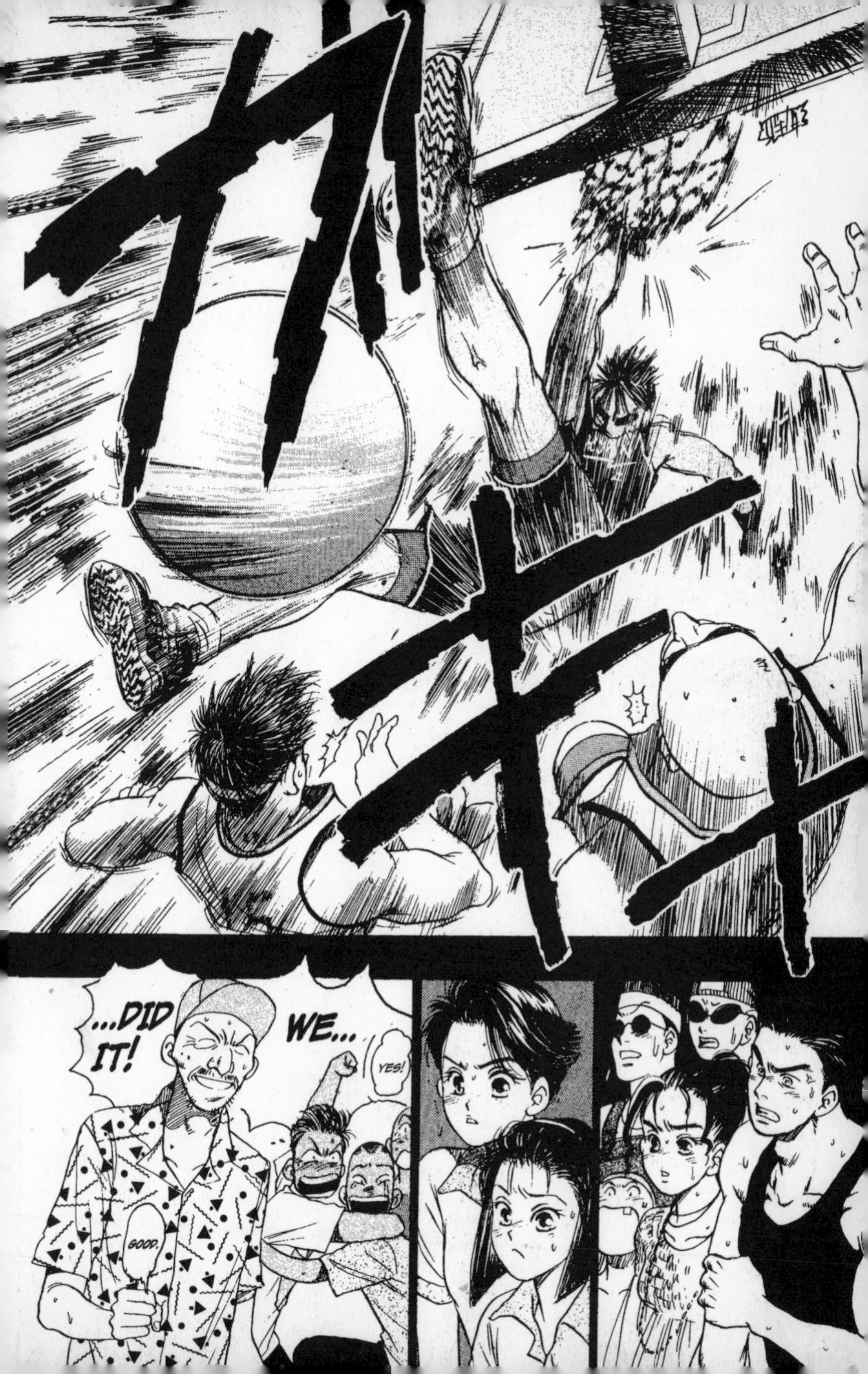
YES!
WE...
...DID IT!
GOOD.

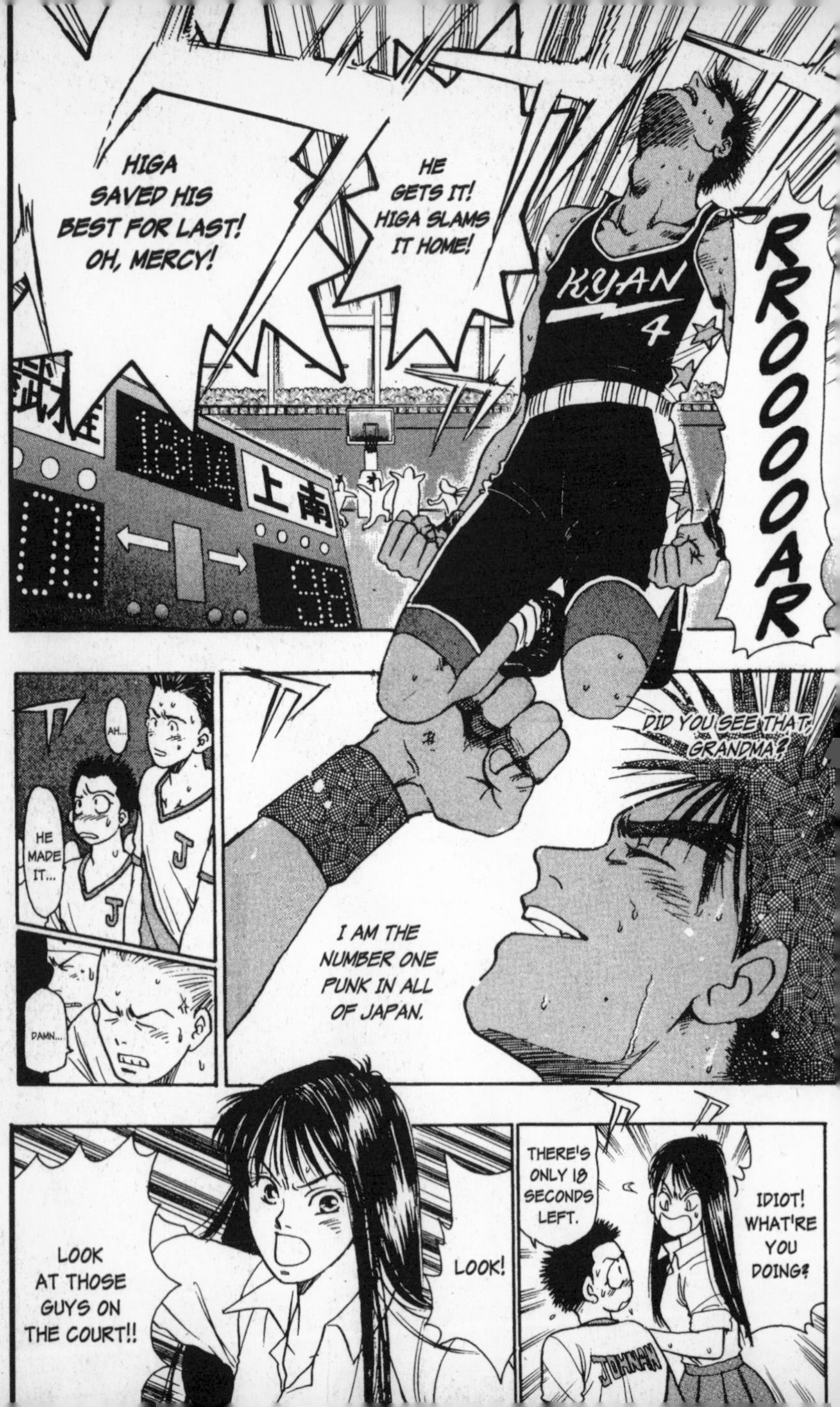
RROOOOOAR
KYAN 4
HE GETS IT! HIGA SLAMS IT HOME!
HIGA SAVED HIS BEST FOR LAST! OH, MERCY!
上南
DID YOU SEE THAT, GRANDMA?
I AM THE NUMBER ONE PUNK IN ALL OF JAPAN.
AH...
HE MADE IT...
DAMN...
IDIOT! WHAT'RE YOU DOING?
THERE'S ONLY 18 SECONDS LEFT.
JOHNAN
LOOK!
LOOK AT THOSE GUYS ON THE COURT!!

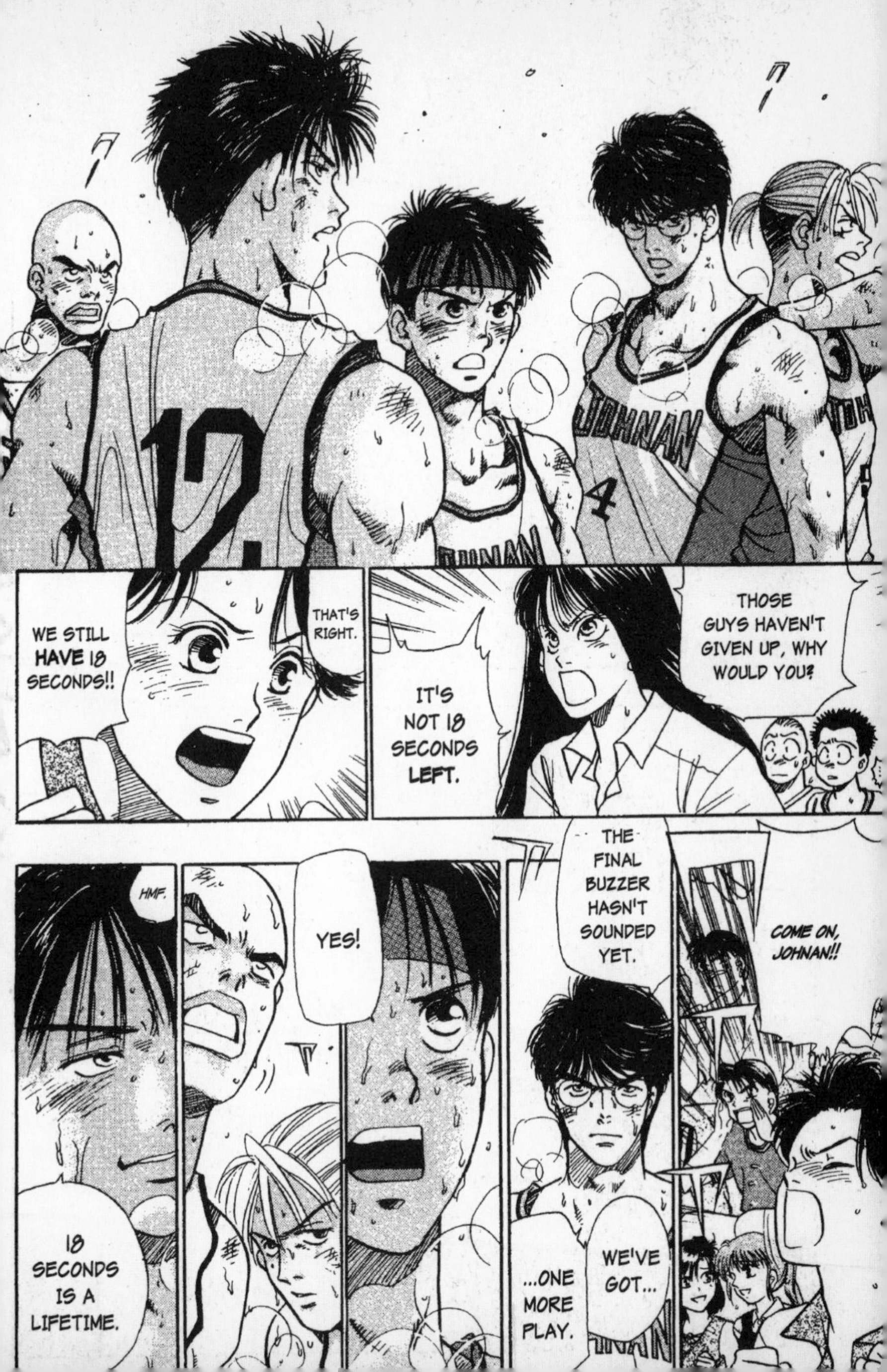
THOSE GUYS HAVEN'T GIVEN UP, WHY WOULD YOU?
IT'S NOT 18 SECONDS LEFT.
THAT'S RIGHT.
WE STILL HAVE 18 SECONDS!!
COME ON, JOHNAN!!
THE FINAL BUZZER HASN'T SOUNDED YET.
WE'VE GOT...
...ONE MORE PLAY.
YES!
HMF.
18 SECONDS IS A LIFETIME.

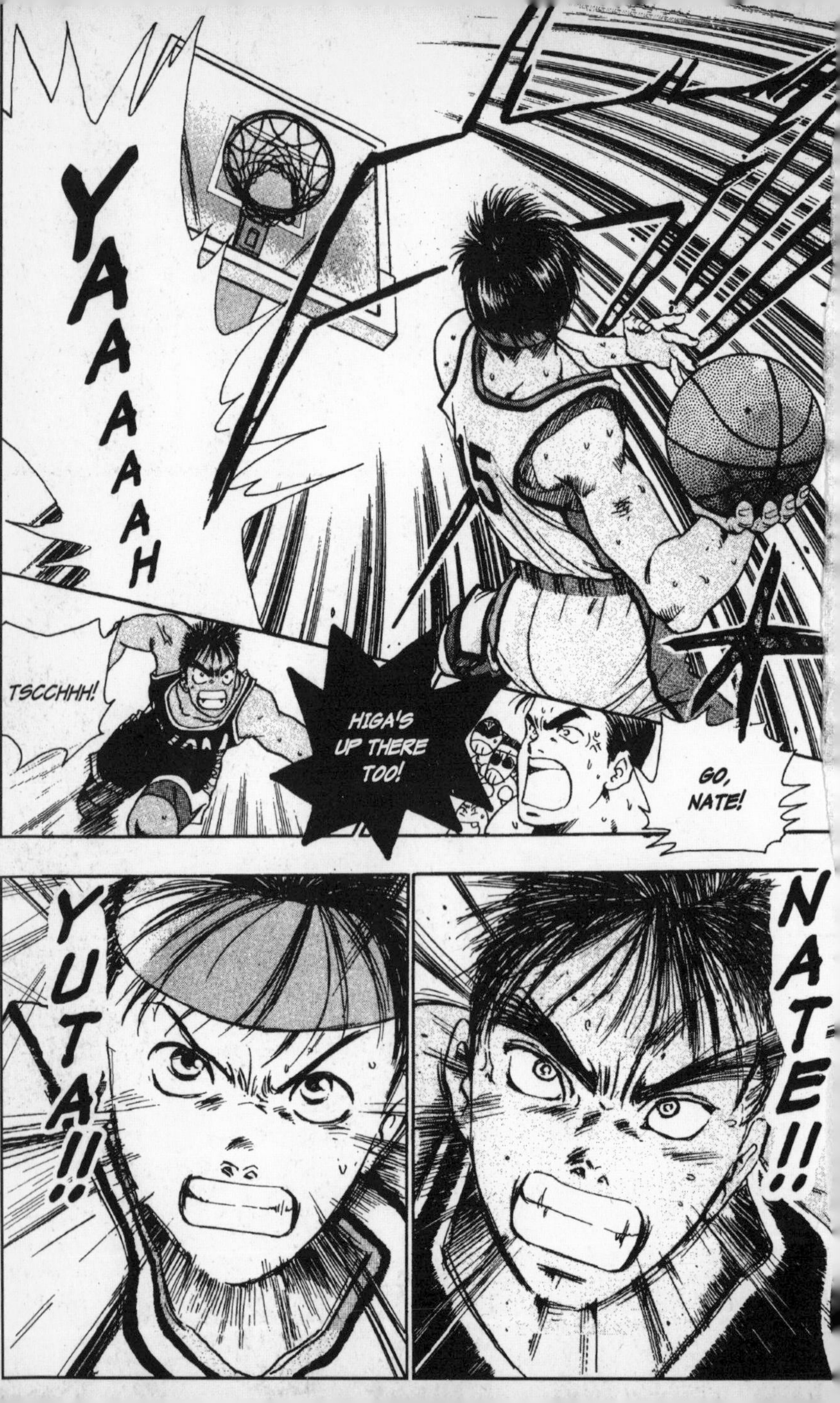
YAAAAAH
GO, NATE!
HIGA'S UP THERE TOO!
TSCCHHH!
NATE!!
YUTA!!

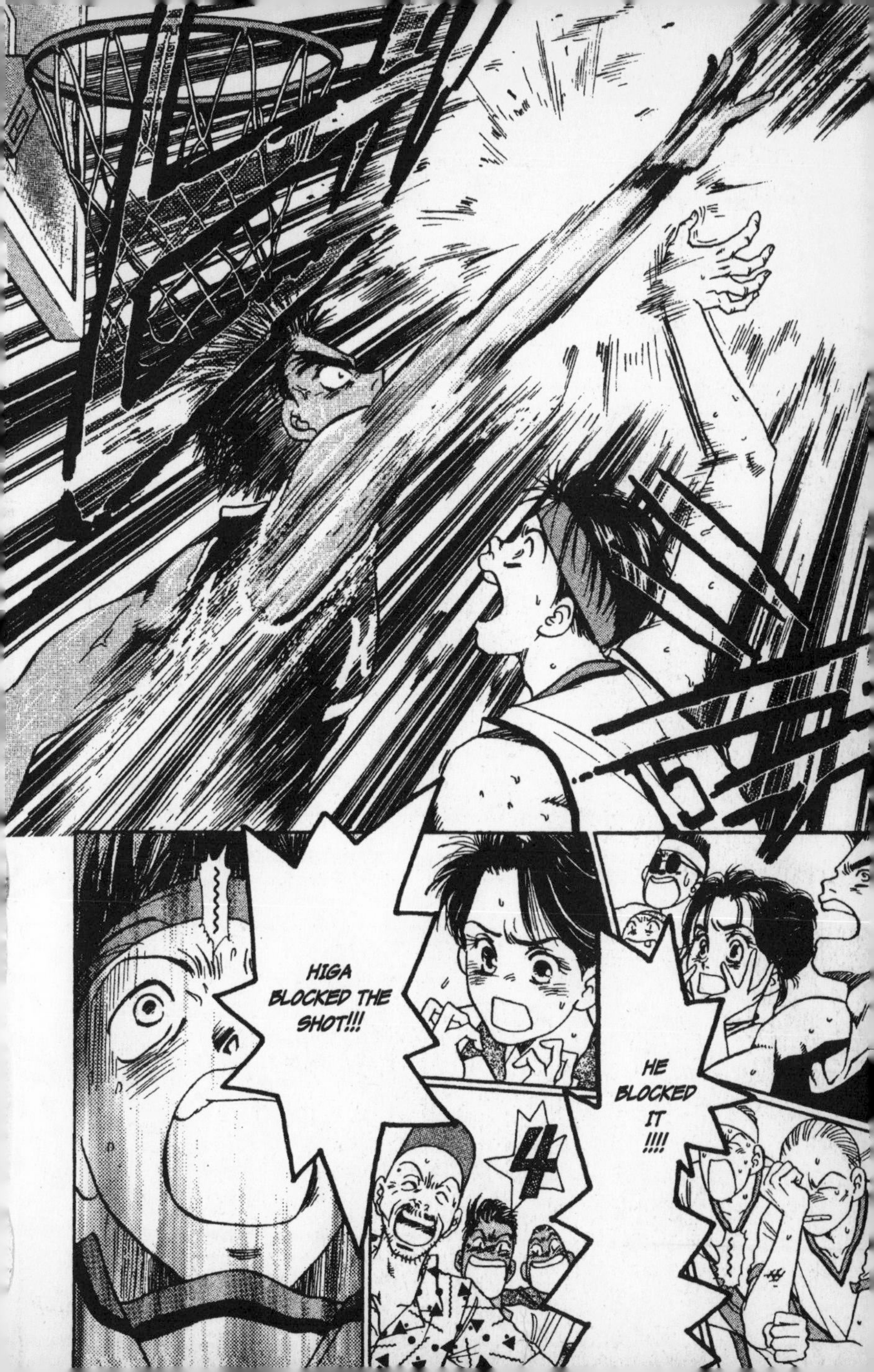
HE BLOCKED IT !!!!
HIGA BLOCKED THE SHOT!!!

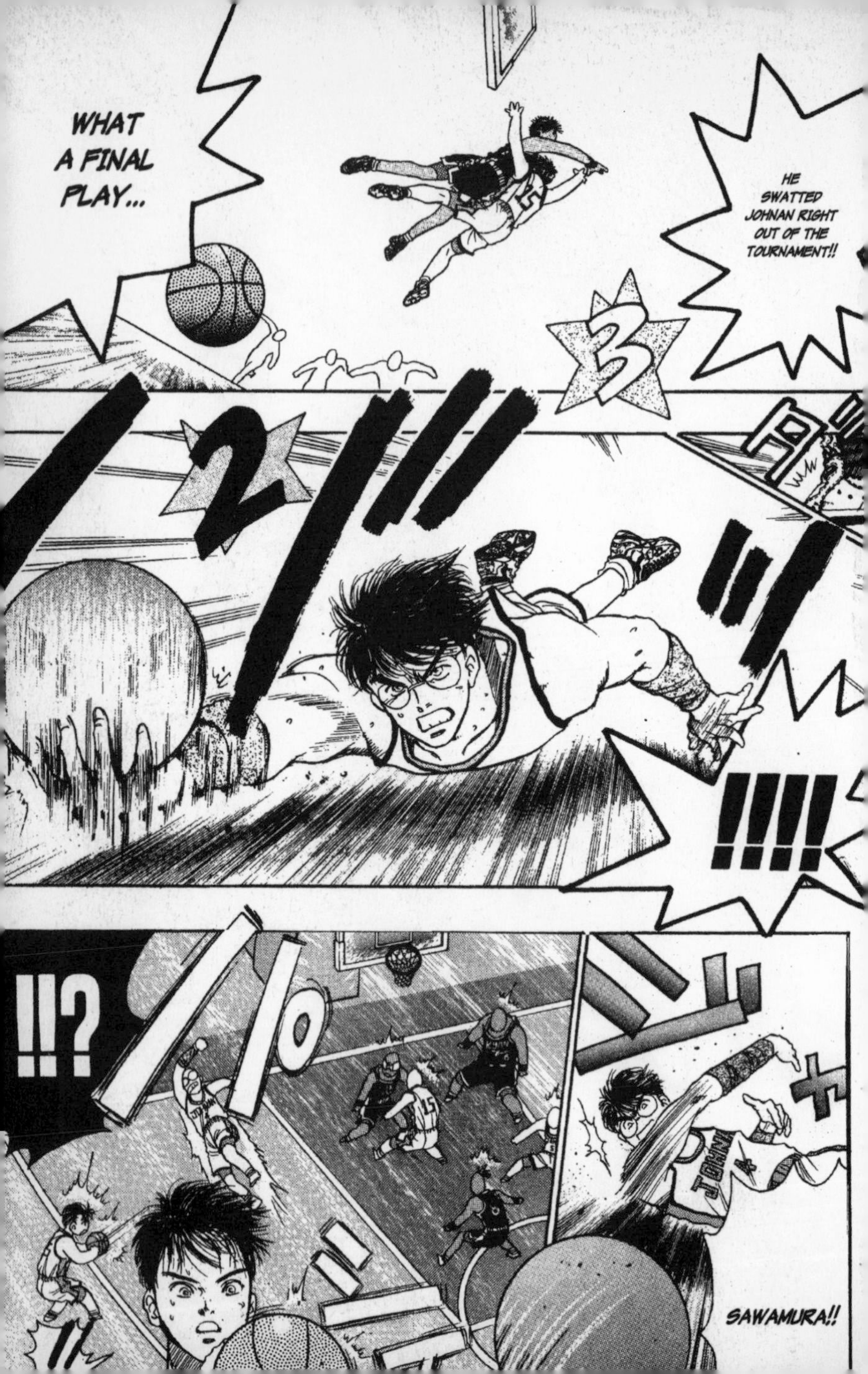
HE SWATTED JOHNAN RIGHT OUT OF THE TOURNAMENT!!
WHAT A FINAL PLAY...
3
2
!!!!
SAWAMURA!!
!!?

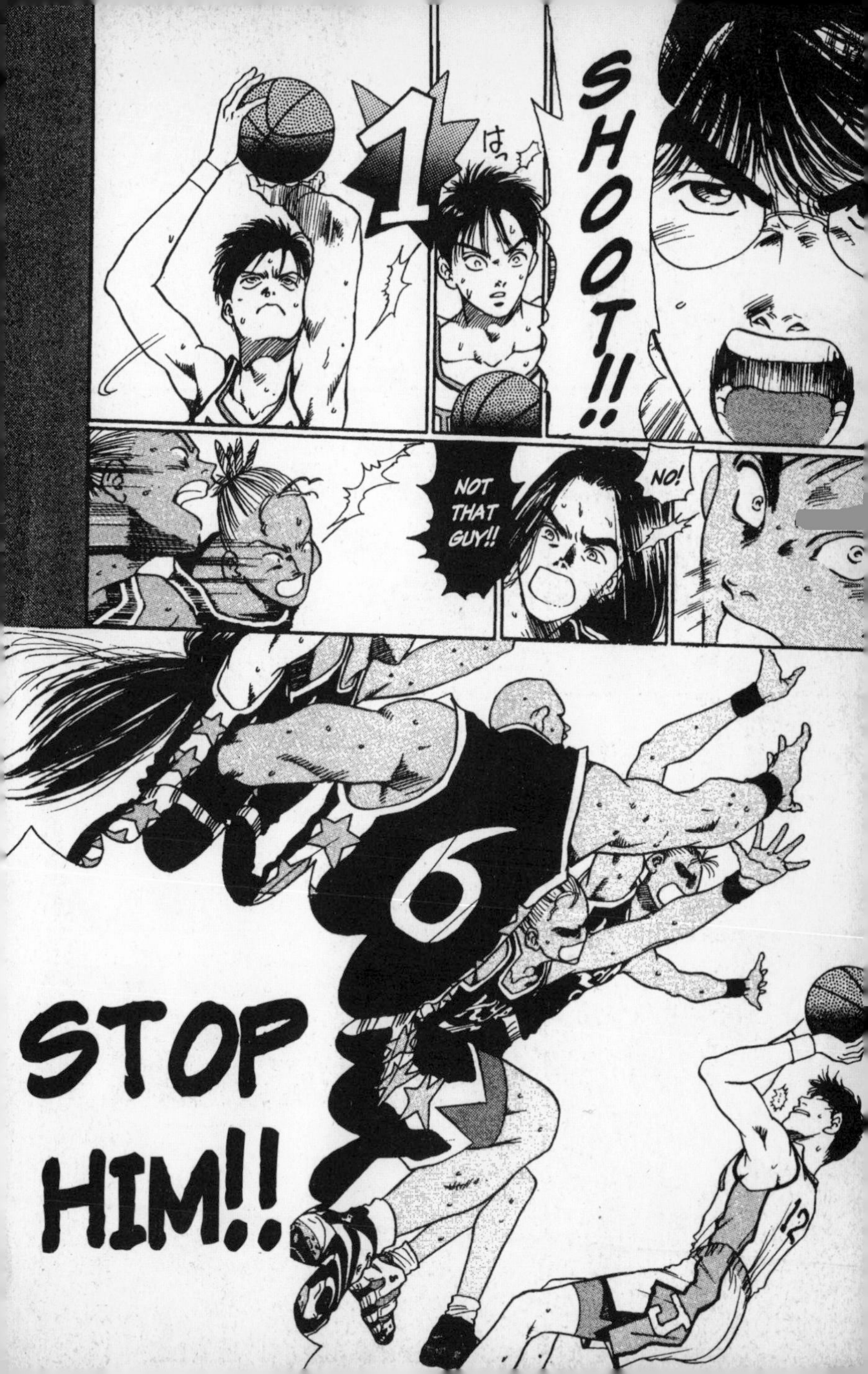
SHOOT!!
1
はっ
NO!
NOT THAT GUY!!
STOP HIM!!

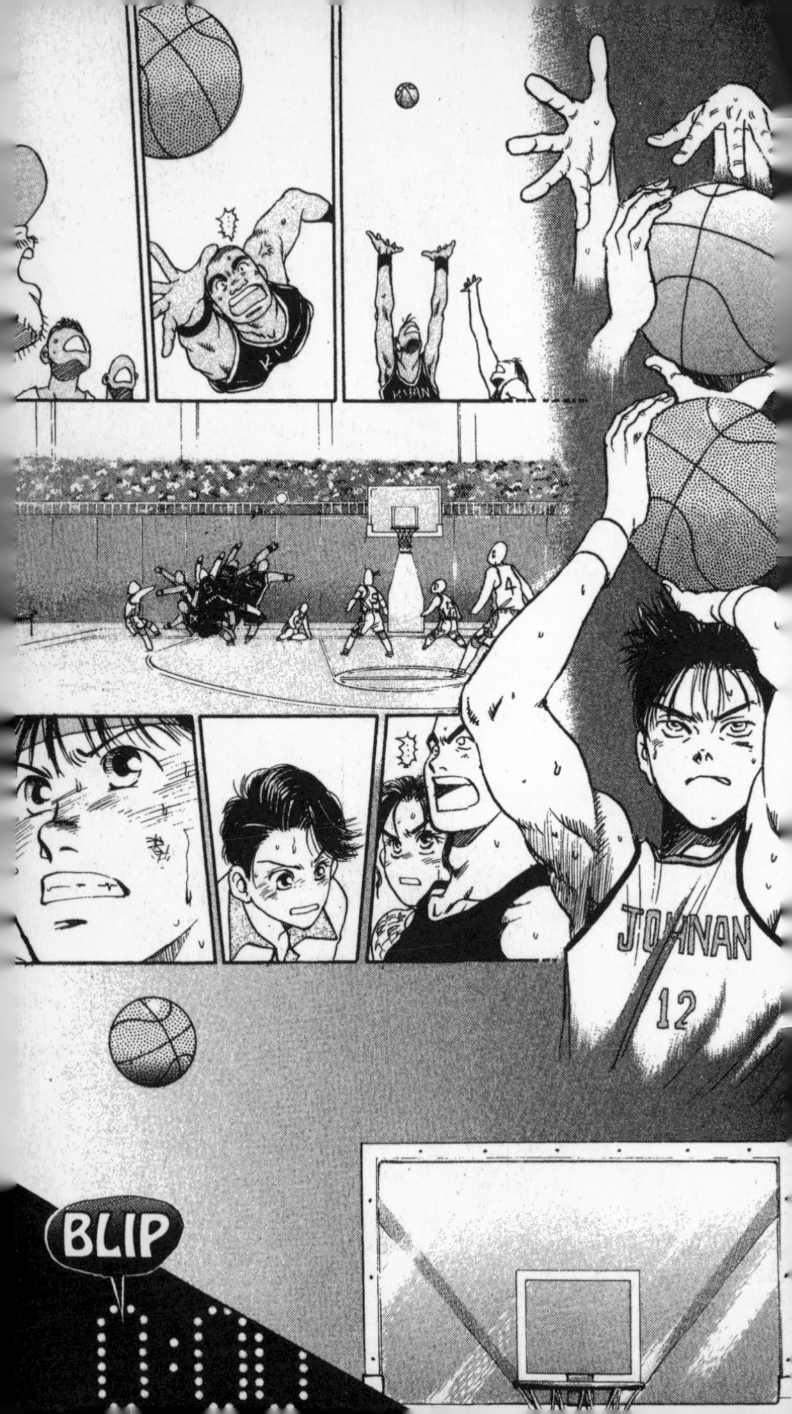
BLIP

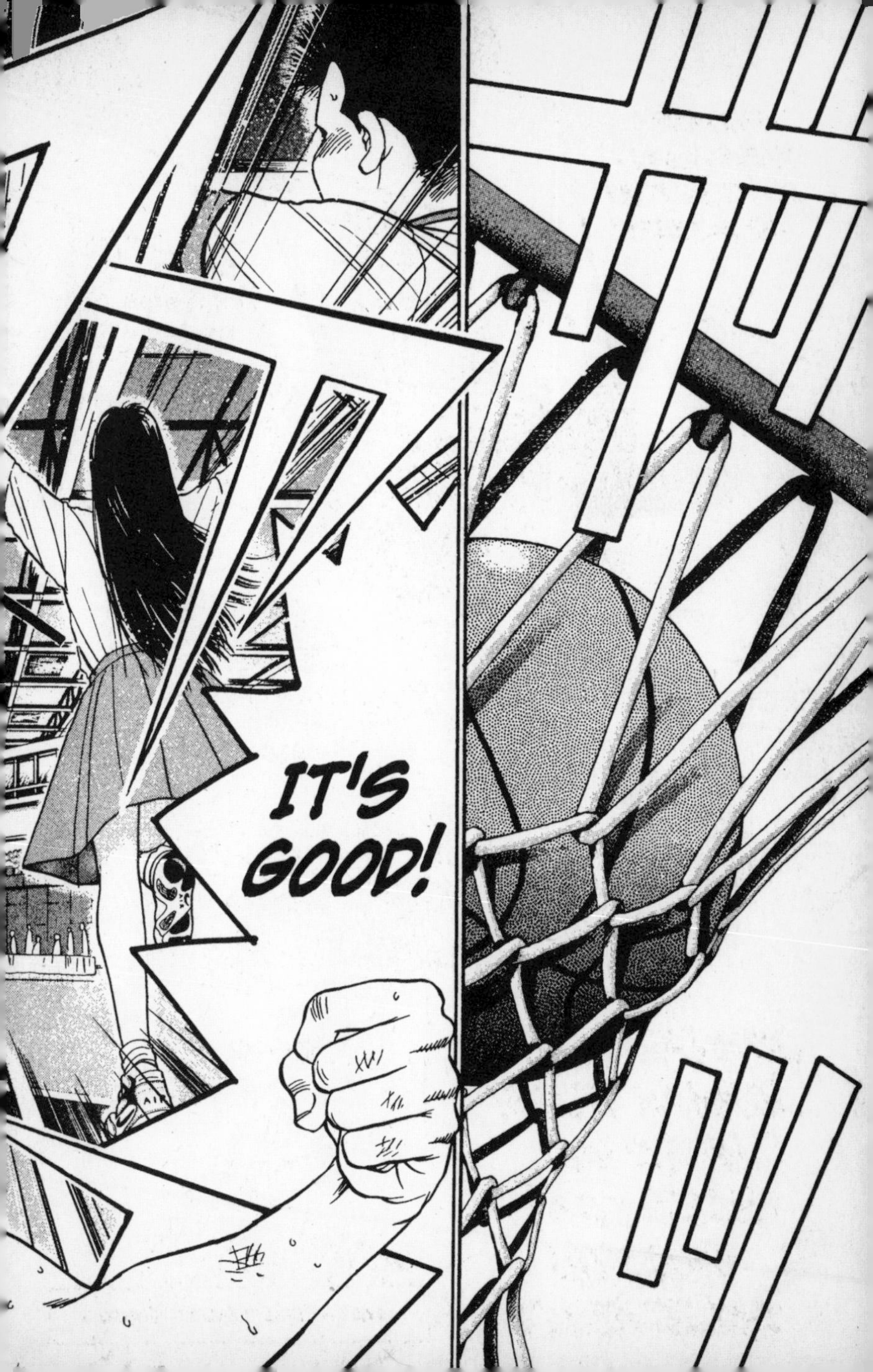
IT'S GOOD!

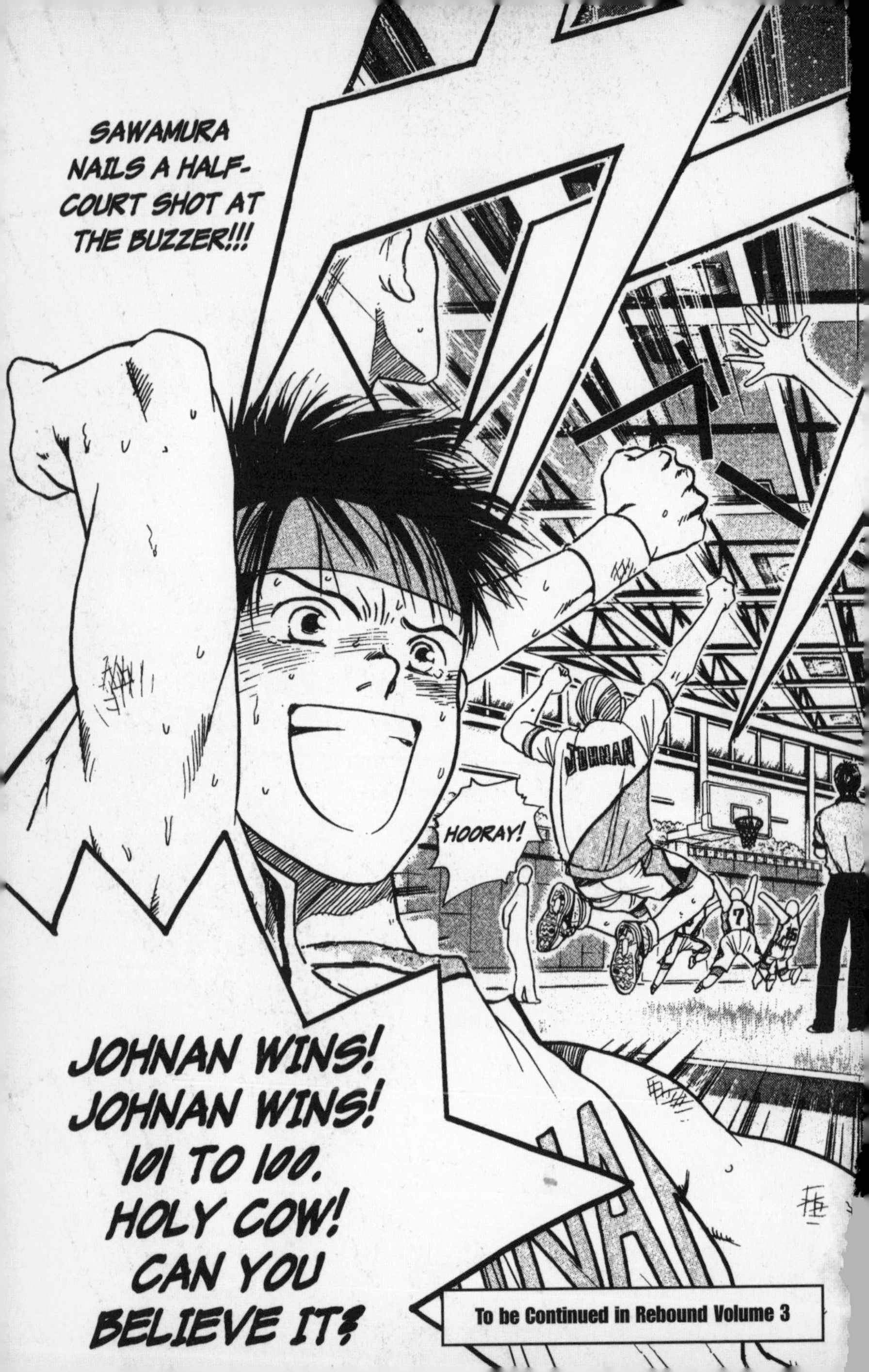
SAWAMURA NAILS A HALF-COURT SHOT AT THE BUZZER!!!
HOORAY!
JOHNAN
JOHNAN WINS! JOHNAN WINS! 101 TO 100. HOLY COW! CAN YOU BELIEVE IT?
To be Continued in Rebound Volume 3

STAY TUNED!!!

We hope you enjoyed your selected manga, *Rebound* Volume 2. Tune in two months from now when the tale continues and Johnan's basketball crew might be in for the basketball blues...

Preview for  Volume 3

Johnan emerges from the first round victorious and will now proceed to the second round against their archrivals, Tsukuba High—the very team that knocked them out of the championships last year by injuring one of Johnan's player, Imagawa, who now bitterly serves as the team's manager. But first the Johnan boys have to face– on a personal level– the Okinawa team, who may turn out to be not as anti-social as they seem on the court. So things are looking up for the Tokyo players, if only personal demons don't threaten their cohesion. When Nate recognizes Sawamura's long lost father working as a doorman in Sapporo, the cool-as-ice pretty boy may not be able to handle the pressure.

And now, a commercial break...

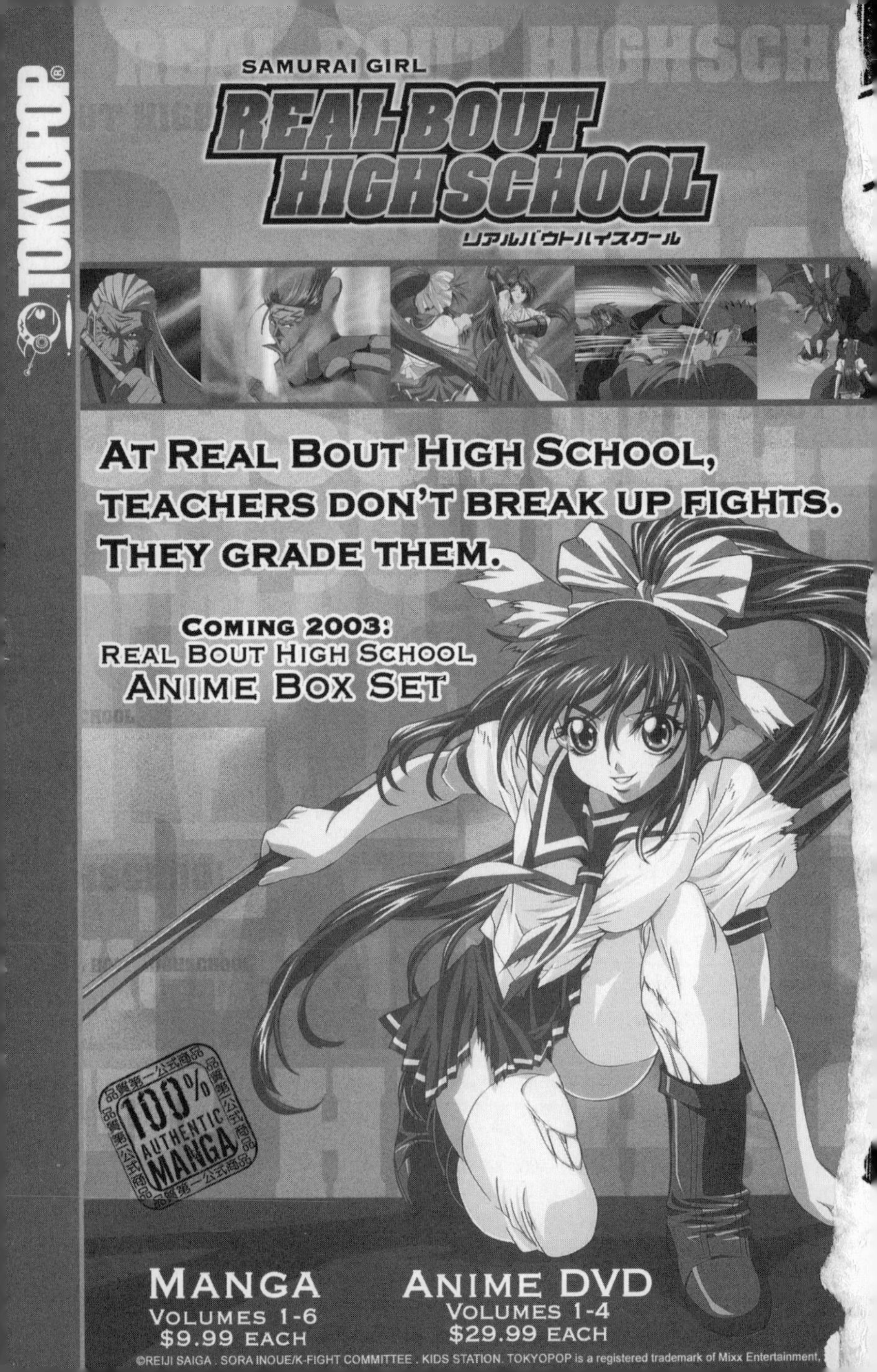
TOKYOPOP®
SAMURAI GIRL
REAL BOUT HIGH SCHOOL
リアルバウトハイスクール
AT REAL BOUT HIGH SCHOOL, TEACHERS DON'T BREAK UP FIGHTS. THEY GRADE THEM.
COMING 2003:
REAL BOUT HIGH SCHOOL
ANIME BOX SET
100% AUTHENTIC MANGA
MANGA
VOLUMES 1-6
$9.99 EACH
ANIME DVD
VOLUMES 1-4
$29.99 EACH
©REIJI SAIGA . SORA INOUE/K-FIGHT COMMITTEE . KIDS STATION. TOKYOPOP is a registered trademark of Mixx Entertainment.

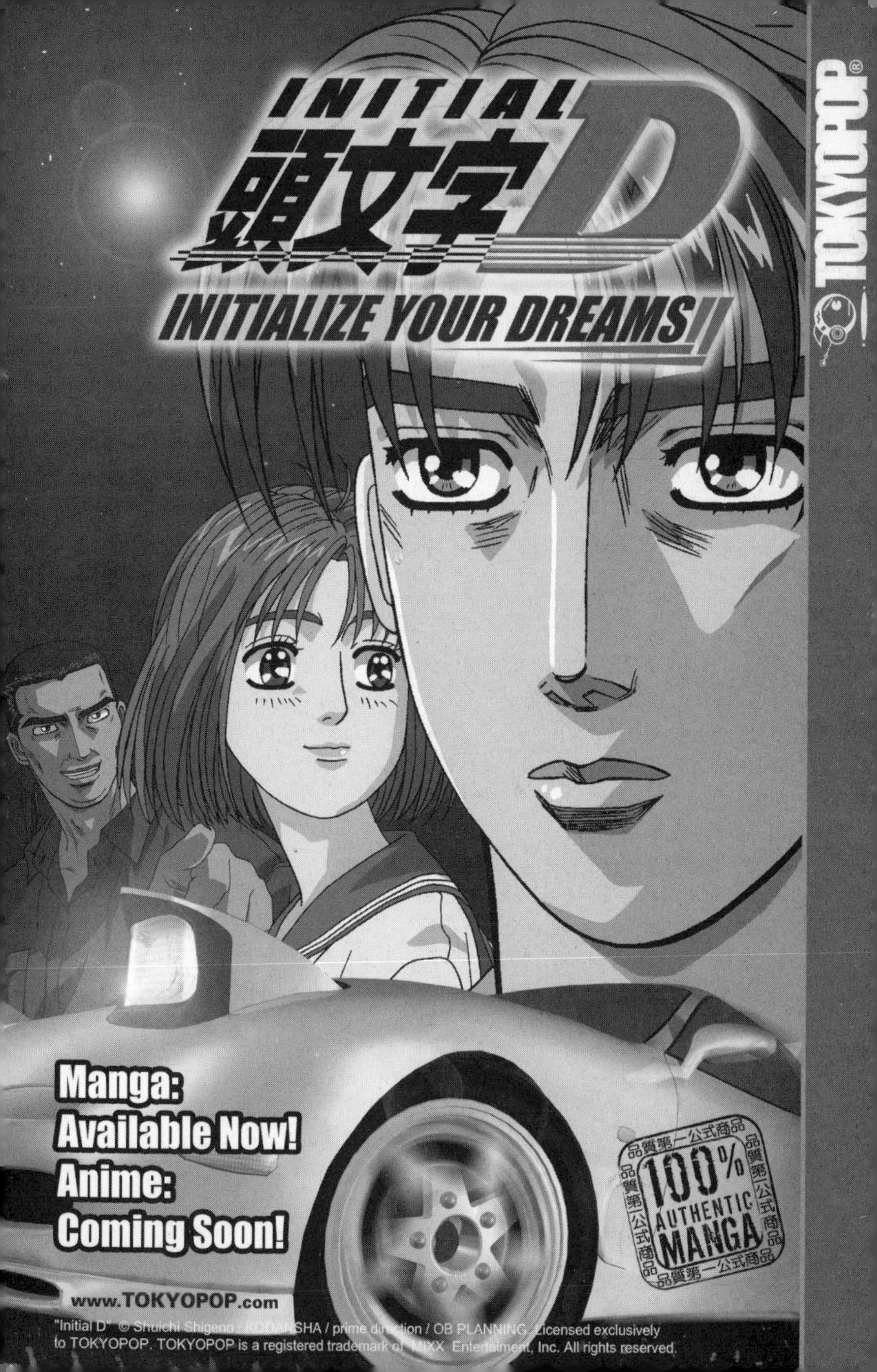
INITIAL
頭文字D
INITIALIZE YOUR DREAMS
TOKYOPOP®
Manga:
Available Now!
Anime:
Coming Soon!
品質第一公式商品
100%
AUTHENTIC
MANGA
www.TOKYOPOP.com
"Initial D" © Shuichi Shigeno / KODANSHA / prime direction / OB PLANNING. Licensed exclusively to TOKYOPOP. TOKYOPOP is a registered trademark of Mixx Entertaiment, Inc. All rights reserved.

BRIGADOON

TWO UNLIKELY ALLIES IN ONE AMAZING ANIME.

BY SUNRISE:
*The Creator of
Gundam and
Cowboy Bebop*

*"Brigadoon is paving the
way for a new fan favourite in the
North American anime community.
...quite possibly, the perfect blend
of wacky humour and intense battles"*
—**Otaku Aniverse**

DVD Vol. 1 Available Everywhere Great Anime Is Sold!
Manga Coming to Your Favorite Book & Comic Stores August 2003!

T
TEEN
AGE 13+

www.**TOKYOPOP**.com

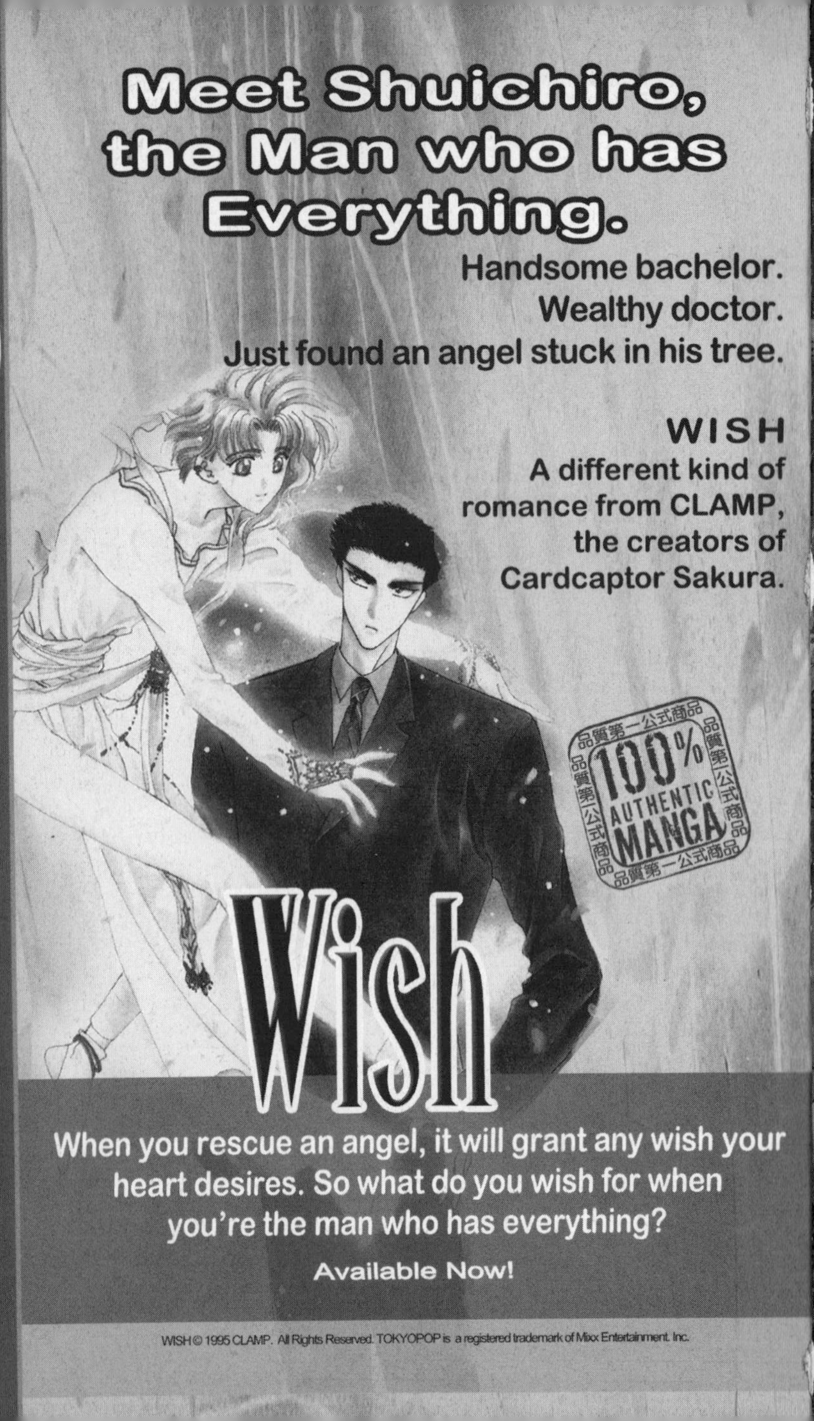
TOKYOPOP
Meet Shuichiro, the Man who has Everything.
Handsome bachelor.
Wealthy doctor.
Just found an angel stuck in his tree.
WISH
A different kind of romance from CLAMP, the creators of Cardcaptor Sakura.
100% AUTHENTIC MANGA
品質第一公式商品
Wish
When you rescue an angel, it will grant any wish your heart desires. So what do you wish for when you're the man who has everything?
Available Now!
WISH © 1995 CLAMP. All Rights Reserved. TOKYOPOP is a registered trademark of Mixx Entertainment, Inc.

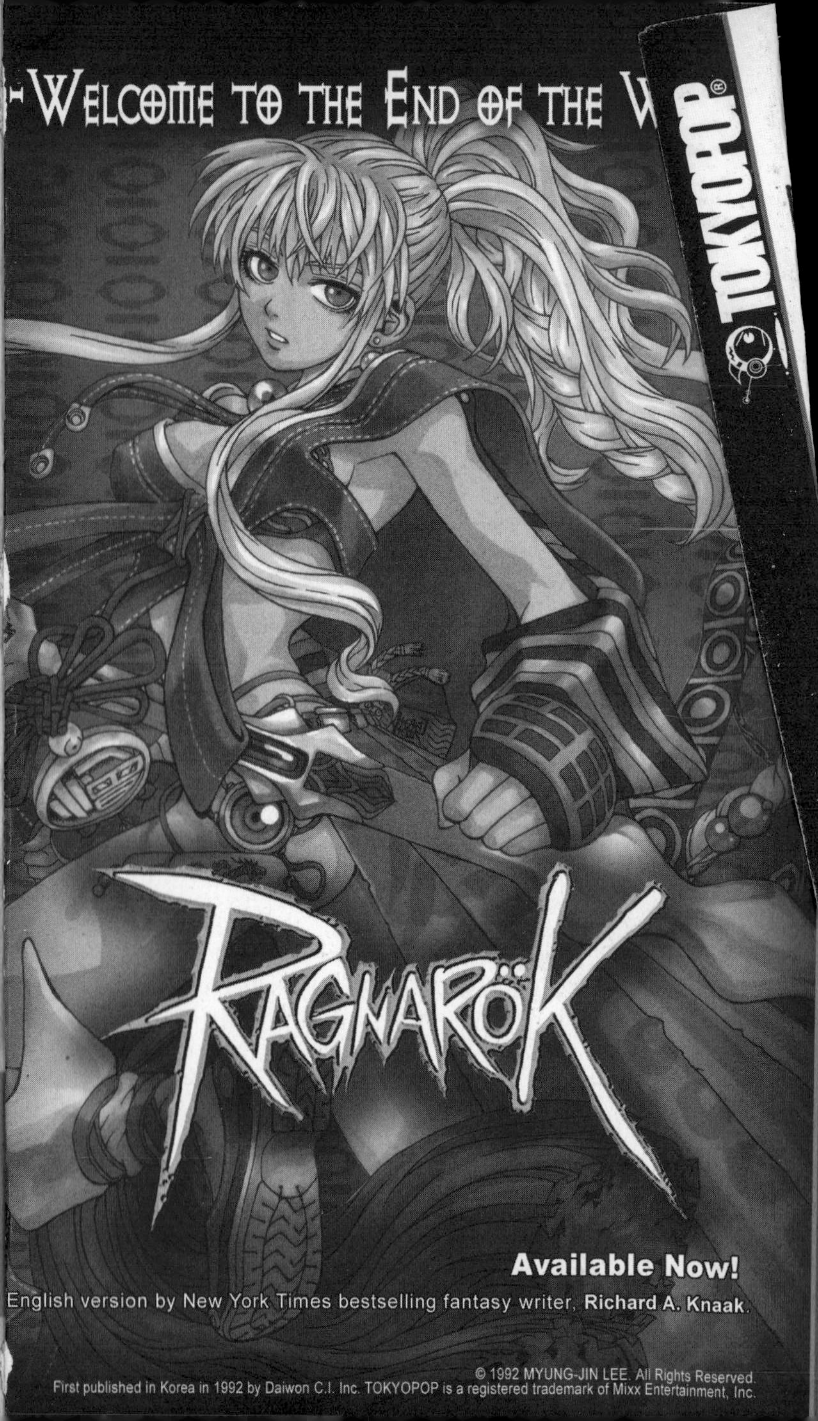
WELCOME TO THE END OF THE W
TOKYOPOP
RAGNARÖK
Available Now!
English version by New York Times bestselling fantasy writer, Richard A. Knaak.
© 1992 MYUNG-JIN LEE. All Rights Reserved.
First published in Korea in 1992 by Daiwon C.I. Inc. TOKYOPOP is a registered trademark of Mixx Entertainment, Inc.

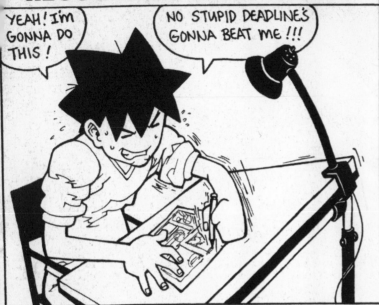

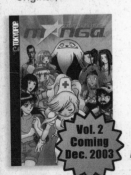

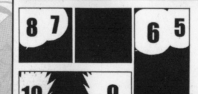

STOP!

This is the back of the book.
You wouldn't want to spoil a great ending!

This book is printed "manga-style," in the authentic Japanese right-to-left format. Since none of the artwork has been flipped or altered, readers get to experience the story just as the creator intended. You've been asking for it, so TOKYOPOP® delivered: authentic, hot-off-the-press, and far more fun!

DIRECTIONS

1
2
3
4
5
6
7
8
9
10

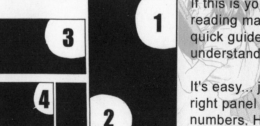

If this is your first time reading manga-style, here's a quick guide to help you understand how it works.

It's easy... just start in the top right panel and follow the numbers. Have fun, and look for more 100% authentic manga from TOKYOPOP®!

100% AUTHENTIC MANGA

S0-BAW-576

IT'S TIME THE WORLD RECOGNIZED YOUR GENIUS!

NO STUPID DEADLINE'S GONNA BEAT ME!!!
YEAH! I'm GONNA DO THIS!

FAME! FORTUNE! GET PUBLISHED!

Everything an aspiring manga-ka hopes for and dreams of. TOKYOPOP wants to make your dreams come true! Beginning June 1, 2003, and running through September 1, 2003, TOKYOPOP will conduct the second "Rising Stars of Manga" Contest, the sequel to America's original, first- ever and best manga competition.

TOKYOPOP
manga
Vol. 2 Coming Dec. 2003

Check www.TOKYOPOP.com for contest rules, and find out if you have what it takes to be included in the second volume of "The Rising Stars of Manga"!

the RISING STARS of MANGA™

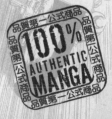